THE FREE NEGRO IN VIRGINIA

1619-1865

BY

JOHN H. RUSSELL, Ph.D.

DOVER PUBLICATIONS, INC.

NEW YORK

Published in Canada by General Publishing Company, Ltd.,
30 Lesmill Road, Don Mills, Toronto, Ontario.
Published in the United Kingdom by Constable and Company, Ltd.,
10 Orange Street, London WC 2.

This Dover edition, first published in 1969, is an unabridged and unaltered republication of the work first published in 1913 by The Johns Hopkins Press, Baltimore.

Standard Book Number: 486-22459-7
Library of Congress Catalog Card Number: 74-92392

Manufactured in the United States of America
Dover Publications, Inc.
180 Varick Street
New York, N.Y. 10014

CONTENTS

PREFACE

The history of the free negro in the slave States forms one of the most interesting chapters in the history of slavery in this country. A number of valuable monographs dealing with the history of the negro or with the institution of slavery in the various States have been published during recent years, but no one of them, so far as the author is aware, has been devoted exclusively to the status or history of the antebellum free negro in a particular Commonwealth of the Union. Such studies are needed, and it is hoped that the present monograph will, as far as Virginia is concerned, supply this need. Moreover, as a study of the free negro in the State in which the African first made his appearance in America, it should supply some of the facts upon which the history of the negro race in the United States must be based. Upon the constitutional side it is hoped that the study will be an aid to a correct conception of the purposes sought to be realized by the adoption of the Fourteenth Amendment.

The author takes this opportunity to acknowledge his indebtedness to Professor W. W. Willoughby for the scholarly guidance and stimulating criticism which were at his service in all stages of the work. It is a pleasure also to acknowledge his obligation to Professor J. C. Ballagh, at whose suggestion the study was undertaken. In the important work of discovery and valuation of the sources Professor Ballagh's generous direction was of particular value. The author is also indebted to Professors J. M. Vincent and G. E. Barnett for helpful suggestions.

Acknowledgment of special obligation is likewise due to Professor Charles Henry Ambler, of Randolph-Macon College, who placed in the author's hands notes of great value which he had made upon the subject of this monograph. For courtesies extended by officials in charge of county and state archives, sincere thanks are here given. From the discussion of various phases of the subject with Dr. H. J. Eckenrode, archivist, and Mr. Earl G. Swem, assistant librarian, of the Virginia State Library, suggestions of great value were received. Mr. William G. Stanard, librarian of the Virginia Historical Society, courteously placed at the author's disposal valuable manuscripts.

J. H. R.

THE FREE NEGRO IN VIRGINIA 1619-1865

CHAPTER I

NUMBER AND DISTRIBUTION OF THE FREE NEGROES IN VIRGINIA

At the beginning of the Civil War there were in Virginia nearly sixty thousand free negroes.[1] This number was far in excess of the number of free colored persons in any other of the great slave States, being about double the number in North Carolina, the State which, south of Virginia, had the largest free colored population. It was in excess of the free negro population in any State, slave or free, with the exception of Maryland. In 1860 the entire number of negroes in New York and New England combined was but little greater than the number of free negroes in Virginia. According to every Federal enumeration from 1790, the aggregate negro population of the State of Pennsylvania was smaller than the free colored population of Virginia, and from 1830 to 1860 the same may be said of New York. At the beginning of the nineteenth century the sum of the free negro populations in New York, New Jersey, and Pennsylvania was only about a thousand more than the number of free negroes in Virginia.[2] Of the free negro population of the United States, Virginia had about one eighth.[3]

---

[1] Except where specific reference is made in footnotes to the sources, the statistical facts in this chapter are based on the United States decennial censuses, 1790–1860.

[2] St. G. Tucker, A Dissertation on Slavery, p. 70 n.

[3] It must be kept in mind that free mulattoes and all other free persons having negro blood are included in the use of the word "free negroes." The term includes the persons enumerated in the census reports under the caption, "all other [than white] free persons except Indians not taxed." In 1771 the general court ruled that negro or mulatto servants and apprentices were to be considered free negroes. It is in this broadened sense that the word is used in this work when used without qualifying words (Howell v. Netherland, Jefferson's Reports, 90).

The condition which made the free negro question in Virginia unique and peculiarly interesting was that in that State only was there so large a free colored population living in a society so vitally connected with and dependent upon slavery. It requires but little imagination to see why a free negro population, numbering from twenty to sixty thousand between 1800 and 1860 and living among a slave population almost as numerous as the dominant white element, created social problems more perplexing than those of New England, where the negroes, few in number, were almost all free, and race problems different from those of other great slave States where the free negroes were too few to constitute a conspicuous factor in the social order. With society in a large area of Virginia composed of about an equal number of masters and slaves, an additional element of free negroes in the proportion of one to about eight slaves acted in no sense as an aid to facilitating the association of the two races.

Prior to a law of 1782 which removed the restrictions upon the right to manumit slaves by will, the number of free negroes relative to the number of slaves or white persons was very much smaller than in any decade after the passage of that act. From 1619 to the end of the century, when custom and the law were fixing the status of the Virginia negro, no satisfactory statistical estimate can be made of the number of free negroes in the colony. In 1670 Governor Berkeley estimated the total number of "black slaves" in the colony at two thousand.[4] Although he made no reference to any free negroes, there is ample evidence to show that there were some in the colony at this time. In 1691 and 1723 laws were enacted which limited the increase of the free negro class to natural means and to manumissions by special legislative acts.[5] These limitations upon manumission remained in force till 1782, when, according to the reliable statement of a contemporary, the free negro class numbered about twenty-eight hundred. Supposing the

[4] W. W. Hening, Statutes at Large of Virginia, vol. ii, p. 515.
[5] Ibid., vol. iii, pp. 87, 88; vol. iv, p. 132.

ninety-one years between 1691 and 1782 to be sufficient time for the numbers of the free negroes to have doubled three times by natural increase, we may judge, by counting backward on the basis of Tucker's estimate in 1782, that in 1691 the number of free negroes in the colony was about three hundred and fifty.[6]

The frequency with which this class of persons is mentioned in church and court records between 1690 and 1782 gives a further appearance of reliability to the above estimate. In 1724 the reports of certain Virginia clergymen to the English bishop mention free negroes among the parishioners, while certain others show that there were none. The report for St. Anne's parish asserted that in the parish there "are many negro slaves," and that "there may be 6 free negroes."[7] The rector of Lawn's Creek parish reported that "there are some Indians, bond and free, and some negroes, bond and free."[8] The answer for Newport parish of Isle of Wight County is, "Both bond and free,"[9] and for Hungar's parish on the Eastern Shore, "There are Infidels, bond and free."[10] The old parish registers, some of which

---

[6] St. G. Tucker, A Dissertation on Slavery in Virginia, published as Appendix to 1803 edition of Tucker's Blackstone, vol. i, note H, p. 66. The edition of the Dissertation on Slavery published in 1796 has 1800 (p. 70) where the later edition has 2800 as representing the author's estimate of the number of free colored persons in Virginia. An indication that the figures of the later edition are the author's true estimate is contained in a statement made by a member of the House of Delegates in discussing manumission in which he cited Tucker as authority for the statement that in 1782 there were 3000 free negroes in Virginia. Evidently the speaker adopted 3000 as a round number for 2800 as given in the edition of Tucker, then only two years old.

[7] W. S. Perry, ed., Papers relating to the History of the Church in Virginia, 1650–1776, p. 315.

[8] Ibid., p. 289.

[9] Ibid., p. 274.

[10] Ibid., p. 273. The word "infidels" in these reports is used somewhat in the sense of "heathen," so that when the answer is made that there are "no infidels that are free," as was made for St. Peter's parish (p. 269), it must be understood to mean that there were no free negroes in the congregation of the minister making the report. One negative answer made to the question as to the number of bond or free infidels declared, "There are none of the latter, especially of those who profess the Church of England worship" (p. 271). Negroes, whether baptized or not, were uniformly reported as infidels.

date back to 1662, bear witness to the existence of a free negro element in the congregations, although it is difficult to ascertain from this source the numerical strength of the free negro population.[11] The register of the old Bruton parish shows that thirty-seven out of eleven hundred and twenty-two colored persons baptized between 1746 and 1797 were free;[12] but the ratio of 37 to 1122, or 1 to 30, is no doubt much too large to show the relative number of free negroes to the slaves in any large section of the State. From about 1762 to 1782 some seventy free colored persons are mentioned in the records of baptisms,—a number larger than could have been found in most areas of the same size included in a single parish.[13]

After 1782 the relative numbers of the three classes of Virginia population are pretty well known. A state census made in 1782,[14] although not classifying free negroes separately, bears out the estimate made by Professor Tucker that twenty-eight hundred[15] would represent fairly accurately the number of free negroes in Virginia at that date. The unparalleled increase of this class, which followed the removal in 1782 of the restrictions on manumission, and also the relative numbers of free colored persons, slaves, and whites in Virginia from 1790 to 1860 will be seen from

[11] By the courtesy of the librarian of the Episcopal Theological Seminary at Alexandria, Virginia, the writer was permitted to examine the manuscript parish records, which contain valuable information not only as to the number of free negroes, but also as to their social position.

[12] Manuscript copy, Williamsburg, Virginia, pp. 24–57. See also W. A. R. Goodwin, Historical Sketch of Bruton Church, p. 153.

[13] The record for a single year reads, with reference to free negroes, as follows: "John, son of Thos. & Sally Pow, a free mulatto was baptized April ye 4. 1762." "Elizabeth, Daughter of Eliza Wallace (a free negro) baptiz'd June ye 6, 1762." "Joseph, Son of Anne Freeman, a free Mulatto, bapt'z'd July ye 4, 1762."

In further illustration of the evidence contained in parish records of the existence of free negroes in the colony is the following entry: "Diego, free negro died Sept. 3, 1741" (MS. Register of Christ's Church, Middlesex County, p. 310).

[14] "State Enumeration of Va., 1782–1785—Heads of Families," published with the First Census of the United States, 1790.

[15] St. G. Tucker, A Dissertation on Slavery, ed. 1803, p. 66.

the following table prepared from the Federal decennial censuses:—

	1790	1820	1840	1860
Free colored........	12,866	36,875	49,841	58,042
Slave................	292,627	425,148	448,988	490,865
White	442,117	603,381	740,968	1,047,299
Total..............	747,610	1,065,404	1,239,797	1,596,206

From these figures one fails to get a correct conception of the significance of the presence of the free colored population in Virginia unless the question of distribution is also taken into consideration. Had the free blacks been equally distributed throughout the white population of the State, the effect would have been different. In the mountainous half of the State, which after 1830 contained half of the white population, free negroes were so scarce as to be an almost negligible social factor. The 58,042 free negroes, together with the slave population, were confined largely to the eastern half of the State, where in 1860 the white population numbered about 600,000.

The State of Virginia was divided north and south on the basis of the elevation of land into four sections: Tidewater, Piedmont, the Valley, and Trans-Alleghany. Of the 12,866 free negroes in Virginia in 1790 only 75 resided in Trans-Alleghany, or what is now West Virginia with several counties of the southwestern part of Virginia. In the Valley district there were 815; in the Piedmont region, 3640, leaving 8330, or about two thirds of the entire number, in Tidewater. In that section the first census recorded 1 free negro to 18 slaves and to 18 white persons. In Trans-Alleghany the figures showed 1 free negro to 30 slaves to 517 white persons.

From the census of 1860 it appeared that the free negroes of Tidewater were between one sixth and one seventh of the colored and about one fourteenth of the entire population of that section. Tidewater contained 32,841 free negroes, over one half of the entire free colored population, while the region beyond the Alleghanies now had 2513, which was about one eleventh of the blacks of that section and 1 to every 160 persons living there. It appears that Tidewater always had from one half to two thirds of the entire free negro class, although after 1830 that section contained less than one fourth of the white people of the State. In 1860 Trans-Alleghany had more than one third of the white population of Virginia and about one twenty-fifth of the free negroes. The two sections west of the Blue Ridge, sometimes called the western half of the State, had in 1860 over one half of the white and but one seventh of the entire free colored class. A few of the lower counties in the Valley contained a large part of the 8354 free colored persons who lived in the western half. Thus it is apparent that an important aspect of the free negro problem in Virginia was the fact that the free negro population was largely concentrated in the eastern half of the State and came in contact with only about one half of the white population.

With respect to the relative numbers of free negroes in smaller localities some interesting observations may be made. As between rural and urban communities the latter had the larger share of free negroes. In 1790, when the average ratio of free negroes to slaves and to whites in the Tidewater section was 1 to 18, in Petersburg the free negroes constituted one fourth of the colored population of the town, and were to the whites as 1 to 4½. In this town of 3000 people there were 310 free negroes. In Richmond, out of a population of 3700 there were 265 free negroes. In Portsmouth, where 1702 persons lived, there were 47 free blacks.

The increase of free negroes in the town populations is best seen by considering the figures of some of the later censuses. Petersburg in 1830 had 2032 free negroes, 2850 slaves, and 3440 white persons. In 1860 this town was the home of 3164 free negroes, 5680 slaves, and a number of white persons about equal to the total black population. In 1860 Winchester, a town of 3000 white inhabitants, had 675 free negroes, only nineteen less than half of the blacks of the town. In 1850, 10,450 free negroes out of a total of 54,333, that is, nearly one fifth, lived in towns, while only about one tenth of the white population lived in cities and towns. In 1860 between a fourth and a third of the whole free colored population lived in towns and cities.[16]

In some counties a large proportion of the black inhabitants were free. In Accomac County 3392 of the 8000 black inhabitants were free. In James City County 926 out of 2764 blacks were free. In Nansemond County there were 2470 free negroes and 581 slaves. Other counties in Tidewater in which from one sixth to one half of the colored population was free were Charles City, Fairfax, Henrico, Isle of Wight, James City, Norfolk, Northampton, Prince William, Richmond, Southampton, Warwick, and Westmoreland. The counties in Piedmont which had the largest free colored population relative to the slave class were Loudoun and Goochland. In the former, one sixth of the negroes were free, in the latter, one ninth.

Occasion may arise for calling attention to other facts relative to the numbers and the distribution of the free negroes in Virginia, but the facts given above will be sufficient for a general conception of the numerical importance of that class at different times and in different places.

---

[16] Census of 1860, Population, p. 516.

CHAPTER II

THE ORIGIN OF THE FREE NEGRO CLASS

The popular misconception of the beginnings of the free negro population in Virginia which this chapter should correct may be stated as follows: The first negroes brought to Virginia in 1619 were from the very outset regarded and held as slaves for life. They and all Africans who came after them experienced immediately upon entering Virginia a perpetual loss of liberty. Unlike the white servant, whose freedom was only temporarily withheld, the freedom of the negro could only be restored by an act of emancipation. This being so, the free negro class was nothing but a divergence from, or a by-product of, slavery, dependent in its origin and existence upon the disintegration of slavery. This erroneous view was expressed by a slavery apologist of the decade immediately preceding the Civil War as follows: "Every negro in this country, or his ancestors, came in as a slave. Every negro, legally free, has reached that condition by his ancestors or himself having been emancipated by a former master."[1]

This popular error is maintained and supported by a large number of writers who have discussed the introduction of negroes into America. Besides Virginia historians such as Burk, Campbell, and Cook, who through thoughtless inference have written the word "slave" where they should, in view of all the evidence before them, have written "negro," there are two classes of writers who have given credence to the theory as a means of supporting some cause of which they were the champions. The first authorities to make use of this historical error were the antebellum

[1] "Calx," Two Great Evils of Virginia. Bound in "Political Pamphlets," vol. xii, p. 5, in Virginia State Library.

proslavery advocates. Judge Tucker of the Virginia supreme court, when delivering an opinion in 1806 in support of the principle of presuming slavery from color, made the following assertion: "From the first settlement of the colony of Virginia to the year 1778, all negroes, Moors, and mulattoes . . . brought into this country by sea, or land, were slaves."[2] The school of proslavery writers in Virginia between 1832 and 1860 made this assumption the basis of an argument for the reduction of all free negroes to slavery: "Every negro in this country or his ancestors came in as a slave." Hence they argued that "the free condition of all negroes in this country is novel or superinduced, artificial and abnormal. The great political problem which is required to be solved, is the recovery of the free negroes from their false position in this slave-holding community."[3]

The other writers whose conclusions have been influenced by their wishes in regard to the early history of the negro in America are historians of sectional bias who desire to assure themselves and their readers that American slavery had its origin in Virginia and not at the North. Thus, Henry Wilson, in his Rise and Fall of the Slave Power in America,[4] assures us that "in the month of August, 1620, a Dutch ship entered James River with twenty African slaves. They were purchased by the colonists, and they and their offspring were held in perpetual servitude." He therefore concludes that "four months before the feet of the Pilgrims had touched the New World, began that system which overspread the land."

Without attempting to say whether slavery had an earlier beginning in Virginia than in the other colonies, and without entering into the merits of the contention of the proslavery advocates that the free negroes should have been universally reduced to slavery, it can be asserted that any contention based solely upon the theory that the first Afro-Virginians and their offspring were slaves from the

---

[2] Hudgins v. Wrights, 1 Hening and Munford, 137.
[3] "Calx," p. 5.
[4] Third edition, vol. i, p. 2.

time of their arrival in the colony is not well founded.[5] Regardless of the bearing upon past or present controversies of the conclusions reached, an examination of the records will be made with the sole object of finding out what was the early status of the negro in Virginia.

If the simple fact of the introduction of negroes into the colony of Virginia is not to be taken as conclusive evidence of the beginning of slavery, upon what facts should its origin or earliest existence be posited? Throughout the seventeenth century there were in the colony persons called servants whose relations to their masters during the time of their service resembled the relations of slavery. Such temporary servitude must be distinguished from slavery. The difference between a servant and a slave is elementary and fundamental. The loss of liberty to the servant was temporary; the bondage of the slave was perpetual. It is the distinction made by Beverly in 1705 when he wrote, "They are call'd Slaves in respect of the time of their Servitude, because it is for Life."[6] Wherever, according to the customs and laws of a colony, negroes were regarded and held as servants without a future right to freedom, there we should find the beginning of slavery in that colony. Dr. J. C. Ballagh, in his History of Slavery in Virginia, very properly treats slavery as a legal status; but by drawing a sharp line between negro servitude and slavery at the date of statutory recognition of slavery he has overemphasized the importance of legislation in determining the origin of the institution.[7] Slavery in Virginia was instituted and developed in customary law, and was legally sanctioned at first by

[5] J. C. Ballagh, in A History of Slavery in Virginia, was the first to point out the error in the assumption that slavery was *introduced* into Virginia. His thesis in the chapter entitled "Development of Slavery" is that "servitude . . . was the historic base upon which slavery, by the extension and addition of incidents, was constructed." Although we are not primarily concerned in this study with the origin of slavery in Virginia, the facts here presented in relation to the origin of the free negro seem to bear out Dr. Ballagh's thesis as above stated.

[6] The History and Present State of Virginia, bk. iv, p. 35. Cf. Ballagh, Slavery in Virginia, p. 28.

[7] Pp. 34, 43.

court decisions. Hence, not in statute law, but in court records and documents which contain evidence of the condition of individual negroes prior to the date of statutory recognition of slavery are to be found, if found at all, the facts relative to the beginning of slavery.

The first act of the Virginia slave code, that is to say, the first act dealing directly with the status of negroes, was passed in 1662.[8] The wording of the act is abundant proof that those who framed it viewed slavery as a practice well established and well understood, the word "slave" being used without an attempt to define its significance. The idea that the act was to establish slavery or to provide the institution with a legal basis seems to have been entirely absent; the sole object was to fix a rule by which the status of mulatto children could be determined. Prior to this act the word "slave" had occurred in the statutes at three different times. In 1655 it was enacted that "if the Indians shall bring in any children as gages of their good and quiet intentions to vs and amity with vs . . . the countrey by vs their representatives do engage that wee will not vse them as slaves."[9] This pledge to the native Indians would seem to justify the inference that some persons, if not some Indians, in the colony had been reduced to slavery. Again, in 1659 in an act concerning commercial relations with the Dutch it was declared "that if the said Dutch or other foreigners shall import any negro-slaves, They . . . shall for the tobacco really produced by the sale of the said negro pay only the impost of two shilling per hogshead, the like being paid by our owne nation."[10] While here the subject of legislation is not even related to status and the reference to slaves is in a conditional clause in the act, it is hardly to be supposed that the persons who drew the act would have used

---

[8] "Whereas some doubts have arisen whether children got by an Englishman upon a negro woman should be slave or free, Be it therefore enacted . . . that all children borne in this country shall be held bond or free only according to the condition of the mother" (Hening, vol. ii, p. 170).

[9] Hening, vol. i, p. 396.

[10] Ibid., vol. i, p. 540.

the word "slave" where "servant" or "negro" was meant. The act came very close to a recognition of the legal possibility of slavery in the colony.[11]

Two years later the wording of an act prescribing certain punishments for runaway English servants shows beyond a doubt that some negroes in the colony were slaves. The act is entitled "English running away with negroes,"[12] and reads as follows: "In case any English servant shall run away in company with *any negroes who are incapable of makeing satisfaction by addition of time,* bee it enacted that the English so running away in company with them shall serve for the time of the said negroes absence as they are to do for their own by a former act."[13] The clause which here refers incidentally to negroes certainly shows that some of them were servants for life, slaves, incapable of compensating for lost time by any addition to their terms; but there is nothing in the act which asserts that all negroes were or should henceforth be slaves.

This is the act which has been interpreted by Dr. Ballagh in his History of Slavery in Virginia as not only a recognition of slavery, but also as a statutory reduction to slavery of all free or servant negroes.[14] As thus interpreted, the law is made to supply a legal basis hitherto lacking upon

[11] There is some indication in the records of the Dutch settlement in New York that the supposition in the act was at times a reality. Four years before this act the Council of the Colony of New York granted to Edmund Scharbuch "permission to sail in his vessel with some purchased negroes from here to Virginia" (Documents Relative to the Colonial History of the State of New York, vol. xii, pp. 93, 94).

[12] Hening, vol. ii, p. 26. Italics my own.

[13] In the repetition of this act the following year the words "if they [the negroes] had not been slaves" are added, showing that a negro who was not a slave was required to make up his own time lost by running away (Hening, vol. ii, p. 117).

[14] At page 71 are used the words, "negro servants reduced to slavery in 1661." The words from which this inference is drawn are quoted thus: "Negroes are incapable of making satisfaction by addition of time" (p. 34). These words as they stand are indeed of universal application, but it will be noticed that two words have been omitted from the text of the act which when supplied give to the clause a restricted meaning and application. The clause should read: "Any negroes who are incapable of makeing satisfaction by addition of time."

which courts might rule against the liberation of negroes suing for freedom. But, manifestly, the act was not intended for such a purpose, and there is abundant evidence that it was not used to alter the status of free or servant negroes then in the colony. The truth is that no attempt was ever made to supply legal grounds for holding negroes in a status of slavery. Custom supplied all the authority that appeared to be necessary, and legislation at first merely performed the part of resolving some uncertainties concerning a well-established institution. "When the progress of the times," wrote Savigny, "calls for new institutions . . . there is necessarily a time of transition in which the law is uncertain, and it is to put an end to this uncertainty that Statute Law is required."[15]

This truth is well illustrated in the growth of slavery in Virginia. The time of transition from slavery sanctioned by customary law to slavery defined by statute law was the decade between 1660 and 1670. A few quotations from the preambles of the acts of this period will reveal the object of the first legislation concerning the Africans in Virginia. In 1662 we read that "whereas some doubts have arisen whether children got by an Englishman upon a negro woman should be slave or free, be it therefore enacted,"[16] and so forth. "Some doubts have [ing] arisen whether negroes that are slaves by birth should by vertue of baptism be made free," the answer was made in 1667 by the enactment of a statute.[17] An act of 1668 begins with the words, "Whereas doubts have arisen whether negro women set free should be accompted tithable,"[18] and another two years later was explained by a preamble which asserted that "it has been questioned whither Indians or negroes manumitted or otherwise free could be capable of purchasing Christian servants."[19] Doubts arose as to whether Indians captured in

[15] Savigny, System, Sec. 13, quoted in J. M. Lightfoot's Nature of Positive Law, pp. 283, 284.
[16] Hening, vol. ii, p. 170.
[17] Ibid., vol. ii, p. 260.
[18] Ibid., vol. ii, p. 267.
[19] Ibid., vol. ii, p. 280.

war should be slaves, and in 1670 was passed an act entitled "An act declaring who shall be slaves."[20]

Even after this decade of legislation the question as to who should or should not be slaves was not fully answered. The act of 1670 merely applied to servants brought in by ship after 1670 the test of Christianity to determine whether they should be servants for a limited time or slaves for life. The status of Africans who came or were brought to Virginia before 1670 was not determined by statute law either before or after that date. Hence, if by statute law slavery was merely regulated and not established or instituted, the only use that can be made of the statutes in determining the origin of the institution is to fix an upper limit to the period in which the beginning was made. Knowing that slavery had its beginning some time before 1661, the date of the first act recognizing it, a study of the period from 1619 to 1661 should throw much light on the question of the earliest beginnings of the free negro class.

From the quaint narrative of Master John Rolfe, who possibly wrote as an eyewitness of the introduction of negroes into Virginia, it is learned that "About the last of August [1619] came in a Dutch man of Warre that sold us twenty negars."[21] In the very year of the arrival of this group of African immigrants a system of labor known as indented servitude received recognition in the laws of the colony.[22] It was not an uncommon practice in this early period for ship masters to sell white servants to the planters;[23] hence, an inference that these twenty negroes were slaves, drawn from the fact that they were sold to the colony or to the planters, would not be justified. Prior to 1619 every inhabitant of the colony was practically "a servant manipulated in the interest of the company, held in servi-

[20] Hening, vol. ii, p. 283.

[21] Works of Captain John Smith, ed. by Arber, p. 541.

[22] The first assembly of the colony provided that all contracts of servants should be recorded and enforced, and thus gave legislative recognition to servitude (Colonial Records of Virginia, 1619–1680, State Senate Document, Extra, 1874, pp. 21, 28; J. C. Ballagh, White Servitude in the Colony of Virginia, p. 27 n.).

[23] Ballagh, White Servitude, p. 45.

tude beyond a stipulated term."[24] The word "freeman" was just beginning to be used to distinguish persons set free from service to the London Company from persons still in a condition of servitude either to the company or to individual freemen.[25] Beyond all question the first twenty negroes brought in were not introduced as freemen. The only question is whether, upon entering the colony, they became servants or slaves. The possibility of their becoming slaves must be recognized because it is conceivable that a status different from that of any person in Virginia at that time was given to persons so different from white settlers as were the Africans.

Since it is the fact that the white population in the colony in 1619 had not been familiar in England with a system of slavery or with a model slave code, and since they had developed in Virginia a system of servitude and were fortifying it by law, it is plausible that the Africans became servants in a condition similar to the status of white servants, who, after a term of service varying from two to eight years,[26] were entitled to freedom. According to the "Lists of living and dead in Virginia"[27] in 1623 and the "Muster Rolls of the Settlements in Virginia,"[28] a census made in 1624–1625, there were in the colony twenty-three Africans. They are all listed as "servants," thus receiving the same class name as many white persons enumerated in the lists.[29] Some had names, as, for instance, "Angelo, a negro woman," and "John Pedro, a neger aged 30." Others apparently had no names, and were designated simply by the word "negro" under the caption "servants." In the opinion of

[24] Ballagh, White Servitude, p. 14.

[25] Hening, vol. i, pp. 126, 128.

[26] Ballagh, White Servitude, p. 49. Two hundred and fifty servants were brought into Virginia in 1619 (ibid., pp. 18, 30).

[27] Colonial Records of Virginia, p. 37 et seq.

[28] J. C. Hotten, Lists of Emigrants to America, passim.

[29] They were distributed as follows: Abraham Piersey, 7; George Yeardley, Kt., 8; Capt. William Piercey, 1; Richard Kingsmall, 1; Edward Bennett, 2; Capt. William Tucker, 3; Capt. Francis West, 1. All these persons held other servants beside the negroes, and some of these masters, being officers in the colony, may have had merely the right of an officer over company servants (Hotten, pp. 218–258).

Thomas Jefferson, "the right to these negroes was common, or, perhaps, they lived on a footing with the whites, who, as well as themselves, were under the absolute direction of the president."[30]

Were any or all of these negroes permitted to realize the freedom to which servants were entitled under the laws and customs of servitude? In the records of the county courts dating from 1632 to 1661 negroes are designated as "servants," "negro servants," or simply as "negroes," but never in the records which we have examined were they termed "slaves."[31] By an order of the general court a negro brought from the West Indies to Virginia in 1625 was declared to "belong to Sir Francis Wyatt (then governor) as his servant."[32] There is nothing in the record which indicates that "servant" meant the same as "slave." Among the twenty-three African "servants" enumerated in 1624 was a negro man named Anthony[33] and a negro woman named Mary,[34] serving under different masters. In the county court records of Northampton, of date February 28, 1652, is the following order:—

> Upon ye humble pet[ition] of Anth. Johnson Negro; & Mary his wife; & their Information to ye Court that they have been Inhabitants in Virginia above thirty years consideration being taken of their hard labor & honoured service performed by the petitioners in this County, for ye obtayneing of their Livelyhood And ye great Llosse they have sustained by an unfortunate fire wth their present charge to provide for, Be it therefore fitt and ordered that from the day of the date hearof (during their natural lives) the sd Mary Johnson & two daughters of Anthony Johnson Negro be disingaged and freed from payment of Taxes and leavyes in Northampton County for public use.[35]

---

[30] Jefferson's Reports, 119 n.

[31] Examples or illustrations may be seen in MS. Court Records of Accomac County, 1632–1640, pp. 55, 152 et seq.; Lower Norfolk County, 1637–1646, 1646–1651.

[32] The case is one which Jefferson noted from the records of the general court (Jefferson's Reports, 119 n.).

[33] Hotten, p. 244. In the second edition the entry referring to Anthony is as follows: "Anthony, negro, Isabell, a negro, and William her child, baptised." In an earlier edition (1874) the entry appeared as follows: "Antony Negro: Isabell Negro; and William theire Child Baptised."

[34] "Mary, a negro Woman [came in] in the Margarett and John, 1622" (Hotten, p. 241).

[35] MS. Court Records of Northampton County, 1651–1654, p. 161.

Subtracting thirty or more years from 1652, the date of this court order, we find that Anthony Johnson and possibly the woman who became his wife were inhabitants of Virginia before 1622.[36] If additional evidence is required to establish the fact that Anthony Johnson and his family were free in 1652, it is contained in a land patent of 1651 assigning to him in fee simple two hundred and fifty acres of land,[37] or in the records of a suit which he maintained in the county court in 1655.[38]

Just what part of the period of over thirty years of Anthony Johnson's residence in the colony was a term of servitude or how long before 1652 he had enjoyed his freedom is not clear. The term of service for white servants was not uniform, being dependent upon the conditions of the contract. Before 1643, servants without contracts generally became freemen after terms of service varying from two to eight years. After 1643 the terms of service for servants "brought into the colony without indentures or covenants to testify their agreements" were fixed by law at four to seven years, the period varying somewhat with the youthfulness of the servant.[39] The variations in the terms of service for negro servants appear to have been greater than the variations for white servants. In 1651 "head rights" were allowed upon the importation of a negro by the name of Richard Johnson.[40] Only three years later a patent calling for one hundred acres of land was issued to this negro for importing two other persons.[41] Hence, it appears that Richard Johnson came in as a free

[36] It is evident from the census of 1624 that the negress Mary, there enumerated, was not then the wife of Anthony; but granting that Anthony and Mary Johnson were in Virginia thirty years before 1652, it is not an unreasonable inference that the only negro man named Anthony and the only negro woman named Mary in the colony thirty years before 1652 were the negroes afterward called Anthony and Mary Johnson.

[37] MS. Land Patents of Virginia, 1643–1651, p. 326.

[38] MS. Court Records of Northampton County, 1651–1654, p. 226; 1655–1658, p. 10; below, p. 32.

[39] Hening, vol. i, pp. 257, 441.

[40] MS. Land Patents of Virginia, 1643–1651, p. 326.

[41] Ibid., 1652–1655, p. 294.

negro or remained in a condition of servitude for not more than three years. A negro who came to Virginia about 1665 was bound to serve Mr. George Light for a period of only five years.[42] It appears from certain indentures to be found on record that the term of service to which a negro might be bound could be for almost any number of years. In the following agreement, for example, the term was for ten years: "Be it thought fitt & assented unto by Mr. Steph. Charlton in Court that Jno. G. Hamander Negro, his servant, shall from ye date hereof [1648] serve ye sd Mr. Charlton (his heyers or assns.) until ye last days of November wh shall be in ye year of our Lord . . . one thousand six hundred Fifty & eight and then ye sd Negro is to bee a free man."[43]

As another example of the contracts of indented negro servants the following extract from the Northampton County court records of 1645 is quoted:—

> This Indenture witnesseth yt I Capt. Francis Pott have taken to service two Daughters of my negro Emanuell Dregis to serve & bee to me my heyers Exors. Adms. or Assigns. The one whose name is Elizabeth is to serve thirteene years whch will be compleat & ended in ye first part of March in ye yeare of our Lord God one thousand six hundred Fifty & eight. . . . And ye other child whose name is Jane Dregis (being about one yeare old) is to serve ye said Capt. Pott as aforesaid untill she arrive to ye age of thirty years old wh will be compleate & ended . . . [May, 1674], And I ye said Francis Pott doe promise to give them sufficient meate, drinke, Apparel & Lodging and to use my best endeavor to bring them up in ye feare of God and in ye knowledge of our Saviour Christ Jesus. And I doe further testify yt the Eldest daughter was given to my negro by one who brought her upp by ye space of eight years and ye younger he bought and paid for to Capt. Robert Shephard (as maye bee made appear). In witness whereof have hereunto sett my hands & seale in ye 27th of May one thousand six hundred forty & five.
>
> MR. FRANCIS POTT.
>
> Witness the names of Thom. P. Powell & John Pott.[44]

It appears from this record that one of the negro children was bound to serve for a period of thirteen years and the other for a term of twenty-nine years. The latter

[42] General Court Records, Robinson Transcripts, p. 161.
[43] MS. Court Records of Northampton County, 1645–1651, p. 150.
[44] Ibid., p. 82.

served, however, only seven years of her term; for in 1652 her father purchased her release from the contract, and upon payment was given the following receipt: "24, May 1652. This day Capt. Pott acknowledged yt hee hath recd of Emanuell Driggs Negro satisfaction & full payment for & in consideration of the present freedome of Jane Driggs daughter of ye sd Emanuell Driggs, the sd girle beinge aged about eight years."[45]

It is quite clear that the children of Emanuel Dregis or Driggs became indented servants and not slaves for life, but a question arises as to their status before this contract was made. Emanuel Dregis may not have been regularly married to the mother of these two daughters of his, and the owner of their mother seems to have claimed some right to dispose of them by gift and sale to their father. But the status of Emanuel Dregis and his wife Frances is fairly well explained in other records. In 1649 Dregis and his wife Frances and one other negro called Bashasor were assigned by Roger Booker to Stephen Charlton.[46] Two years later the following record was made concerning the property rights of these negroes:—

> Whereas Emanuel Driggs and Bashasar Farnando negroes now servants unto Capt. Franc Pott have certain cattle, Hoggs & poultry now in their possession ye wch they have honestly gotten and purchased in their service formerly under ye sd Capt. Pott & since augmented and increased under the service of Capt. Steph. Charlton now we, sd Pott & Charlton, doe hereby declare yt ye said cattle, hoggs, & poultry (with their increase) are ye proper goods of the above sd Negroes; and yt they may freely dispose of them either in their life tyme or att their death. In witness our hands 30th December 1652.
>
> FRANCIS POTT.[47]

The fact that these negroes had an absolute right to this property, a right which was not destroyed by the death of the property owner, is convincing that their status was higher than the status of the slave, whose loss of liberty was absolute. Bills of sale recording the transfer of property to

[45] MS. Court Records of Northampton County, 1651–1654, p. 82.
[46] Ibid., p. 28.
[47] Ibid., p. 114.

these negroes were recorded by the county court, which shows that the negroes were regarded as capable of making and enforcing a contract.[48] It may be of some significance in this connection to note that later in that century there was a Dregis or Driggus family of free negroes living in Northampton County.[49]

An instance very similar to the case of Emanuel Dregis is found in the records of the general court of Virginia for 1640–1641. The example is of special importance because there is very little specific information of earlier date concerning the condition of negroes. An order of the court runs as follows: "It appeareth to the court that John Geaween being a negro servant unto William Evans was permitted by his said master to keep hogs and make the best benefit thereof to himself provided the said Evans might have half the increase which was accordingly returned unto him by the said negro and the other half reserved for his own benefit."[50] Geaween, like Dregis, accumulated property, and purchased from Lieutenant Robert Sheppard his child's freedom; by order of the court the child was declared to "be free from the said Evans," its father's master, and "to be and remain at the disposing and education of the said Geaween and the child's god-father," Robert Sheppard.

The status of negroes like John Geaween, Emanuel Dregis, and Farnando fits precisely the description of servitude written in 1656 by John Hammond. "There is no master almost," says Hammond, "but will allow his Servant a parcell of clear ground to plant some Tobacco in for himself . . . which in time of shipping he may lay out for commodities, and in Summer sell them again with advantage, and get a Sow-Pig or two, which anybody almost

[48] Bill of sale by Francis Pott to Emanuel Dregis of "a black cow and a red calf" (MS. Court Records of Northampton County, 1645–1651, p. 83). In 1647 Tony Kongo, a negro, was compelled in court to make good a debt, due Lewis White, amounting to three hundred and eighty-two pounds of tobacco. By the order of the court, he was allowed thirty days to guarantee payment out of "ye next croppe" (ibid., p. 131).

[49] MS. Court Records of Northampton County, 1689–1698, p. 463.

[50] General Court Records, p. 30. Published in Virginia Magazine of History, vol. xi, p. 281.

will give him and his Master suffer him to keep them with his own . . . and with one year's increase of them may purchase a Cow-Calf or two and by that time he is for himself."[51]

Upon the completion of a term of servitude negro servants were sometimes granted a written discharge, as was Francis Pryne in 1656. The court record of the discharge of this man reads as follows:—

> I Mrs. Jane Elkonhead . . . have hereunto sett my hand yt ye aforesd Pryne [a negro] shall bee discharged from all hinderances of servitude (his child) or any [thing] yt doth belong to ye sd Pryne his estate.
>
> JANE ELKONHEADE.[52]

The priority of the origin of the free negro class over the origin of the slave class and the continuity of the free negro class will appear as plainly when historical evidence of the beginning of slavery is sought as when examples of negro servitude are looked for. When the court records are examined with a view to finding the earliest beginnings of slavery, it appears that between 1640 and 1660 slavery was fast becoming an established fact. In this twenty years the colored population was divided, part being servants and part being slaves, and some who were servants defended themselves with increasing difficulty from the encroachments of slavery.

In 1640 the general court[53] rendered in a singular case a judgment which is very instructive as to the earliest development of slavery. "Three servants" of Hugh Gwyn, to wit, a Dutchman called Victor, a Scotchman named James Gregory, and John Punch, a negro, having run away from their master, were overtaken in Maryland and brought back to Virginia to stand trial for their misbehavior. The verdict of the court was "that the said three servants shall

---

[51] P. Force, Tracts and Other Papers, no. 14, p. 14. Cited as Force Tracts.

[52] MS. Court Records of Northampton County, 1654–1655, p. 100.

[53] "The General Court so called because it trys the Causes of the whole Country, is held twice a Year by the Governors and Council as Judges at Jamestown; viz: in the Month of April and October" (Hartwell, Blair, and Chilton, The Present State of Virginia, and the College, p. 44).

receive the punishment of whipping and to have thirty stripes apiece." Thus far there was no discrimination in penalty, but the court went on to order that the Dutchman and the Scotchman should "first serve out their times with their master according to their Indentures and one whole year apiece after the time of their service is expired . . . in recompence of his loss sustained by their absence," and that then they should serve the colony for three years. But "the third, being a negro . . . shall serve his said master or his assigns for the time of his natural life."[54] While there is no mention of an indenture or contract in the case of the negro, it must be remembered that not all white servants had formal contracts. If John Punch was not merely a servant with a future right to freedom, his punishment was much less severe than that of his white accomplices. If he was such a servant, his penalty was greater than the penalties inflicted upon the white men. The most reasonable explanation seems to be that the Dutchman and the Scotchman, being white, were given only four additional years to their terms of indenture, while "the third, being a negro," was reduced from his former condition of servitude for a limited time to a condition of slavery for life.[55]

[54] General Court Records, pp. 9, 10. Printed in Virginia Magazine of History, vol. v, p. 236.

[55] A case which came up for trial before the general court at the July session of 1640, three months later than the case above cited, indicates that some negroes were being held as slaves as early as 1640. The record reads: "Six servants and a negro of Mr. Reginald's has plotted to run away unto the Dutch plantation." In addition to the fact that the negro is not here called a servant, the nature of the penalties inflicted indicates that the negro was a slave. The "prime agent" in the plot was a white man named Miller. His punishment was to be thirty stripes, burning of the letter R on the cheek, the wearing of shackles on his leg for one year, and seven years' service to the colony when his term to his master should expire. The punishments ordered for the other five white men were less severe, but none of them escaped with less than two years' additional service. When the court came finally to the negro, he was given a penalty exactly equal to that of the prime agent, except the addition to his time of service. These facts indicate that the negro was a slave "incapable of making satisfaction by addition of time," and that such discriminations as were made because of his race or color were made by inflicting upon him a severer corporal punishment than his white fellow-conspirators received (General Court Records, p. 11. Printed in Virginia Magazine of History, vol. v, p. 236).

Some time before 1644 Thomas Bushrod, assignee of Colonel William Smith, sold a mulatto boy named Manuel "as a slave for-Ever, but in September, 1644, the said servant was by the Assembly adjudged no Slave and but to serve as other Christian servants do and was freed in September, 1665."[56] By "Christian servants" here is meant covenant or indented servants. This case makes possible the statement that although some negroes were being treated as slaves, others retained their right to freedom and were not reduced to a state of slavery, not even by the statutes of 1661 and 1662 recognizing slavery. Another case in point is that of a negro set free in 1665 by order of the general court, "after serving seven years."[57] A similar ruling of this court in the same year was transcribed by Robinson simply as "a judgment of a negro for his freedom."[58]

Even these cases decided in court favorably to individual servants are no better evidence of the continuity of the free negro class than they are of the encroachments which slavery was making upon the freedom rights of negro servants. It was estimated in 1649 that there were in Virginia at that time three hundred Africans.[59] A majority of this number had been imported in the decade immediately preceding this date, and it appears certain that the greater part of the negroes brought in after 1640 were not permitted to realize freedom. Most of them had no indentures or contracts, and the difficulty with which such as had no contracts could have defended any rights that they possessed under the laws and customs may be inferred from the success with which some who had indentures were reduced to perpetual servitude.

[56] Journal of House of Burgesses, October, 1666, in Randolph MS. in Virginia Historical Society, and printed in Virginia Magazine of History, vol. xvii, p. 232.

[57] General Court Records. Printed in Virginia Magazine of History, vol. viii, p. 237.

[58] General Court Records. Printed in Virginia Magazine of History, vol. viii, p. 243.

[59] "There are in Virginia about fifteen thousand English, and of negroes brought thither, three hundred good servants" (A Perfect Description of Virginia, printed for Richard Wodenoth, 1649. Reprinted in Virginia Historical Register, vol. ii, no. ii, p. 62).

A very instructive and interesting case in point is that of John Casor,[60] a negro of Northampton County, who came to Virginia about 1640. Strange to relate, John Casor's master was the negro Anthony Johnson, who, as we have seen, came in before 1622, and who owned a large tract of land on the Eastern Shore. According to the records made of the case, John Casor set up the claim in 1653 "Yt hee came unto Virginia for seaven or eight years of Indenture, yt hee had demanded his freedom of Anth. Johnson his Mayster; & further sd yt hee had kept him his serv[an]t seaven years longer than hee should or ought." Casor appealed to Captain Samuel Goldsmith to see that he was accorded his rights. Goldsmith demanded of Johnson the servant negro's indenture, and was told by Johnson that the latter had never seen any indenture, and "yt hee had ye Negro for his life." Casor stood firmly by his assertion that when he came in he had an indenture, and Messrs. Robert and George Parker confirmed his declaration, saying that "they knewe that ye sd Negro had an Indenture in one Mr. [Sandys] hand, on ye other side of ye Baye & . . . if the sd Anth. Johnson did not let ye negro go free the said negro Jno. Casor would recover most of his Cows from him ye sd Johnson" in compensation for service rendered which was not due. Whereupon Anthony Johnson "was in a great feare," and his "sonne in Law, his wife, & his own two sonnes persuaded the old negro Anth. Johnson to set the sd Jno. Casor free."

The case would be interesting enough and very instructive if it had ended here, but the sequel is more interesting still. Upon more mature deliberation Anthony Johnson determined to make complaint in court[61] "against Mr. Robert Parker that hee detayneth one Jno. Casor a negro the plaintiff's Serv[an]t under pretense yt the sd Jno. Casor is a free-

[60] MS. Court Records of Northampton County, 1651–1654, p. 226; 1655–1658, p. 10. The spelling of the servant negro's name is not quite clear. As it appears in some places in the records it looks as if it might be Fasor.

[61] MS. Court Records of Northampton County, 1651–1654, p. 226; 1655–1658, p. 10.

paid £25 sterling, but from whom he had had only twenty-one years of service. Hence it would seem that £25 was regarded as a price too high for servants except those whose terms were for life.

In the inventory of the estate of William Burdett, recorded in 1643, Nehemia Freenton, aged twenty-two years, having eight years to serve, was rated at a thousand pounds of tobacco, while "Caine the negro boy, very Obedient," was rated at three thousand pounds of tobacco. Edward Southers, "a little Boy having seaven years to serve," was valued at seven hundred pounds of tobacco, while "one negro girle about 8 years old" was put down at two thousand pounds.[69] The inventory of Major Peter Walker's estate, recorded in 1655, shows that two good men servants having four years to serve were worth thirteen hundred pounds of tobacco each, and that a woman servant having two years to serve was worth eight hundred pounds of tobacco. Two negro boys with no term limit specified were rated at forty-one hundred pounds of tobacco each, and a negro girl was rated at fifty-five hundred pounds.[70] The valuation put upon the servants of Thomas Ludlowe of York County in 1660 reveals the fact that a white boy, a "seasoned hand," with six years to serve, was worth less than an old negro man and just half as much as Jugg, a negro woman.[71] The only reasonable explanation of the wide difference in the valuation of white servants having long terms of service and negroes whose terms of service were not specified is that the negroes were servants to whose service no limit was set, that is, slaves.

Thus it appears that before legislation affected in any way the development of slavery the institution had grown up, and without doubt included within its scope a large part of the African immigrants who arrived after 1640. Be it remembered, however, that the legislative recognition and

[69] MS. Court Records of Northampton County, 1640–1645, p. 225.
[70] Ibid., 1654–1655, p. 110.
[71] MS. Court Records of York County, 1657–1662, pp. 275, 278, in Virginia State Library.

man." His complaint was received, and the court, "seriously considering & weighing ye premises," rendered the following verdict, than which there are none stranger on record: "The court . . . doe fynd that ye sd Mr. Robert Parker most unrightly keepeth ye sd Negro John Casor from his r[igh]t Mayster Anthony Johnson & . . . Be it therefore ye Judgment of ye court & ordered that ye sd Jno. Casor negro shall forthwith return into ye service of his sd Mayster Anthony Johnson and that the sd Mr. Robert Parker make payment of all charges in the suite and execution."

This record is quoted at length because in itself it supports a number of important propositions: (1) Before the middle of the seventeenth century some negroes in the colony were servants by indenture under the laws of servitude. (2) Some negro servants who had become freemen owned indented negro servants. The act of 1670 forbidding free negroes to own Christian servants but conceding them the right to own servants of their own race[62] is thus given a concrete explanation. (3) By the middle of the century it was with difficulty that an African immigrant escaped being reduced to slavery. If by the aid of a county court one negro could reduce to slavery another who unfortunately was unable to produce his indenture, this proceeding taking place prior to any statute supporting slavery, it can readily be seen how difficult it had become for negroes to escape being made slaves for life by white masters into whose hands they came.

It is noteworthy that all the records after the middle of the century indicate that slavery was fast becoming the rule. An entry upon the minutes of the general court in 1656 shows that a "Mulatto was held to be a slave and appeal taken."[63] Negro servants were sometimes compelled by threats and browbeating to sign indentures for long terms after they had served out their original terms. In 1675

[62] Hening, vol. ii, p. 280.
[63] General Court Records. Printed in Virginia Magazine of History, vol. viii, p. 163.

complaint was made by Philip Cowen, a negro, that Charles Lucas, "not being willing that he should enjoy his freedom, did with threats and a high hand and by confederacy with some other persons" compel him to set his hand to a writing which Lucas claimed was an indenture for twenty years, and to acknowledge it in the county court of Warwick.[64]

Fifteen years before the passage of the first act in the Virginia slave code, white persons were making assignments of negroes as slaves, and county courts were recording and recognizing the validity of contracts involving the service of negroes for life, and, in the case of female negroes, the service of the female and her offspring. In 1646 Francis Pott, preparing to return to England, sold to Stephen Charlton a negro woman called Marchant and a negro boy called Will, to be "to ye use of him . . . his heyers etc. forever."[65] A contract was made and recorded in Northampton County in 1652 according to the terms of which William Whittington "bargained & sold unto Jno. Pott . . . his heyers, Exors. Adms. or Assigns one negro girle named Jowan, aged about ten years, with her Issue and produce . . . and their services forever."[66]

[64] MS. in Virginia State Archives, at one time on exhibition in a glass case; compare Calendar of Virginia State Papers, vol. i, p. 10. The petitioner says that at the expiration of his term of service he was entitled to "enjoy his freedom & be paid three barrels of corn and a suit of clothes." This illustrates the statement of P. A. Bruce that upon the close of the negro servant's term he was entitled to the same quantity of clothing and corn as the white servant (Economic History of Virginia, vol. ii, p. 53). The practice is clearly stated in a petition made by a servant to the governor and council in 1660: "yor petins lately servid Henry Sprat of ye County of Lower Norff. who refuseth to pay him Corn and Cloths according to custome for wh ye petins obtained order of ye aforesaid Court against ye sd Mr. Sprat & C" (Calendar of Virginia State Papers, vol. i, p. 4. See also Hening, vol. iii, p. 451).

[65] MS. Court Records of Northampton County, 1651–1654, p. 28. Six years later the woman was living with Charlton, although during the six years since her sale by Francis Pott she had run away from her new master to go and live with John Pott, and later left his service to return to Charlton. She apparently exercised some liberty in the choice of her master (MS. Court Records of Northampton County, 1651–1654, p. 81).

[66] MS. Court Records of Northampton County, 1651–1654, p. 124. See also MS. Records of Lower Norfolk County, 1646–1651, p. 23, for the deposition of Cornelius Loyd concerning "a little black negro boy" and his mother. The boy was given as a present to Thomas Silsey. See also Records of Northampton County, 1654–1655, April, 1654, for record of sale "unto Henry Armsteadinger one negro girle named patience to him . . . and his heyers . . . forever with all her increase both male and female."

Some time before 1660 Jane Rookins and Henry Randolph jointly purchased a negro woman called Maria, with the understanding that she and her children should belong to William Rookins and William Randolph and their heirs. William Randolph died, and his father, Henry Randolph, by deed gave to William Rookins all his right and title to the negro woman and her children. A creditor of William Randolph obtained an order against the estate of the deceased, and the Surry County court adjudged one half of the negroes, the negroes being Maria and her children, to belong to the estate of William Randolph.[67]

If further evidence is required to show that some negroes were regarded and held as slaves between 1640 and the date of the statutory sanction of slavery, it may be found in inventories of estates of some persons who held negroes. From the records of various counties it appears that negroes for whose service no limit is mentioned are valued in inventories at £20 to £30 sterling, while white servants of the longest terms of service receive a valuation of not more than £15 sterling.[68] In the journal of the House of Burgesses is recorded a petition of William Whittaker, an ex-member of the House, that he might be reimbursed from the public treasury for a loss incurred by an act of the House which set free a negro for whom the petitioner had

[67] Petitions to the Governor and Council, in Virginia State Archives; also printed in Calendar of Virginia State Papers, vol. i, pp. 2, 3.

[68] MS. Court Records of York County, 1657–1662, p. 195, in Virginia State Library. In 1668 two servants, one having four and a half and the other three years to serve, were valued at £12 each, but a negro woman whose term was not specified was valued at £27 (ibid., 1664–1672, p. 291, in Virginia State Library). In an inventory of the latter part of the century an Indian woman was valued as follows: "1 Indian Woman, if a slave for life £25" (MS. Court Records of Elizabeth City County, 1684–1699, p. 223, in Virginia State Library). Compare P. A. Bruce, Economic History, vol. ii, pp. 51, 52.

sanction so abundantly given to slavery between 1660 and 1670 did not broaden the institution to include all Africans. The first slave laws reduced to a status of slavery no free negroes or negroes who were servants by covenant or contract. On the contrary, these first laws dealing with the status of the Africans in Virginia recognized the free negro as amply as they did the slave. The first one of these acts, passed in 1662, provided that the status of offspring should follow the status of the mother.[72] Far from reducing free negroes to slavery, this act provided for the perpetuation of the free negro population in the provision which, as applied to this class of persons, guaranteed to free colored females the right to extend their free status to their offspring. The act of 1668 dealing with the condition of the colored population related solely to the tax obligations of a free negro woman,[73] and two years later an act guaranteed to "negroes manumitted or otherwise free" the right to own servants of their own race, and expressly denied to them the right to purchase or to own white or "Christian" servants.[74] Here again we see in the first laws which recognized and sanctioned slavery a guaranty of the continuity of the free negro class.

Proof of the persistence of a free negro population, however, is not confined to inference from statutes. The county court and church records continue without a break the record of the free and servant negro through the period when slavery was given the legislative sanction. In December, 1656, Benjamin Doyle, a negro, was granted a patent for three hundred acres of land in Surry County, "due . . . by and for the transportation of six persons into the colony."[75] In addition to the free negro landowners of Accomac County already mentioned, the records specify a few others. In 1651 John Johnson, a negro, received as head rights for the importation of eleven persons a tract of

[72] Hening, vol. ii, p. 170.
[73] Ibid., vol. ii, p. 267.
[74] Ibid., vol. ii, p. 280.
[75] MS. Land Patents, 1655–1664, pp. 71, 72.

five hundred and fifty acres adjoining the tract granted to Richard Johnson.[76] There is also a record of a grant in 1651 of fifty acres to John Johnson, sr.[77] A few years later John Johnson, a negro, entered suit against John Johnson, sr., to recover four hundred and fifty acres of land.[78] Certainly this land owned by free negroes remained, for many years at least, in their possession or in the possession of their descendants.[79] In 1667 Emanuel Cambew, a negro, received a grant of fifty acres in James City County.[80] The next year a deed calling for fifty acres was executed by Robert Jones, a tailor of Queen's Creek, to "John Harris negro his heyers, Executrs, Admtrs, & Assigns forever."[81] Some time after 1676 a lease of two hundred acres for a period of ninety-nine years was issued by John Parker to Philip Morgan, a negro.[82] In one instance at least a negro servant became the overseer of his master's servants. Beverly defines an overseer as "a man who having served his time has acquired Skill and Character of an experienced Planter and is, therefore, intrusted with the Direction of the Servants and Slaves."[83] In 1669 Hannah Warwick, probably a white servant, on trial before the general court, produced in extenuation of her case convincing evidence that her overseer was a negro.[84] In 1673 a judgment was rendered by the general court against Mr. George Light, who had unlawfully detained in servitude beyond his contract term of five years a negro indented servant. It was ordered that

---

[76] MS. Land Patents, 1652-1655, p. 101.

[77] MS. Court Records of Northampton County, 1651-1654, pp. 17, 18.

[78] Ibid., p. 200.

[79] J. C. Wise, Ye Kingdome of Accawmacke, p. 285.

[80] MS. Land Patents, no. 6, p. 39.

[81] MS. Court Records of York County, 1664-1672, p. 327, in Virginia State Library.

[82] MS. Court Records of Accomac County, 1676-1690, p. 185, quoted in P. A. Bruce, Economic History, vol. ii, p. 127 n. See MS. Records of Northampton County, 1683-1689, p. 258, for a judgment against the estate of a mulatto.

[83] Book iv, p. 37; compare P. A. Bruce, Economic History, vol. ii, p. 18.

[84] General Court Records. Printed in Virginia Magazine of History, vol. viii, p. 163.

the negro should "be free from his said master and that the said Mr. Light pay him Corne and Clothes according to the Custome of the Country and four hundred pounds tobac & Caske for his service Done him since he was free and pay costs."[85]

The upper limit of the period in which it was possible for negroes to come to Virginia as servants and to acquire freedom after a limited term is the year 1682. A law of 1670 was intended to enslave all negroes brought in after its enactment, but in practice it permitted a few to escape. In 1678 two men of African blood were sold for terms of seven years by inhabitants of Boston to residents of Virginia.[86] Under the provisions of the law of 1670 "all servants not being christians imported into this colony by shipping" were to be slaves for their lives, but such servants as came by land were to "serve, if boys and girls until thirty years of age, if men or women, twelve years and no longer."[87] After this act had been in force twelve years, the preamble of a new act asserted that "many negroes, Moors, mulattoes and others" born in a heathen country and of heathen parents had, before coming to Virginia, been converted to the Christian faith, and that such persons, when sold in Virginia, had to be sold as servants for a limited term. Hence an act was passed repealing the law of 1670 and making slaves of all persons of non-Christian nationalities thereafter coming into the colony, whether they came by sea or land and whether or not they had been converted to Christianity after capture.[88]

After the enactment of this law the free negro population

---

[85] General Court Records, p. 161.

[86] Bill of Sale: "I, John Indicott, cooper, Inhabitant of Boston in New England, have sold unto Richard Medlicott A Spanish Mulatto, by name Antonio. I having full power to sell him for his life time. But at the request of William Taylor, I doe sell him But for seven years from the day that he shall Disembark in Virginia" (MS. Court Records of Middlesex County, Virginia, March 5, 1677–1678. See also ibid., May 18, 1678. Cited in William and Mary College Quarterly, vol. vi, p. 117).

[87] Hening, vol. ii, p. 283.

[88] Ibid., vol. ii, pp. 490, 491.

in Virginia received from imported negroes no more recruits of which we have any record until after the non-importation act of 1778.[89] By 1662 other means of growth had been opened up to this class. For the next two hundred years the free colored population was increased by five classes of colored persons springing from the population already existing. The classes may be enumerated as follows:—

(1) Children born of free colored parents. The rule of partus sequitur ventrem was applied consistently from 1662 to 1865, and natural increase or procreation was throughout this period an important factor in the growth of the free negro population.

(2) Mulatto children born of free colored mothers.

(3) Mulatto children born of white servant or free women.

The most numerous class of the mulattoes was of slave-women parentage, but such children were slaves. Both classes of free mulattoes were the product of illegitimacy, since the laws prohibited the intermarriage of whites and negroes, bond or free.[90] Under the provisions of the law of 1691 free mulatto bastards were bound by the church wardens as apprentices to responsible white persons for a term ending upon their attaining the age of thirty years.[91] In the revision of this act in 1705 one year was added to the period of apprenticeship.[92] By 1774 this long-term apprenticeship had come to be regarded as bearing "an unreasonable severity toward such children," and it was shortened to twenty-one years for males and eighteen years for females.[93] After the disestablishment of the Anglican

---

[89] The last clause of the act of this date for preventing the further importation of slaves into Virginia declared: "That every slave imported into this commonwealth, contrary to the true intent and meaning of this act, shall upon importation become free" (Hening, vol. ix, p. 471; vol. xii, p. 182). Under the operation of this provision a few negroes occasionally recovered their freedom (5 Call, 425; MS. Petitions, A 2880, A 2882).

[90] Hening, vol. iii, p. 87.

[91] Ibid.

[92] Ibid., vol. iii, p. 453.

[93] Ibid., vol. viii, pp. 134, 135.

church in 1785 this class of persons were bound out by the overseers of the poor as they had been previously by the church wardens.[94]

(4) Children of free negro and Indian mixed parentage. If such children had no visible means of support, they were bound out as apprentices, just as were free mulatto children. The offspring of all colored apprentices born during the apprenticeship became, by the mere force of the law, apprentices to the masters of their mothers on terms similar to those under which the mothers were bound.[95] All colored apprentices were counted with the free colored population even during their apprenticeship.

(5) Manumitted slaves. Manumission was the most important of all the methods by which the free colored population was increased in numbers. In an act of 1670 occurred the words "negroes manumitted and otherwise free." Having considered in this chapter the "otherwise free," the following chapter will be devoted to those who were manumitted.

---

[94] Hening, vol. xii, pp. 27, 28.

[95] Gwinn v. Bugg, Jefferson's Reports, 87 (1769); Howell v. Netherland, Jefferson's Reports, 90 (1770).

CHAPTER III

MANUMISSION

Manumission is the term which may be applied to all the various processes by which negroes in Virginia were taken from a condition of slavery and legally raised to a status of freedom, saving only that act of the nation by which slavery was abolished in all the States and to which is properly applied the term emancipation.[1] There are three general methods by which slaves in Virginia were manumitted or legally set free during the life of the institution of slavery: (1) by an act of the legislature, (2) by last will and testament, and (3) by deed. A still more general classification recognizes only two kinds of manumission—public and private, the first of the three methods above being classed as public manumission and the last two of the three bearing the name of private manumission.

According to strict legal theory and the conception of slavery maintained by the courts in Virginia in the nineteenth century, there were no private manumissions. A so-called private manumission, that is, a manumission by will or deed, was not in fact the act of the slave-owner, but was "the conjoint act of the law and the master."[2] "The question of emancipation," said the Virginia supreme court of appeals in 1830, "is a question of statutory law and can only be resolved by referring to the terms of the statute."[3] In theory, a master who freed a slave exercised a power dele-

[1] Emancipation in Virginia came as a result of the Civil War, and was an accomplished fact at its close in the spring of 1865. Emancipation was formally accepted by the General Assembly in a joint resolution of February 6, 1866 (Acts of the General Assembly of Virginia, 1865–1866, p. 449, cited as Acts; Richmond Whig, August 11, 1865; J. P. McConnell, Negroes and their Treatment in Virginia from 1865 to 1867, p. 11).

[2] Wood v. Humphreys, 12 Grattan, 333 (1855).

[3] Thrift v. Hannah, 2 Leigh, 319.

gated to him by statute. To regulate or determine the status of individuals was a sovereign power. By manumission, individuals who were "in truth *civiliter mortuus*"[4] and who had the character of property rather than of persons were raised to life and personality within the State and accorded civil rights and civil liberty. The power to do this was of such a high and sovereign character that not even the legislature could exercise it except by delegation from the constituent legislative authority. Indeed, a practical application was made of the theory in 1849, when the constitutional convention expressly denied to the General Assembly the power to manumit a slave.[5]

Viewing slavery as a legal status imposed upon persons by the laws, it is not surprising that the colonial legislature, which enacted the first slave laws and freely imposed the slave status upon certain persons, should assume that it had the power to set slaves free. The first use in Virginia of the legislative power to break the bonds of a slave was made in 1710. A negro slave named Will had been "signally serviceable in discovering a conspiracy of divers Negroes for levying war in this colony," and in recognition and reward of this public service an act was passed conferring freedom upon him.[6] However, it was never the policy of the colonial legislature to exercise its power to manumit slaves except for some such special service or merit as that for which the slave Will received his freedom. In 1723 it delegated to the governor and the council the power to pass upon the merit of any claims to freedom based upon meritorious service performed by a slave.[7] But upon an occasion which arose out of circumstances connected with the Revolutionary War the legislature deemed it expedient to resume the exercise of its right to pass a private act of

[4] Peter v. Hargrave, 5 Grattan, 12.

[5] Constitution of Virginia, 1851, sections 19, 20, 21; Journal, Acts, and Proceedings of a General Convention, 1850, appendix, p. 8.

[6] "The said Negro Will is and shall be forever hereafter free from his slavery . . . and shall enjoy and have all the liberties, privileges, and immunities of or to a free negro belonging" (Hening, vol. iii, p. 536).

[7] Hening, vol. iv, p. 132.

manumission. The circumstances were that while Lord Dunmore, the royal governor, who had deserted his office and fled the province, was absent from the seat of government, application was made for permission to manumit the slaves of John Barr, of Northumberland County, who had in his will expressed the desire that they should be free. In the absence of His Excellency the consent of the governor and the council obviously could not be obtained. Fortunately for the petitioners, the Assembly considered that the peculiar circumstances justified a special legislative dispensation. An act was passed confirming Barr's will, but specifying that the act should establish no precedent except in cases exactly similar.[8]

The act did, however, become a precedent in one respect, namely, as to the location of the power to pass upon applications for permission to manumit slaves. The Assembly continued to perform the function, previously exercised by the council, of receiving and passing upon the merit of applications. "Application having been made" in 1779, a special act of the legislature was passed manumitting three slaves,—John Hope, a mulatto named William Beck, and Pegg.[9] Upon similar application made in 1780 the legislature set free Ned, the property of Henry Delony, and Kate, who belonged to Benjamin Bilberry.[10]

As indicative of the policy of the legislature with reference to the use of this power of freeing persons from slavery, as well as in illustration of the form of such acts, we quote from the laws the following specimen of acts of manumission:—

An act for the manumission of a certain Slave.

WHEREAS a negro man slave named Kitt the property of Hinchia Mabry, of the County of Brunswick, hath lately rendered meritorious service in this commonwealth, in making the first information and discovery against several persons concerned in counterfeiting money, whereby so dangerous a confederacy has been in some measure broken, and some of the offenders have been discovered and

[8] Hening, vol. ix, p. 320.
[9] Ibid., vol. x, p. 211.
[10] Ibid., vol. x, p. 372.

brought to trial; and it is judged expedient to manumit him for such service; *Be it therefore enacted by the General Assembly,* That the said Kitt be, and is hereby declared to be emancipated and set free; any law or usage to the contrary notwithstanding.[11]

From the Revolutionary War onward a more extensive and general use was made of this form of manumission than merely to reward acts of public service. The legislature became a sort of court of equity for granting relief to masters who were confronted with legal or other difficulties in freeing their slaves as well as for extending mercy to slaves of a deserving or piteous character.[12] In more than one instance special legislative acts were obtained to give legal validity to wills of manumission recorded before the act of 1782 authorizing this procedure.[13] Hundreds of colored petitioners sought special acts that they might not be deprived of freedom because of mistake or oversight or fraud in the execution of a will or of an expressed intention of a master to set them free.[14] Among the acts of a private nature passed in the period of the Commonwealth down to about 1825 are to be found a large number of acts setting slaves free or granting such as were already liberated a legal right to reside in the State.[15]

The method of manumission by an act of the legislature is not the method the genesis of which requires the more detailed explanation. The colonial House of Burgesses, the sovereign legislative body in Virginia, inferred from its right to make, its right to unmake, a slave. But what was

---

[11] Hening, vol. x, p. 115 (1779). It was further enacted that the treasurer of the Commonwealth "pay to Hinchia Mabry . . . the sum of one thousand pounds [of tobacco] out of the publick treasury, as a full compensation for the said slave." In all cases where the special act of manumission was in reward of a public service, provision was made for compensating the owner of the slave for his loss. Cf. Hening, vol. iii, p. 619; vol. xi, p. 309.

[12] See, for example, an act of 1792 manumitting Rosetta Hailstock and her three children, who had been barred from freedom by a legal technicality (Hening, vol. viii, p. 618). See also ibid., vol. xi, p. 363.

[13] Hening, vol. xii, pp. 611–613; vol. xiii, p. 619.

[14] For example, see MS. Petitions, Henrico County, 1818, A 9290.

[15] Acts of a private character, 1811–1812, p. 131; 1813–1814, p. 153; 1814–1815, p. 151. The private acts of almost any year within the above-named period will afford examples.

the origin of the right of an individual slave-owner to bestow civil rights and civil liberties upon a slave, which in the eyes of the law was a thing? Manumission by a will or a deed cannot be regarded as merely a transfer of the property rights in the slave from the master to the slave, because in the eyes of the law there existed "no right in the slave to acquire property."[16] "Manumission," said Judge Tucker, "is not strictly speaking a gift of property. It is the exoneration of a human being from the bonds which our institutions have fastened upon him."[17]

Now, the first law which could be construed as delegating to or conferring upon slave-owners any right to make free men of their slaves was enacted in 1691,[18] but it appears from the records of the county courts that manumissions had been taking place several decades before this act was passed. In fact, the act itself, which was a rigid restriction upon the right of private manumission, shows that the act did not originate the right. The first wills of manumission in the colony were made and recorded not only prior to the statute of 1691, but also in advance of any statute in regard to slavery. To reconcile these facts with the nineteenth century theory of manumission, Judge Brooks, speaking for the court in Thrift v. Hannah, said, "Although it had been the practice of owners of slaves to emancipate their slaves before the act of 1691, that *practice* gave no perfect right to owners, of their own will to emancipate their slaves."[19]

The origin of that practice has its explanation in the close relations of indented servitude and slavery in the seventeenth century. Before slavery as an institution had fully diverged from indented servitude it borrowed from that system the practice of manumission by individual masters. Under the system of indented servitude the time or term of service for which a servant was bound was, though the

[16] Ruddle's Executors v. Ben, 10 Leigh, 480 (1839).
[17] Parks v. Hewlett, 9 Leigh, 511 (1838).
[18] Hening, vol. iii, p. 87.
[19] 2 Leigh, 319. See also argument of council in Phoebe et al. v. Boggess, 1 Grattan, 129 (1844).

servant himself was not, regarded as property. The unexpired time of a servant could be alienated, like other property, by gift, sale, or bequest.[20] The servant, unlike the slave of the eighteenth and nineteenth centuries, was capable of contracting and of holding property. If the master of a servant chose to sell or make a gift of the servant's unexpired time to the servant himself, the servant was capable of receiving the same and would thereafter owe service to no man. For example, the will of Samuel Thacker, of Essex County, contained this item: "I give unto my servant, John Glary, one year of his time."[21] It has been noted in the chapter on negro servitude that evidence of the discharge of a negro servant was sometimes recorded in a written instrument. Now, in the seventeenth century the processes by which masters set negroes free, whether they were servants for a time or for life, were more like discharges from servitude than manumissions from slavery.

In 1655 Richard Vaughan, of Northampton County, had recorded by the county court the following declaration respecting one of his negroes: "These testify that Mr. Rich Vaughan doe hereby acquitt & discharge one negro Boye known by the name of James from all Claymes or Demands of service for myself, heyers, Exors., Adms. provided the negro do not covenant with any person but shall keepe himselfe free."[22]

Two years later Anne Barnhouse, of York County, executed an instrument of writing which in form was quite similar to the deeds of manumission of the eighteenth and nineteenth centuries. It reads as follows: "Mihill Gowen

[20] As an example of the transfer of the time of servants by bequest, note the following will, of date 1657: "I Francis Jones Widdow of ye county of York Doe freely give unto my Loving Sonne Francis Townshend these servants and cattle . . . Five Servants & one child their names John Reeves, John Keech, Richard Poutry, John Swillinante & one negro woman named sarah and his child Francis two years old" (MS. Court Records of York County, 1657–1662, p. 88. Compare Ballagh, White Servitude, pp. 43, 44).

[21] Essex County Records, 1713, abstracts printed in Virginia Magazine of History, vol. xviii, p. 329.

[22] MS. Court Records of Northampton County, 1655–1658, p. 3.

negro late servant of my brother Xopher Stafford Deced . . . had his Freedome given him by his last will & Testament—1654—after expiration of four years service unto my Uncle Robert Stafford therefore know that I absolutely quitt & discharge the said Mihill Gowen from any service and forever set him free."[23]

In a similar writing of the same date Anne Barnhouse assigned as a gift to Mihill Gowen a child of his, born of a negro woman belonging to Anne Barnhouse during Gowen's four-year term of service. The writing binds Anne Barnhouse "never to trouble or molest the said Mihill Gowen or his said son William or demand any service of Mihill or his son."[24] Even if the negroes discharged by these legal instruments were slaves prior to their discharge, it is perfectly clear that the conception which their owners had of slavery was not such as prevailed at a later time. A slave, in the seventeenth century conception, was merely a person serving for life. If such slave, who was then regarded as a person and not as a thing (as he later came to be), were discharged and given a pledge by his master that no further service would be demanded, he went as a free man, just as did a servant freed at the expiration of a period of contract servitude. In the nineteenth century the gift or assignment of a slave child to its free father, as in the case of the gift by Anne Barnhouse of the child William to its father, would have rendered the child a slave to its father; but in the seventeenth century the result of such a process was the complete freedom of the child.

Not only in such of these early writings as took the form of deeds of manumission, but also in the earliest recorded wills bequeathing freedom we see the analogy between manumission as first practiced and the discharge from servitude of indented servants. As was shown in a former chapter, it was the custom and later the law of indented servitude that the servant, white or colored, receive from his master

[23] MS. Court Records of York County, 1657–1662, p. 45, in Virginia State Library.
[24] Ibid.

at the time of his discharge from servitude a certain amount of property called "freedom dues."[25] Nearly all of the seventeenth century wills of manumission contained grants of property to the liberated negroes. The earliest of which we have any record is that of Richard Vaughan, written in 1645 and recorded in 1656, making bequests of a considerable amount of property to each negro set free.[26] In 1657 Nicholas Martin, of York County, left a will setting free two negroes, and providing that "each of them have . . . one Cow and Three Barrells of Corne Clothes & Nayles to build them a house."[27] Thomas Whitehead of the same county died about 1660, leaving a will which shows that the testator believed that he was merely releasing his negro from further obligations of service or simply shortening a servant's term. The item of the will giving to the negro the right which the testator had had to his service reads: "I sett my negro free . . . he shall be his own man from any person or persons whatsoever."

This negro was considered by his master as having the

---

[25] See above, p. 34 n.

[26] "The last will and testament of Mr. Richard Vaughan planter in Ocohamocke, in Accomacke. . . .

"And for my old Negro woman (after my decease) to remayne with her Dame, till her Dames decease; and then bee free; and to receive twoe Cowes wth calfe (or calves by their side) two suits of clothes, a bedd & a Rugge, a chest & a pott with foure Barrells of Corne & a younge breedinge Sowe; Likewise my Negro girle Temperance (after my decease) to bee possessed of two Cowes and to have their increase male and female; and she to remayne with her Dame . . . to be brought up in the Fear of God & to be taught to read & make her owne clothes, and after her Dames decease [and when] she come to twenty yeares of age . . . to receive two cows with calves (or calves by their side) Two good suits of clothes, a good Bedd & Bowlster & a Rugg & two Blanketts & a pott and one great Brass Kettle with Four Barrells of corne & a younge breeding sowe."

The rest of the negroes, three in number, were provided for in a similar way, and then there was appended the clause "that ye three Negro girls be possessed of the plantacon of Jno Walthome beinge to this plantacon some hundred & forty & four acres of land; and he to build them a Home twenty-five feete in length and twenty feete broad, with one chimney" (MS. Court Records of Northampton County, 1654–1655, pp. 102, 103).

[27] MS. Court Records of York County, 1633–1694, p. 108, in Virginia State Library.

capacity to receive the property rights in the negro's time and also certain of the master's personal effects; for other items of the will provided as follows: "I give my negro man named John all my wearing clothes, my shirts & hatts & shoes and stockings and all that I used to weare. I give unto my negro named John Two Cows One called gentle and the other a black heifer & I give him house & ground to plant upon as much as he shall tend himselfe & peaceably to enjoy it his life time without trouble." A short time after this will was recorded the county court of York decided that the instrument had the effect of making the negro a free man, and that he was legally entitled to come into possession of the property bequeathed to him by his master.[28]

All the instances of manumissions by individual masters above cited occurred before the institution of slavery had reached the legislative phase of its development. The first slavery legislation, in 1662, in no way interrupted the practice of manumission. Whether the frequency of private manumissions in the seventeenth century was a result more of a strong body of sentiment favorable to freedom than of an imperfect, immature development of the system of slavery is a question that may not be answered with certainty. Probably the freedom of some negroes was due to the one and the freedom of others due to the other of these conditions, but the evidence points clearly to the fact that up to 1691 the class of "negroes manumitted" was becoming noticeably larger. The tax obligations of this class formed a subject of legislation in 1670.[29] In 1684 John Farrar, of Henrico County, wrote in his will the following item: "I give unto my negroe Jack his freedom after Christmas day next & in ye meantime he continue on my plantation & use his endeavors with the rest of my hands to make a Cropp."[30] Daniell Parke, of York County, in 1687, "considering the time and ffaithful Service" of one of his ne-

---

[28] MS. Court Records of York County, 1657–1662, p. 217, in Virginia State Library.

[29] Hening, vol. ii, p. 280.

[30] MS. Court Records of Henrico County, 1677–1692, p. 299, in Virginia State Library.

groes, willed that he should be free at the time of the testator's death, and should have an annual allowance of provisions.[31] The will of Nathaniel Bacon, sr., in 1691, bequeathed to "Molatto Kate her freedome, Itt being formerly promised by my deceased wife."[32] The will of John Carter, proved in Lancaster, June 11, 1690, gave freedom to "several negroes."[33]

By the year 1690 the free negro class had become an object of suspicion and fear. The increasing frequency of manumissions created apprehensions as to the consequences of allowing the practice to continue, and restrictive legislation was deemed expedient. The preamble of the restrictive act, which was passed in 1691, declared a law to be necessary to prevent manumissions, because "great inconvenience may happen to this country by setting of negroes and mulattoes free by their either entertaining negro slaves or receiving stolen goods or being grown old bringing a charge upon the country."[34] Under the provisions of this act no negro or mulatto was to be set free unless the person so doing should pay the charges for transporting the manumitted negro beyond the limits of the colony. Thus was devised a scheme which would offer three obstacles to the increase of the free negro class: A charge of transportation would restrain the master; the prospect of banishment would restrain the desire of the slave to be free. Should both of these restraints fail in any case, removal would prevent addition to the free colored class.[35]

---

[31] The will bound the executors to "allow unto the said negro fifteene Bushells of Clean shilled Corne and fifty pounds of dryed beif to be delivered him annually as long as hee shall live. Also one Kersey Coat and Britches, two pair of yarne stockings two white or blew shirts one pair of blew drawers an Axe a Hoe and to pay his leavies" (MS. Court Records of York County, 1687–1691, p. 278, in Virginia State Library).

[32] MS. Court Records of York County, 1690–1694, p. 154, in Virginia State Library.

[33] Virginia Magazine of History, vol. xi, p. 237.

[34] Hening, vol. iii, p. 87.

[35] Under the provisions of this law Richard Trother, of York County, near the close of the century made his will which reads: "I will that old negro Peter and negro Tom have their true and

The conduct of the legislature in 1710 in manumitting by special act a negro slave might appear to be inconsistent with the restrictive policy begun in 1691, unless the legislative purpose in both instances be kept in view. The policy of the colonial legislature, begun in 1710, of rewarding with freedom any acts of special merit in slaves was no indication of the growth of freedom sentiment. Its real intent was a more perfect disciplining of negroes in slavery. Freedom in the case of the negro Will was awarded as an example to discourage in slaves that which most free negroes were suspected of encouraging, namely, insubordination and any disposition to plot mischief. Danger from conspiring and plotting negroes was the common object at which both laws were designed to strike.

Notwithstanding the effort made to prevent servile insurrection, new conspiracies were discovered within the next dozen years, and the fears of the people were again much aroused. "Tumultuous and unlawful meetings," "secret plots and conspiracies carried on among" all classes of negroes, "dangerous combinations," the exchange of advice "to rebel and make insurrection," brought the colonial legislature to declare existing laws "insufficient."[36] The free negroes, suspected and accused upon every occasion of an outbreak, became in this instance the objects of restrictive legislation. By an act passed in 1723 they were forbidden to visit or meet with slaves and to carry or own a firelock.[37] They were deprived of the right to vote at elections and discriminated against in the levying of taxes;[38] but still, despairing of success in restraining the free negro by drastic police measures, the legislature determined to prohibit entirely manumission by individual slave-owners. In 1723 an act was passed which declared that under no pretense

perfect liberty and freedome six days after my wife's decease and 15 pounds sterling money to be paid apiece for their transportation" (MS. Court Records of York County, 1694–1702, p. 194, in Virginia State Library).

[36] Hening, vol. iv, p. 126.

[37] Ibid., vol. iv, p. 131.

[38] Ibid., vol. iv, p. 133.

whatsoever could a master, without the license of the governor and the council, manumit a slave.[39] Moreover, "meritorious service" was made the sole ground upon which permission might be obtained for setting free a slave.[40] If this law prohibiting manumission were violated, it became the duty of the churchwardens of the parish in which the violation occurred to apprehend and sell the negro "by public outcry," and to apply the receipts to the use of the vestry.

From this time till near the end of the colonial period, or, in other words, for nearly half a century, the policy of prohibiting voluntary manumission met with little opposition.[41] The provisions of 1723 were reenacted in 1748 with no alterations that indicate a desire to allow to the free negro class wider liberty or possibility of increase.[42] Under the enforced prohibitions of these laws, manumissions were few and widely separated.[43] The "meritorious service" for which a slave could expect to be rewarded with freedom was something more than faithfulness of service. In 1729 the discovery by a slave of an herb medicine by which wonderful cures could be effected merited favorable action by the governor and the council.[44] Rev. Charles Greene de-

---

[39] Hening, vol. iv, p. 132.

[40] Cf. J. B. Minor, Institutes of Common and Statute Law, vol. i, p. 167.

[41] That "the manumission of slaves was never popular in the colony" was the opinion of a writer so careful of statement as H. B. Grigsby (Collections of the Virginia Historical Society, vol. x, p. 133. Cited as Virginia Historical Collections).

[42] Hening, vol. vi, p. 112.

[43] "The number of manumissions under such restrictions must necessarily have been very few" (St. G. Tucker, A Dissertation on Slavery, ed. 1796, p. 71).

[44] Governor Gooch asserted in a letter to the Board of Trade that he had "met with a negro, a very old man who has performed many wonderful cures of diseases. For the sake of his freedom he has revealed the medicine, a concoction of roots and barks. . . . There is no room to doubt of its being a certain remedy here & of singular use among the negroes—it is well worth the price (£60) of the negro's freedom since it is now known how to cure slaves without mercury" (Sainsbury Transcripts from the British Public Record Office, vol. ix, p. 462).

sired to manumit his slave woman, Sarah, in 1767, but under the laws in force he could not carry out his desire.[45]

Up to 1763, the date of the close of the struggle between the English and the French colonies in America, wars and troubles with the Indians had occupied so much of the attention of the people that there was little opportunity for the growth of an enlightened sentiment favorable to freedom for the negroes, whose labor was proving so valuable in the development of the resources of the colony. Jefferson once wrote that at the time when our controversy with England was still "on paper only, few minds had yet doubted but they [the negroes] were as legitimate subjects of property as their horses or cattle."[46] Andrew Burnaby, travelling in Virginia from 1759 to 1760, asserted that "their [the people's] ignorance of mankind and of learning exposes them to many errors and prejudices, especially in regard to Indians and Negroes, whom they scarcely consider of the human species."[47]

This statement was written at about as late a date as it could have been truthfully made, for the principles of the rights of man and freedom by nature could not effect a revolution against foreign oppression and not ameliorate the hard situation of Virginia's black population. An article in the Virginia Gazette in 1767 began with the following significant words, "Long and serious reflections upon the nature and consequences of slavery," and went on to say that "now, as freedom is unquestionably the birth-right of all mankind, Africans as well as Europeans, to keep the former in a state of slavery is a constant violation of the right and

[45] MS. Petitions, Fairfax County, 1785, A 5460.

[46] To Edward Coles, August 25, 1814, in H. S. Randall, Life of Thomas Jefferson, vol. iii, p. 643. W. Goodell erroneously used this sentence from Jefferson's letter to describe the condition or state of sentiment in Virginia at the time the letter was written (The American Slave Code in Theory and Practice, p. 48). The time of which Jefferson was writing was when he "came into public life" before the war with England. The statement would not have been true had it been made with reference to conditions in 1814.

[47] Travels through the Middle Settlements of North America, p. 54.

therefore justice."[48] Two years later Thomas Jefferson became a member of the legislature, and upon his initiative and with his aid Colonel Bland, one of the oldest, ablest, and most respected members of that body, pressed forward a proposition to remove the restrictions which for forty-six years the laws had imposed upon voluntary manumission. "I seconded his motion," wrote Jefferson, "and as a younger member was more spared in the debate, but he was denounced as an enemy to his country and was treated with the greatest indecorum."[49] Opposition to the measure was as yet overpowering, but the kind of support it received augured well for a later victory. Even a legislature as conservative as this one declared that the discriminatory tax levied upon free negroes and mulattoes since 1668 was "derogatory to the rights of free born subjects," and, therefore, that it stood repealed.[50] A new antislavery spirit which was nation-wide in its operation was powerfully affecting sentiment in Virginia. While that spirit was rising at the North which was to culminate from 1777 to 1785 in acts of emancipation in Vermont, Pennsylvania, Massachusetts, New Hampshire, Connecticut, and Rhode Island, and in a manumission act in Maryland, it was destined to grow and spread in Virginia till it effected the repeal of the old restraints upon manumission, and strongly threatened the existence of the institution of slavery in that State.

The movement in Virginia kept a remarkably even pace with the American Revolution. Since both were applications of the principles of natural equality and individual liberty, they must indeed be viewed as two parts of the same current of progress. "The glorious and ever memorable Revolution," argued many petitioners of the legislature, "can be justified on no other principles, but what do plead with still greater force for the emancipation of our slaves

---

[48] Virginia Gazette, March 19, 1767, quoted in Views of American Slavery, Taken a Century Ago, p. 109.

[49] Jefferson to Edward Coles, August 25, 1814, in Randall, Life of Jefferson, vol. iii, p. 643; G. Tucker, Life of Thomas Jefferson, vol. i, p. 46.

[50] Hening, vol. ii, p. 267; vol. viii, p. 393.

in proportion as the oppression exercised over them exceeds the oppression formerly exercised over the United States by Great Britain."[51]

This logical application of the Revolutionary philosophy, though not quite convincing to the legislature, was freely and conscientiously accepted by many individuals.[52] From the beginning of the war it became quite common among slave-owners to apply the doctrine; for example, John Payne, of Hanover County, in the year of the Declaration of Independence freed his slave because he was "persuaded that liberty is the natural condition of all mankind."[53] Some slave-owners ignored the laws, as did Charles Moorman, a Quaker, of Louisa County, who in 1778 executed a deed of manumission relinquishing his right to thirty-three slaves as if there were no laws forbidding such action.[54] Joseph Mayo, of Henrico County, owner of nearly a hundred slaves, was more desirous that his act be in conformity with the laws, and expressed in his will a "most earnest request that the executors petition the General Assembly for leave to

---

[51] MS. Petitions, Hanover County, 1785; Frederick County, 1786, A 6340.

[52] In 1814 Thomas Jefferson expressed his disappointment that the generation who had received "their early impressions after the flame of liberty had been kindled in every breast, and had become, as it were, the vital spirit of every American" had not gone even to the extent of making possible a general emancipation of slaves (Jefferson to Edward Coles, in Randall, Life of Jefferson, vol. iii, p. 644).

[53] See quotation of the original will in R. A. Brock's prefatory note to "The Fourth Charter of the Royal African Company," in Virginia Historical Collections, vol. vi, p. 18. In 1771 Jonathan Pleasants, a large slave-owner, attempted to provide that his slaves be set free by a will beginning thus: "and first believing that all mankind have an undoubted right to freedom and commiserating the situation of my negroes" (2 Call, 270). William Binford, of Henrico County, set free twelve youthful slaves in 1782 because he was "fully persuaded that freedom is the nat'l right of all mankind" (MS. Deeds of Henrico County, no. 1, p. 421). In 1790 Colonel William Grason manumitted all of his slaves "born after the Declaration of Independence" ("History of the Virginia Federal Convention, of 1788," in Virginia Historical Collections, vol. ix, p. 211). For similar expressions see MS. Deeds of Henrico County, no. 3, p. 378; no. 7, p. 131.

[54] Hening, vol. xii, p. 613.

set free all" his slaves.[55] Some masters made their wills in anticipation of an act permitting manumission. A notable instance was the devise made in 1777 by John Pleasants, a Quaker, whose will, when later held valid by the supreme court of appeals, set free several hundred slaves.[56] The contingency upon which this devise of freedom in futuro was based was that "the laws of the land . . . admit them to be set free without their being transported out of the country."

A still more novel instance of anticipating action by the legislature was the devise by Gloister Hunnicutt, of Sussex County, of six slaves to the Monthly Meeting of the Society of Friends, to be manumitted by such members as the meeting should appoint. In passing upon the validity of this will, recorded two years prior to the act of 1782 permitting manumission, the supreme court said: "He knew the existing laws forbade it and that his society had been anxiously endeavoring to procure an enabling statute for that purpose from the legislature; which was generally believed would shortly be obtained." Counsel, in defending the legality of the will, observed that the testator must have known "that a sentiment existed in the country very favorable to the passage of such a law."[57]

In the forefront of the movement which culminated in the repeal of restrictions upon the right of private manumission were two religious sects—the Quakers and the Methodists. Many Quakers in Virginia had been owners of slaves up to the period of the Revolutionary War, but they were among the first to recognize and admit fully the humanity of the negro and the injustice of depriving him of his right to freedom. Committees of their meetings were appointed "to labor with such Friends as still hold their negroes in bondage, to convince them, if possible, of the

---

[55] Hening, vol. xii, p. 612; MS. Petitions, Henrico County, 1886, A 8990. By special acts of legislation in 1787 both the above-mentioned wills were made effective (Journal of the House of Delegates, 1786, p. 23. Cited as House Journal).

[56] 2 Call, 270; Brock, p. 17.

[57] Charles et al. v. Hunnicutt, 5 Call, 311, 312.

evil of that practice and inconsistency with our Christian profession."[58] The few members who clung to their slaves did so at the price of being disowned by their society.[59] The growing body of Methodists likewise showed themselves the friends of the negro, and many of them, like the Quakers, refused to own or sell slaves. In the Methodist annual conference held at Baltimore in 1780 this question was put to the conference: "Does this Conference acknowledge that slavery is contrary to the laws of God, man, and nature, and hurtful to society; contrary to the dictates of conscience and pure religion, and doing that which we would not others should do to us and ours? Do we pass our disapprobation on all our friends who keep slaves, and advise their freedom?" The answer was, "Yes."[60] Philip Gatch, a slave-owning Methodist of Powhatan County, was one among many of these people who acted according to the advice of their society in a very short time after it was given.[61] The Methodists as well as the Friends exerted an influence upon legislation by memorials to the legislature reiterating their opposition to slavery.[62]

Probably these two societies, the Friends and the Methodists, deserve to rank first in the work of advancing the cause of manumission from genuine altruistic motives. They sought to make manumission lawful because they were willing to take the negro within the scope of the doctrine of equal rights and natural freedom. But the Baptists and Presbyterians were then striving to gain for the whites freedom of religion and freedom of conscience; hence they too were consistent advocates of the measure by

[58] MS. Minutes of Fairfax Monthly Meeting, 1776–1802; MS. Minutes of Warrenton and Fairfax Quarterly Meeting, 1776–1787, passim; S. B. Weeks, Southern Quakers and Slavery, p. 211 et seq.

[59] MS. Minutes of Hopewell Monthly Meeting, 1777–1791, p. 184; MS. Minutes of Fairfax Monthly Meeting, 1777–1791, pp. 42, 65.

[60] W. W. Bennett, Memorials of Methodism in Virginia, p. 131.

[61] Ibid.

[62] Letters and Other Writings of James Madison, vol. iii, p. 124; cited as Madison's Writings. See Weeks on the prominence of Quakers and Methodists among the eighty members of the Virginia Abolition Society in 1791 (Southern Quakers and Slavery, p. 213).

which restraints were to be removed from the will and conscience of a slave-owner who felt moved to set free his slave for conscience' sake. Furthermore, without regard to church affiliations, there was a class of young men who, according to a distinguished French traveller, "were almost all educated in principles of sound philosophy and regarded nothing but justice and humanity."[63] To this younger set of men, who represented the liberal ideas of the English and French thought of that time, and prominent among whom was Thomas Jefferson, is due much of the credit for the support in the legislature of the proposition which was enacted into law in May, 1782, bearing the title, "An act to authorize the manumission of slaves."[64]

To a certain class of those persons who demanded a revision of the laws respecting the negroes the law of 1782 was only a partial victory. The object sought by persons of that class was the freedom of the negro and not the greater freedom of the white master; hence they were now as ready to support a plan of general emancipation as they had been to promote the progress of manumission. In 1785 a petition was presented to the legislature asserting it to be the firm conviction of the petitioners that slavery is contrary to the principles of the Christian religion and an express violation of the principles upon which our government was founded.[65] Several months later seventeen citizens of Frederick County petitioned for the gradual emancipation

---

[63] F. J. Chastellux, Travels in North America in the years 1780–82, vol. ii, pp. 196, 197.

[64] "Be it enacted That it shall hereafter be lawful for any person by his or her last will and testament, or by any other instrument in writing, under his or her hand and seal attested and proved in the county court by two witnesses, or acknowledged by the party in the court of the county where he or she resides, to emancipate and set free his or her slaves, or any of them, who shall thereupon . . . enjoy as full freedom as if they had been particularly named and freed by this act" (Hening, vol. xi, pp. 39, 40).

[65] House Journal, November 8, 1785, p. 27. This petition urged not only emancipation, but also "the strengthening of our government by attaching to its support by ties of interest and gratitude" the freedmen. Apparently, enfranchisement of the freedmen was within its scope.

of slaves, reasoning that "liberty is the birthright of mankind, the right of every rational creature."[66]

These propositions met with very strong protest from those who had opposed the passage of the manumission act and who were already preparing to make a fight for its repeal. Counter petitions and remonstrances were received by the Assembly as soon as were the petitions.[67] In addition to remonstrating against proposed plans of emancipation, the petitioners urged the repeal of the law authorizing manumission.[68]

In the issue thus joined the balance of power was held by the class of persons who had supported the passage of the law of 1782 with the view to removing restraints upon the will of the master for the sake of the master's freedom. Neither the proposition for emancipation nor the project for the repeal of the law authorizing manumission could command their support. Persons of this class were as much opposed to hampering the property rights of the master by denying to him the right to dispose of slaves at will as they were to compelling him to relinquish his title to slaves. The emancipation schemes and the projects to prohibit again the manumission of slaves failed of enactment. Hence, on compromise ground between two extreme views, the act authorizing manumission remained on the statute book, and represented the policy to which the State remained for many years firmly committed.[69]

---

[66] MS. Petitions, Frederick County, 1786, A 6340. Madison, in a letter to Jefferson of January 22, 1786, says that "several petitions (from Methodists, chiefly) appeared in favor of a gradual abolition of slavery" (Madison's Writings, vol. i, p. 217).

[67] MS. Petitions, Brunswick County, 1785, A 2901; House Journal, 1785, p. 30; Madison to Washington, November 11, 1785, in Madison's Writings, vol. i, p. 200.

[68] Petitions of this kind were received by the legislature from the counties of Brunswick, Amelia, Mecklenburg, Halifax, and Pittsylvania (House Journal, 1785, p. 91; MS. Petitions, A 2901). A petition from Hanover County, signed by one hundred and forty-four citizens, and one from Henrico, signed by one hundred and twenty citizens, praying for the repeal of the act of 1782, were sent to the legislature in 1784 (MS. Petitions, Hanover County, A 8124; Henrico County, A 8971).

[69] House Journal, 1785, p. 91. The vote against repeal was 53 to 35.

The removal in 1782 of restraints upon manumission was like the sudden destruction of a dam before the increasing impetus of a swollen stream. The free negro population in the State at that time—probably less than 3000, but the product of a century and a quarter's growth—was more than doubled in the space of two years. Instances of manumission, often of large numbers of slaves, became frequent.[70] In eight years after the act became effective the number of free colored persons rose from less than 3000 to 12,866.[71] By 1800 the number had increased to 20,000; and according to the census of 1810 it was over 30,000.

The principles of natural rights and the consent of the governed had only a year before the passage of the enabling act received a triumph in the victory of the American and French armies at Yorktown, and many a slave-master now seized the opportunity to follow those principles to their logical conclusion by manumitting every slave in his possession, whether one or one hundred. In 1782 William Binford and Robert Pleasants, of Henrico County, manumitted respectively twelve and ninety slaves. Most of them were of an age to be very valuable, but young and old were set free because of a "conviction and persuasion that freedom is a natural right."[72] Joseph Hill, of Isle of Wight County, gave expression to his views in his will of March 6, 1783, as follows: "I . . . after full and deliberate consideration, and agreeable to our Bill of Rights, am fully persuaded that freedom is the natural life of all mankind . . .

---

[70] Cf. Brock, p. 19.

[71] In 1835 William Jay wrote as follows: "In 1782, Virginia repealed her restraining law and in nine years 10,000 slaves were manumitted" (Slavery in America, p. 101). In 1796 St. George Tucker called attention to the fact that "there are *more* free negroes and mulattoes in Virginia alone than are to be found in the four New England states and Vermont in addition to them. The progress of emancipation in this state is, therefore, much greater than our *Eastern* brethren may at first suppose. There are only 1087 free negroes and mulattoes in the states of New York, New Jersey, and Pennsylvania more than in Virginia" (A Dissertation on Slavery, p. 72 n.).

[72] MS. Deeds of Henrico County, no. 1, p. 42.

do hereby emancipate and set free all and every of the above-named slaves."[73]

Every negro who fought or served as a free man in the late war was given in 1783 a legislative pledge of the utmost protection of the State in the enjoyment of the freedom he had helped to gain;[74] and a slave who could prove any honorable service rendered by him to the American cause was freed by special act and at the expense of the State.[75] Aberdeen, a slave who had helped forward the cause of liberty "by his long and meritorious service in the lead mines,"[76] and "Caesar, who entered very early into the service of his country and continued to pilot the armed vessels of the state during the late War,"[77] were set free at public expense. Slave-owning Quakers who were reluctant to manumit their slaves were urged by their society to extinguish their titles in human chattels.[78] The labor supply being abundant from 1782 to the end of the century, mercenary masters were

[73] MS. Deeds of Isle of Wight County, no. 15, p. 122. Quoted from B. B. Munford, Virginia's Attitude toward Slavery and Secession, p. 105. In 1797 Richard Randolph, jr., of Prince Edward County, manumitted his slaves "in whom my countrymen by their iniquitous laws in contradiction of their own Declaration of Rights have vested me with absolute property" (MS. Wills of Prince Edward County, 1797; H. A. Garland, The Life of John Randolph, of Roanoke, vol. i, p. 67).

[74] Hening, vol. xi, p. 308; St. G. Tucker, A Dissertation on Slavery, p. 20. Compare below, pp. 110, 111, 111 n.

[75] William Boush and Jack Knight, and Saul, "who avoided the rocks upon which so many negroes wrecked when the trumpet call pronounced his freedom if he would turn upon his master," were all set at liberty by the State because of their services in the cause of liberty (Hening, vol. xiii, pp. 103, 619). The slave James, a spy or secret agent of Marquis Lafayette in his Virginia campaign, received favorable consideration by the Assembly (MS. Petitions, New Kent County, 1786, B 4051).

[76] Hening, vol. xi, p. 309 (1783).

[77] Ibid., vol. xiii, p. 102 (1789).

[78] In 1788 it was inserted in the Friends' Discipline "that none amongst us be concerned in importing, buying, selling, holding, or overseeing slaves, and that all bear a faithful testimony against the practice." In 1785 the following query was put before the delegates to the Upper Quarterly Meeting: "Do any Friends hold slaves and do all bear a faithful testimony against the practice?" In 1796 it was reported at a meeting that there was no longer complaint of Friends' holding slaves when they could be lawfully liberated (Weeks, Southern Quakers and Slavery, pp. 212, 214).

often easily induced by the slaves themselves, or by a philanthropic person in behalf of the slaves, to grant deeds of manumission in consideration of a money payment. This period from 1782 to 1806 was the time when manumission was most popular in Virginia, and is unique in the history of slavery in the State as being the only period when manumission went on at a rapid rate without legal restraint.

Public opinion, however, was by no means unanimous as to the wisdom of manumission or as to the expediency of permitting the practice to go on without some legal restriction. Very soon after the act of 1782 took effect, lessons learned from experience with a free negro element began to cast a tremendous weight in the balances on the side of the reactionaries, who lost no opportunity to point out the evil results of manumission.[79] Almost a hundred years previously, manumission was for the first time restricted by law, because free negroes were unproductive and because they incited slaves to steal and to rebel.[80] Throughout the long period which intervened between that experience and the close of the Revolutionary War the free negro was almost a negligible social factor, and afforded little reminder of the real character of a large and growing free negro element in a population constituted as was that of Virginia. With the old restraints upon manumission removed, two years trial of the freedmen was sufficient to convince many persons that "free negroes are agents, factors and carriers to the neighboring towns for slaves, of property by them stolen from their masters and others."[81] Three years later the opponents of manumission declared it to be "a very

[79] MS. Petitions, 1784, A 8124; A 8971; A 2901. A petition from Accomac County, in June, 1782, signed by forty-five persons, assigned four reasons why the slaves of persons who had made their wills before 1782 should not be set free: (1) Manumitted slaves had helped unmanumitted slaves to join the British; (2) It would depreciate the value of slave property and thus lessen revenue; (3) Manumission should be preserved solely as a means of rewarding slaves for good conduct; (4) Free negroes easily become charges upon the public (MS. Petitions, Accomac County, 1785, A 11).

[80] See above, p. 51.

[81] MS. Petitions, Hanover County, 1784, A 8124; Henrico County, 1784, A 8971.

great and growing evil," and, failing to get a prohibitive measure passed, they proposed the plan of compelling every negro to leave the State within twelve months after the date of his manumission.[82] The plan was not adopted, but free negroes were forbidden by an act of 1793 to come into the State.[83]

Much difficulty was soon experienced in discriminating between slaves fraudulently passing as free negroes and negroes actually free. The right of free negroes to go and come and to pass to and fro in a community without hindrance or question proved to be a cloak behind which runaway slaves escaped detection.[84] An attempt to regulate the evil by strict registration requirements only augmented it;[85] free negroes treated their registers or "free papers" as if they were transferable, and escaping slaves used them to conceal their identity.[86] Enterprising slaves even forged such papers, or secured them from white persons who made a practice of forging freedom certificates and supplying slaves with the means of escape.[87]

All these things had been operating to effect a change in sentiment adverse to manumission when an attempted insurrection of slaves in Richmond, led by a slave named

---

[82] K. M. Rowland, The Life of George Mason, vol. ii, p. 201. For failure to leave they were to be sold at public auction. The proposition followed closely the law passed in 1691. Unlike that law, however, it contained no provision for requiring the master to pay the expenses of transporting the manumitted slave.

[83] Hening, vol. xiv, p. 239. Any citizen might arrest a violator of this law and take him before a justice, who was empowered "to remove every such free negro or mulatto . . . into that state or island from whence it shall appear he or she last came."

[84] Virginia Gazette and the American Advertizer, July 5, 1783. "Reward: Ran away from the subscriber a mulatto man slave named Jack a crafty fellow . . . he has a forged pass to pass for a free man" (ibid., October 16, 1784).

[85] Hening, vol. xiv, p. 238.

[86] Ibid., vol. xv, p. 78.

[87] Ibid., vol. xiv, p. 365. Any person "aiding or abetting in forgery of writings whereby a slave or servant of another may go free" was liable to a penalty of two hundred dollars and one year's imprisonment. Ishmael Lawrence was indicted, found guilty, and fined only ten dollars by a Henrico County court in 1795 for "forging uttering and distributing freedom papers or Deeds of emancipation to runaway slaves" (MS. Orders, no. 6, p. 514).

Gabriel, set the white people of the State to thinking on the dangers from a partial subjection of a servile race.[88] While the evidence showed but little direct or criminal connection of free negroes with the plot,[89] it revealed the fact that barbacues, fish-feasts, and "preachings," at which the free negro was known to be a prominent figure, had furnished the occasion for arranging the plot. This fact and testimony that Methodists, Quakers, and Frenchmen, all of whom had been favorable to manumission, were to be spared by the insurgents[90] were convincing that the mere presence in a community of a manumitted negro was a source of danger.

On December 31, 1800, the year of the Gabriel insurrection, the legislature, behind closed doors, passed the following resolution: "That the Governor be requested to correspond with the president of the United States on the subject of purchasing lands without the limits of the United States whither persons obnoxious to the laws or dangerous to the peace of society may be removed."[91]

The obnoxious and dangerous persons described here were not criminals or seditious aliens, as might be supposed, but "free negroes and mulattoes including those who may hereafter be emancipated."[92] At the time this resolution was passed there were upwards of twenty thousand persons in Virginia included within its scope; hence persons who viewed the growth of the free negro population with alarm

[88] This attempt to massacre the white inhabitants of Richmond was called the Gabriel Insurrection. See The Richmond Recorder, April 6, 9, 1803; R. R. Howison, A History of Virginia, vol. ii, pp. 390, 391.

[89] "A man named Samuel Bird, a free mulatto of Hanover town was arrested on suspicion of being concerned in the conspiracy of the negroes; he . . . was finally discharged for want of evidence, it being decided that people of his own color, in slavery, could not give testimony against him. His son, a slave, was condemned and executed yesterday" (Writings of James Monroe, ed. by Hamilton, vol. iii, p. 215).

[90] Richmond Recorder, April 9, 1803.

[91] Documents of the House of Delegates, no. 10, 1847–1848, cited as House Documents; A. Alexander, A History of Colonization on the Western Coast of Africa, p. 63.

[92] Writings of Monroe, vol. iii, p. 20.

began to realize that restrictions upon the manumission of slaves could not now afford complete relief from the menace of the free negro. The resolution of the legislature was the starting-point of the colonization movement in Virginia and, in fact, in the United States. Governor Monroe, acting upon the request made of him by the resolution, promptly communicated with President Jefferson, and in a lengthy correspondence which followed, opinions were given and received of the comparative value of the southwestern frontier, the West Indies, and Africa as a place for a colony of these persons who were obnoxious to the laws and the peace.[93]

While colonization ideas were being born, new and unusually stringent measures for keeping watch over and controlling the actions of free negroes were enacted. They were forbidden to move from one county or town to another on penalty of being arrested and imprisoned as vagrants.[94] The laws concerning the migration of free negroes into the Commonwealth were declared defective and in need of revision, and more exacting registration requirements were enacted.[95] The laws of evidence were changed so that a slave was a good witness in pleas of the Commonwealth against a free negro.[96] A strong public guard to be stationed at Richmond was considered by the Assembly to be expedient for the public safety "in the present crisis of affairs."[97]

The prospect of removing the free negroes was, however, not yet deemed so promising as to cause persons to lose sight of the necessity of reducing the enormous rate of increase in the free negro population by closing the avenue of escape from slavery to freedom. In the legislative session of 1804–1805 the state of public opinion upon the sub-

[93] Writings of Monroe, vol. iii, pp. 201–217, 292; The Writings of Thomas Jefferson, ed. by Ford, vol. iv, pp. 419–422; House Documents, no. 10, 1847–1848.

[94] Hening, vol. xv, p. 301 (1801).

[95] Ibid., vol. xv, p. 301.

[96] Ibid., vol. xv, p. 300.

[97] Ibid., vol. xv, pp. 295, 296; Howison, vol. ii, pp. 388–393; House Journal, 1800–1809, pp. 47, 48.

ject of manumission was reflected in a vigorous debate on the floor of the House on the merits of a proposition to abolish the right of private manumission altogether.[98] The speakers who favored a restriction of the privilege seemed to recognize the difficult task before them of overcoming a strong presumption against legislative interference with an individual right enjoyed since the close of the Revolution. "It is not the natural rights of individuals," they asserted, "to dispose of his own property in every case. . . . It is a moral maxim that no man can appropriate his property to any purposes which may injure the interest of others. . . . Whoever emancipates a slave may be inflicting the deadliest injury upon his neighbor. He may be furnishing some active chieftain of a formidable conspiracy." Vivid illustration of and support for the argument were freely taken from the recent insurrections in Santo Domingo as well as from those in the State.[99] An additional "power of combining," it was said, was placed in the hands of slaves by giving to them the "right of locomotion." "What should we say of a man who having his mortal foe bound at his feet sets him at liberty and plants a stiletto in his hand?"

A second ground of attack was occupied by matching against the property-rights defense of manumission an argument for economizing revenue by checking a reckless destruction of property in slaves. The members of the House were asked to consider the loss to the State in revenue incurred by the manumission of twenty thousand slaves since 1782. A third argument was in refutation of the strongly entrenched opinion that the proposed measure would violate "the rights of conscience." "What respect is due," asked Smyth, of Wythe County, "to the conscience of that man who, after having made all the use he could of his slaves does not hesitate to deprive his wife and children of their labor?"

---

[98] Richmond Enquirer, January 15, 1805.

[99] A speaker in debate before the House read portions of the history of the insurrection of Santo Domingo (Richmond Enquirer, January 15, 1805).

With equal skill the defenders of the privilege of manumission matched arguments with the opposition. They affirmed that the loss in revenue incurred by manumission was smaller than would be the loss of a single day occupied by the legislature in considering the mass of petitions which would pour in upon that body, as they poured in upon the legislatures before the act of 1782, should the restrictive measure carry. They emphasized also the fact that there was "a vast number of people who labor under scruples of conscience and think it wrong to keep their fellow creatures in slavery. . . . These men consider their religion as the law of God; and if we pass this bill we shall place them between two contrary and conflicting laws."

Moreover, the proposed measure, they said, would not only be unwise policy, but would also be in violation of the constitution. "The first clause says that all men are by nature equal and independent. Already we have violated this declaration, but the present measure will do so still more; for . . . the last clause declares that conscience ought to be free."

Finally, what better safeguard against insurrection could there be than the power in the hands of every slave-master to reward with freedom his faithful and loyal slaves? "What reward is more seductive than the acquisition of freedom? . . . Suppose a servant knows that some harm is to happen to his master, can he have a stronger incitement to inform him of it and put him upon his guard than the prospect of emancipation?"[100]

When the vote which determined the fate of the bill was taken, it stood 77 against and 70 in favor of its becoming law. The editor of the Enquirer avowed his disappointment that the measure, "in spite of the imperious policy which dictated its adoption was rejected," and expressed a hope "that some future Legislature will have the prudence to administer the suitable remedy."[101]

---

[100] Richmond Enquirer, January 15, 1805.
[101] Ibid.

In the next annual session of the legislature there were not lacking those who shared the views of the editor on the matter of reopening the question in another effort to administer a remedy. Fears were expressed by some members that free and open discussion was dangerous, but in spite of these warnings a bill for taking from masters the right to free slaves was introduced and debated with much zest.[102] The events connected with the Gabriel attempt at insurrection were again recalled and associated with the idle and vicious habits of free negroes. A friend of the bill declared that "these blacks who are free obtain a knowledge of facts by passing from place to place in society; they can thus organize insurrection. . . . It may be proven that it is the free blacks who instil into the slaves ideas hostile to our peace."[103] Principles of policy and considerations of safety were no longer to be brushed aside by arguments based upon the rights of man.[104]

When the division came, the bill was lost by a vote of 75 to 73.[105] But the full strength of the party in favor of restricting manumission was not shown in this vote, which was a test only upon the question of abolishing the right altogether. There was apparent agreement that drastic police measures were necessary, and but very little objection to placing free negroes under any surveillance and restriction that seemed to be necessary for the safety of society; but a majority was held intact against abolishing the right of manumission only because it believed that the measure infringed the rights of private property and "that the conscience of a dying man ought not to be deprived of the momentary comfort emancipation of his slaves would produce."[106] The objectionable features could, however, be avoided by approaching the question from its other side,

---

[102] Virginia Argus, January 17, 1806.

[103] Ibid.

[104] A speaker affirmed that he was not less friendly to "the rights of man" than others who opposed the bill, but that he advocated it from policy (Virginia Argus, January 17, 1806).

[105] House Journal, 1805–1806, pp. 68, 77.

[106] Virginia Argus, January 17, 1806.

that is, by leaving unrestrained the will of the master and restraining the will of the slave with an imposition of such conditions upon freedmen as would make liberty undesirable. Such a plan had been adopted in 1691, and had been proposed in 1787. The device met with the approval of this Assembly, and an act was passed by which all slaves manumitted after May 1, 1806, were required to leave the State within twelve months from the time their freedom accrued, or, if under age, from the time they reached their majority.[107]

In 1784 a vote taken in the House of Delegates showed that only one third of the members of that House were then in favor of the absolute prohibition of the manumission of slaves. By 1806 this minority had made such gains that an accession of only two votes would have transformed it into a majority. It is a significant fact that when the opponents of the policy of permitting private manumissions seemed so near to victory, almost all concerted efforts to repeal the law of 1782 came to an end. The law of 1806 was the last important change in the policy of the State respecting the slave-owner's right to free a slave. The absence after 1806 of a strong demand to curb the power of a master to convert his slave into a free negro was due chiefly to two causes.

In the first place, the act of 1806 prescribing banishment for any slave thereafter set free was regarded as an indirect restriction upon the will of the master; hence it afforded to those who had been urging the repeal of the act of 1782 a measure of satisfaction. It promised to bring about the results which the opponents of manumission desired without

[107] The act, being a restriction in disguise upon manumission, was included as section 10 in an act concerning slaves. It declared that "if any slave hereafter emancipated shall remain within this Commonwealth more than twelve months after his or her right to freedom shall have accrued he or she shall forfeit all such right and may be apprehended and sold by the overseers of the poor for any county or corporation in which he or she shall be found for the benefit of the poor of such county or corporation" (Hening, vol. xvi, p. 252). Section 10 was a Senate amendment to the act concerning slaves, and was agreed to by the House by a vote of 94 to 65 (House Journal, 1805–1806, p. 77).

a direct interference with jealously guarded property rights and without hindrance to freedom of conscience.[108]

In the second place, the act of 1806 represented a new idea—that of removing free negroes from the State. As the free negro population increased, a prohibition upon manumission was seen to be of diminishing importance as a means of coping with the problem. From 1782 to 1806 strenuous efforts were made to limit the power of masters to recruit the free negro population from the slave class. After 1806 the strength of the opposition to the growth of the free colored class was directed mainly to removing or colonizing that class of the population. The question of colonization, as we have seen, assumed an aspect of importance as a consequence of a resolution of the state legislature in 1800. The act of 1806 was the first actual law of a long succession of laws enacted with a view to realizing the ideas set forth in the House resolutions of the first years of the century.

A fundamental defect in the law of 1806 was its failure to provide any definite place to which the freed slaves might go. As an immediate consequence of spasmodic attempts to enforce the law and of fears on the part of manumitted slaves that the law would be enforced against them, a noticeable egress of negroes took place from Virginia to the Northern States and to the States bordering on Virginia on all sides. Citizens of Maryland soon began to make loud complaint to their legislature. "Virginia," they said, "has passed a law [expelling certain free negroes] and many of her beggarly blacks have been vomited upon us."[109] Within

---

[108] "That Government would be justly chargeable with the extreme of despotism that should attempt, without necessity, to interfere with the kind and generous feelings of the human heart," asserted a committee of the House of Delegates in its report in 1829 favorable to the expediency of continuing the policy of removing free negroes and of permitting masters to manumit slaves (African Repository and Colonial Journal, vol. iii, p. 54. Cited as African Repository).

[109] MS. Petitions to House of Delegates, in Maryland Historical Society, portfolio 7, no. 28; J. R. Brackett, The Negro in Maryland, pp. 176, 177.

a year after the Virginia act was passed the legislatures of three different States—Maryland,[110] Kentucky,[111] and Delaware[112]—had passed countervailing acts forbidding free negroes to come in from other States to take up permanent residence. Other States followed the lead of the three already named, and passed laws excluding free negroes or imposing upon their admission such rigid requirements as to render their coming impracticable. Ohio,[113] Indiana,[114] Illinois,[115] Missouri,[116] North Carolina,[117] and Tennessee[118] had passed some such law within twenty-five years after the Virginia act of 1806. The people of Mercer County, Ohio, refused to allow John Randolph's three hundred and eighty-five negroes, who left Virginia in compliance with the laws, to remain even for three days upon land purchased for them in that county, although these negroes could comply with Ohio's law requiring of emigrant free negroes bond for good behavior.[119] In no State was a cordial welcome held out to Virginia's expatriated negroes. A refugee slave was far more likely to meet with hospitality in the Northern States than was a free negro.[120]

When that portion of the population of Virginia which viewed the residence of the free blacks among them as "an intolerable burden"[121] saw that the removal laws were being

[110] Laws of Maryland, 1806, ch. 56; 1823, ch. 161; Brackett, p. 176.

[111] Acts of Kentucky Legislature, 1807–1808, sec. 3; J. C. Hurd, The Law of Freedom and Bondage in the United States, vol. ii, pp. 15, 18; MS. Petitions, Cumberland County, 1815, A 4728.

[112] 4 Delaware Laws, 108; Hurd, vol. ii, p. 77.

[113] Ohio Sessions Laws, ch. 8; Hurd, vol. ii, p. 117.

[114] Hurd, vol. ii, p. 130.

[115] Ibid., vol. ii, p. 135.

[116] Ibid., vol. ii, p. 170.

[117] Revised Code of North Carolina, 107, sec. 54–58, 75–77; J. S. Bassett, Slavery in the State of North Carolina, in J. H. U. Studies, ser. xvii, nos. 7–8.

[118] Hurd, vol. ii, p. 92. See also The Richmond Enquirer, February 19, 1832, speech of Mr. Goode.

[119] The Liberator, August 7, 21, 1846.

[120] "If there is one fact established by steadily accumulating evidence it is that the free negro cannot find a congenial home in the United States. He is an exotic among us" (quoted in De Bow's Commercial Review, vol. xxvii, p. 731, from Philadelphia North American).

[121] MS. Petitions, Prince William County, 1838.

"frustrated by the action of sister states"[122] as well as by the inactivity of local officials in enforcing the banishment provisions, efforts were made to seek a place beyond the United States where free negroes could be colonized. On December 14, 1816, a resolution was adopted in the House of Delegates which strongly urged the importance of colonization, and requested the governor to "correspond with the President of the United States for the purpose of obtaining a territory upon the shores of the North Pacific, or some other place not within any of the States or territorial governments of the United States to serve as an asylum for such persons of color as are now free and may desire the same and for those who may be hereafter emancipated within this Commonwealth."[123] Within a short while after the adoption of this resolution there was organized in Washington the American Colonization Society, and throughout the counties and cities of Eastern Virginia auxiliary organizations sprang up.[124] A state colonization society had headquarters at Richmond in 1831, and had various branches throughout the State.[125] The two most important duties of these societies and their agents were to procure, first, funds for the transportation of free negroes[126] to Africa, and, secondly, free negroes who were willing to be transported there.[127]

From 1820 to 1860 these societies were very active in propagating the colonization ideas. In 1833 they procured from the legislature an annual appropriation of eighteen

---

[122] MS. Petitions, Dinwiddie County, 1838, A 5090.

[123] House Journal, 1816–1817, p. 90.

[124] Address of the Rockbridge Colonization Society, in African Repository, vol. iii, p. 274; Report of Managers of the Lynchburg Auxiliary Colonization Society, in ibid., vol. iii, p. 202; Memorial of the Richmond and Manchester Auxiliary Colonization Society, in MS. Petitions, Henrico County, 1825, A 9358.

[125] Petition of the Colonization Society of Virginia, in MS. Petitions, Henrico County, 1831, A 9431.

[126] African Repository, vol. iii, pp. 280, 281.

[127] "Difficulty has been apprehended in obtaining a sufficient number of emigrants. . . . Many of the free people are either ignorant of the scheme or prejudiced against it. They are suspicious of white men" (Address of Rockbridge Colonization Society, in African Repository, vol. iii, p. 279).

thousand dollars for five years to be used in colonizing free negroes in Africa. From this time on for a quarter of a century the state legislature was committed to the plan of colonization as a solution of the free negro problem; and although that plan resulted in repeated failure, it was sufficiently promising to absorb the greater part of the interest of nearly all who wished to check the growth of the free colored class.[128] Between 1836 and 1856, propositions for limiting the power of masters to manumit their slaves were pressed forward with some energy, but were uniformly defeated.[129] The constitutional convention of 1850 evaded the question of limiting manumission by granting to the legislature the power to " impose such restrictions and conditions it shall deem proper upon the power of slave-owners to emancipate their slaves," a power which the legislature had always been understood to have.[130] The law of 1806 was reenacted at various times after its first enactment, with such changes as were deemed necessary to improve its effectiveness, and in 1850 it was embodied in the new constitution and remained a part of the constitutional law of the State till the overthrow of the slavery regime.

The adoption in 1806 of a new policy respecting manu-

[128] Acts, 1832–1833, p. 14. Large appropriations ($30,000) were made by the legislature in 1850 and 1853 for the purpose of colonizing the free colored population (ibid., 1849–1850, p. 7; 1852–1853, p. 58). But so few were the numbers of Virginia negroes actually colonized in comparison with the entire free negro population of the State that Virginia colonization may be said to have been an absolute failure. During the three years in which the law of 1850 was in operation only 419 free blacks and slaves were sent from Virginia to Africa, and of the $90,000 available for colonization purposes only $5410 was used. Prior to 1854 only 2800 colored persons in all had been sent from Virginia to Africa. After 1853 the annual appropriation of $30,000 was never consumed upon the transportation of emigrants. For the fiscal year ending October 1, 1858, only $2100 was expended by the colonization board and only 42 negroes were sent out (Message of Governor Johnson, in House Journal, 1853–1854, p. 15; House Documents, 1859–1860, no. 5, p. 407).

[129] House Journal, 1839, p. 247; 1842–1843, p. 28; 1852–1853, p. 83; 1855–1856, pp. 112, 436; 1857–1858, p. 262; Journals of the Senate of the Commonwealth of Virginia, 1857–1858, p. 668, cited as Senate Journal.

[130] Journal, Acts and Proceedings of the Convention of 1850, p. 327; Constitution of 1850, sec. 3 on Slaves and Free Negroes.

mitted slaves should be considered as the point of division between two stages in the progress of manumission in Virginia. The actual operation of the law was, however, only one of several causes of the decline which occurred about that time in the frequency of manumissions. First among the causes which resulted in a decreased disintegration of slavery early in the century was the growth of an anti-free-negro sentiment which acted as powerfully to determine the action of individual slave-owners as it did to determine legislation. Not a few of these persons were becoming converted to the opinion expressed in the editorial columns of the Richmond Recorder that "there never was a madder method of sinking property, a method more hostile to the safety of society than the freak of emancipating negroes."[131] Even from the point of view of the slave's welfare, honest reflection upon the hard conditions—economic, social, and legal—of free negroes, whether they remained in the State or attempted to emigrate, caused masters of benevolent intentions to hesitate long before surrendering a slave to his own care. The feeling of this class of slave-owners was well expressed by Thomas Jefferson in 1814: "Men of this color are by their habits, rendered as incapable as children of taking care of themselves and are promptly extinguished whenever industry is necessary for raising the young. In the meantime they are pests in society by their idleness and the depredations to which this leads them."[132]

In the second place, among the causes of the decline in the frequency of manumissions must be reckoned the restraining effect of the law annexing banishment as an attendant condition. "This law," wrote the Powhatan Colonization Society, "has restrained many masters from giving freedom to their slaves and has thereby contributed

[131] Richmond Recorder, November 10, 1802. This issue contains a lengthy and animated discussion of the vicious character of the free negro and the dangers of manumission.

[132] Randall, Life of Jefferson, vol. iii, p. 644. Compare also John Burk's statement in 1804 that "the first loss to be sustained by an emancipation is not the greater bar to this desirable end" (The History of Virginia, vol. i, p. 212 n.).

to check the growth of an evil already too great and formidable."[133] Richard Hildreth, writing in 1856, asserts that under the act of 1782 manumissions were very numerous, "and but for the subsequent re-enactment [in 1806] of restrictions upon it, the free colored population of Virginia might now exceed the slaves."[134] A petition to the legislature from the Richmond Colonization Society attributed entirely to this law the decline of four thousand in the decennial increase in the free negro population from the first to the second decade of the century.[135]

The Virginia slaves felt keenly their dependence upon those by whom they were reared and for whom they labored. Many of them preferred to continue as slaves in their master's household rather than incur the risk of being sent homeless into a strange land. Lucinda, a negro woman manumitted about 1812 by the last will of Mary Mathews, refused to be moved to Tennessee with other negroes set free by the same will, deliberately remaining in the State long enough to forfeit her freedom and petitioning the legislature to vest the title to her in William H. Hose.[136] Sam, a negro petitioner, declared to the legislature in 1808 that he preferred slavery to being forced to leave his wife and family, all of whom were slaves.[137] There were many slave-owners who considered the question of manumission solely from the standpoint of the welfare of their slaves, and who were therefore temporarily or permanently prevented from conferring upon them a freedom which would deprive them of their only hope of a lawful support. John Randolph of Roanoke, writing in his will in 1819 concerning his slaves, said, "It has a long time been a matter of deepest regret to me that . . . the obstacles thrown in the way by the laws

[133] Memorial to Virginia Legislature, in MS. Petitions, Powhatan County, 182(5?), uncatalogued.

[134] The History of the United States, vol. iii, p. 392.

[135] MS. Petitions, Henrico County, 1825, A 9358.

[136] MS. Petitions, King George County, 1813, B 1109.

[137] MS. Petitions, Essex County, 1808, A 5385.

of the land have prevented my emancipating them in my life-time."[138]

Furthermore, many free negroes who owned as slaves in a legal sense their wives and children or their brothers, sisters, and other relatives were after 1806 deterred from setting them free when they contemplated the prospect of seeing their dearest friends banished from the State by an enforcement against them of the limited residence law. For example, a colored man named Frank, who resided in Amelia County, had purchased his wife and three children, and, according to the statement of his white neighbors, had "always intended that they should be *virtually* free, although the law prohibited him from making them actually so without subjecting them to removal from the state."[139] Bowling Clark, a free negro of Campbell County, purchased his wife a few years after the act of 1806 went into operation; but both were declining in years, and both preferred the existing arrangement to one which would have given the wife freedom at the cost of parting husband and wife or of sending both from their home together.[140] Numerous instances could be cited to show that the law annexing banishment as a condition of manumission exerted a powerful effect in restraining the will of black slave-owners.[141]

The third of the causes which deserve notice here in connection with the general decline in the frequency of manumissions in the nineteenth century is a noteworthy change in the economic aspects of slaveholding. The invention of

---

[138] The last will and testament of John Randolph of Roanoke set free about three hundred and eighty-five slaves. The document is printed in Garland, vol. ii, p. 150.

[139] In 1809 Frank died, and the only means that remained of saving "Patience, the wife, and Philemon, Elizabeth and Henry, the children of the free black man" from sale into slavery was legislative intervention by private act. The legislature intervened in this case because the purchase by Frank of his family took place before the enactment of the law of 1806. Legislative action was refused in many similar cases of later date (MS. Petitions, Amelia County, 1809, A 768; Acts, 1809–1810, p. 54).

[140] MS. Petitions, Campbell County, 1815, A 3412.

[141] See MS. Petitions, Fauquier County, 1837, A 5859; and below, pp. 92, 93. The imperfect enforcement of the act of 1806, a subject treated elsewhere in this monograph, did not relieve negroes of the fear of the consequences following violation of it.

the cotton gin in 1793 made possible the expansion of the cotton industry in the South. The result of this industrial expansion created a demand for slaves to work in the cotton fields. The abolition of the foreign slave trade in 1808 produced the final condition for the rapid growth of a domestic slave trade which eventually resulted in a rise in prices of Virginia slaves. About 1790, "when slave prices reached the bottom of a twenty years' decline,"[142] the maximum frequency of manumissions was attained, with the exception of the first few months after the manumission act took effect. Conditions in 1794 were such as to lead Washington to say that he believed that slaves would be "found to be a very troublesome species of property ere many years pass over our heads."[143] Any slave-owner having a limited number of acres for tillage might readily become overstocked with slaves and be forced to the alternative of manumitting or selling some of them.[144] In various ways household slaves made demands upon or appeals to their owners for freedom. In competition with these demands was the demand of the slave market. When the competition of the market was weak, as it was in the last quarter of the eighteenth century, the slave had a better opportunity to purchase, or to induce a friend to purchase, his freedom, or to appeal with success to the charity of his owner, than when attractive prices were being offered to owners for their surplus property.[145]

---

[142] U. B. Phillips, "The Economic Cost of Slaveholding in the Cotton Belt," in Political Science Quarterly, vol. xx, p. 257.

[143] Washington to Alexander Spottswood, November 23, 1794, in New York Public Library Bulletin, vol. ii, pp. 14, 15.

[144] Delegates representing slave-owning interests in the constitutional convention of 1829–1830 feared that delegates from western Virginia desired to see slavery taxed out of existence. If slaves were to be taxed more heavily, thought Richard Morris, "Either the *master* must run away from the slaves or the *slave* from the master." Here we see a recognition of the relation between the freeing of slaves and the paying character of slave property (Proceedings and Debates of the Convention, p. 116).

[145] In 1792 a negro man living in King William County died, leaving a will which directed that so much of his estate as was necessary be used to purchase the freedom of his son, the property of Benjamin Temple. This illustrates a phase of manumission directly affected by the market price of slaves (Hening, vol. xiii, p. 619).

It is important, however, to keep in mind that the change in economic conditions was not a sudden one, and that it was not the sole cause of the decline in the frequency of manumissions. John Fiske overrated the economic phase when he wrote, "After the abolition of the slave-trade in 1808 had increased the demand for Virginia-bred slaves in the states further south the very idea of emancipation faded out of memory."[146] This statement is erroneous both as to the facts and as to the inference that the cause of the change was wholly economic. The personal and human element in the relations of the master and his slaves so often overshadowed the property relation that the disposition which a master would make of his slaves could not be foretold by reference to economic laws.

The change in the economic value of slaveholding ascribed by Fiske to the early part of the century was in fact more potent in producing the second stage in the decline of manumission, which began about 1830, than it was in ushering in the first period of decline in the first decade of the century. No great rise in slave prices came about in Virginia before 1830 as a result of the growth of the cotton industry.[147] As a result of the decided improvement in slavery as an economic system and of the increasing vehemence of attacks made upon slavery by abolitionists, there arose soon after the great slavery debate in the Virginia legislature in 1832 a new school of slavery apologists whose outspoken defenses of slavery as a beneficial economic and political institution represented a new stage in the development of sentiment adverse to manumitting. The man who may be called the founder of this school of proslavery writers was Thomas R. Dew, professor of history and metaphysics in William and Mary College, who reviewed the slavery debate of 1832 and wrote an elaborate defense of slavery entitled "Essay on Slavery." Other writers who followed Dew in defend-

---

[146] Old Virginia and Her Neighbors, vol. ii, p. 191.

[147] W. H. Collins, The Domestic Slave Trade of the Southern States, p. 26 et seq.; W. Jay, Miscellaneous Writings on Slavery, pp. 266, 267.

ing slavery upon its merits were George Fitzhugh,[148] Alfred T. Bledsoe, professor of mathematics in the University of Virginia,[149] Rev. Dr. Thornton Stringfellow,[150] and Edmund Ruffin.[151]

The theory advanced by these writers was that the negro occupied his true and proper economic and political sphere in slavery, and that the correct solution of the race problem was not a plan of gradual emancipation, as was urged by a large minority in the legislature of 1832, but a reduction and continued subjection of the members of the black race to slavery. This view differentiates the part of the nineteenth century before 1832 from the part which came between 1832 and 1860, and serves to show by contrast how considerable was the freedom sentiment in Virginia up to 1832. The increase of the free negro population during the decade of 1820–1830 was 10,474. From 1830 to 1840 the increase in that class of the population was only 2500. Prior to the Southampton insurrection and the consequent discussion of the slavery question, prevailing opinion regarded slavery as an evil system to be removed as soon as a feasible method could be devised. It was hoped that by manumission the problem of drawing off a certain part of the colored class for colonization would be solved, and that this plan would finally remove the negroes to Africa. A stronger and more general antislavery sentiment existed in Virginia prior to 1832 than some writers are disposed to admit. The earnestness of the debate and the closeness of the vote on an emancipation project in the legislature in 1832 is wrongly regarded by Edward Ingle[152] as a sort of wild expression of fear created by the Southampton insurrection, and not as an expression of normal sentiment. It is true that the insurrection furnished the occasion for the debate of 1832, but the antislavery sentiments expressed fairly represented

[148] "Sociology for the South," and "What Shall be done with the Free Negroes?"

[149] "Liberty and Slavery."

[150] "The Bible Argument."

[151] "African Colonization Unveiled."

[152] Southern Sidelights, pp. 265, 266.

honest views which had persisted up to that time. Anti-slavery sentiments had been uttered in the constitutional convention of 1829–1830 by such men as James Monroe.[153] In 1821 Madison declared that the free negroes were "increasing rapidly from manumissions and from offsprings."[154] Again in 1826 he wrote to La Fayette that "manumissions more than keep pace with the outlets provided and that the increase of them is only checked by their [the freedmen] remaining in the country.[155] This obstacle removed and all others would yield to the emancipating disposition." In Madison's opinion, "the tendency was favorable to the cause of universal emancipation."

In contrast with this view expressed by Madison, which is representative of an attitude toward the slavery question quite extensively held before 1832, we may consider the opinion of a pamphlet writer of the decade of the fifties as indicative of the change in sentiment since 1832. Speaking of the mistaken philanthropy of the slave-owners of the period of the Commonwealth prior to 1832, he declared that the soil was then especially favorable to the growth of manumission sentiment. "For slavery had come to be generally considered as an economical and political evil by a large portion of the intelligent slaveholders in Virginia. It was not until after abolition fanaticism of the Northern people had become both active and malignant, and that Professor Dew's excellent 'Essay on Slavery' (the first important defense of the system offered in modern days) had been published that the revulsion began. At the present time, there are few intelligent and well informed persons in all Virginia who do not deem negro slavery to be in every respect a beneficial institution."[156]

---

[153] Debates of the Convention, p. 172; Richmond Enquirer, November 5, 1829.

[154] Madison's Writings, vol. iii, p. 240.

[155] Madison's Writings, vol. iii, pp. 275, 540. For petitions signed by large numbers of citizens pleading, in 1827, in the interest of "citizens who may feel disposed to emancipate their slaves," see MS. Petitions, Frederick, Jefferson, and Berkeley Counties, 1827, A 6495.

[156] "Calx," pp. 4, 5.

From what has already been said it should appear clear that the periods in the history of manumission from 1782 to 1865 were marked rather by changes in sentiment than by changes in laws. The act of 1782 authorizing manumission by the will or other instrument of writing remained in full force to the close of the Civil War.[157] By way of comparing the three stages in manumission sentiment under the act of 1782 it may with tolerable accuracy be stated that the chances of manumission of a slave living in Virginia through the generation preceding 1800 were about ten in a hundred; of one living through the period from 1800 to 1832, about four or five in a hundred; and of one living after 1832, about two in a hundred.

On a basis of sentiment or of the frequency with which manumissions occurred there may be said to be three stages in the progress of manumissions during the period of the Commonwealth, but from the standpoint of legal processes and regulations of manumission the period from 1782 to 1865 is but one period.

The act of 1782 imposed upon slave-owners who manumitted slaves over forty-five years of age the duty of providing for their maintenance, in order that they might not become charges upon the public.[158] In 1792 a revision of the act of 1782 was deemed necessary to the proper protection of creditors. A qualifying clause was appended to the provisions of the original act which made any manumitted slave liable to be taken by execution to satisfy the debts contracted by his former master previous to the date of manumission.[159] In several important cases the supreme

[157] It seems an inexcusable error on the part of Henry Wilson that he should have asserted in his History of the Rise and Fall of the Slave Power that the act of 1782 remained in force for only ten years, and that after its provisions were repealed, "that source of just and humane individual action being forcibly stopped, gradually dried up and ceased to flow" (vol. i, p. 20). See Code (1849), 459 n., for a statement by the compiler that "the right to emancipate has continued ever since [1782]; and the validity and effect of instruments of emancipation have been passed upon in many cases."

[158] See deed executed by Samuel Tinsley, 1792, in MS. Deeds of Henrico County, no. 4, p. 212.

[159] Hening, vol. xiv, p. 128.

court of appeals held that "the right to emancipate slaves is subordinate to the obligation to pay debts previously contracted by express will of the statute."[160] In 1805 certain negroes set free by a deed of gift from their owner were, in pursuance of a decision of the supreme court of appeals, taken in execution for the satisfaction of the debts of the slave-owner's wife, notwithstanding the fact that the negroes belonged to their owner before he married the wife for whose debts the negroes were held.[161] All other forms of property, personal or real, had to be applied to the payment of debts before execution could be made upon liberated slaves; and if the amount of indebtedness remaining could be paid by hiring out the liberated negroes of the debtor, they were deprived of freedom only as long as was necessary to raise the required amount. No statute of limitations could be appealed to by negroes who had been in peaceful possession of their freedom for five, ten, or apparently any number of years to stop an execution upon them for the debts of their owner contracted before the liberation.[162]

Under the provisions of the act of 1782 and of every later revision of that act, manumissions could be made by last will and testament or by other instrument of writing properly attested and proved. Written instruments of manumission other than wills were generally called "deeds of manumission" or "deeds of emancipation." Strictly speaking, such instruments were not deeds, because they imported no transfer of property from one to another, but they bore a close analogy to deeds. Referring to this analogy, a judge of the supreme court of appeals in Thrift v. Hannah said: "A deed is a writing *sealed* and *delivered*. *Proof* or *acknowledgment* in court is to an instrument of emancipation what delivery is to a deed at common law."[163] In imitation

[160] Dunn v. Amey, 1 Leigh, 465 (1829); Jincey et al. v. Winfield Administrators, 9 Grattan, 708 (1853).

[161] Woodley v. Abby, 5 Call, 336. See also Patty v. Colin, 1 Hening and Munford, 519 (1807).

[162] Woodley v. Abby, 5 Call, 336; Patty v. Colin, 1 Hening and Munford, 519 (1807).

[163] Thrift v. Hannah, 2 Leigh, 330.

of deeds or indentures conveying property from one to another, such instruments of manumission usually stipulated a pecuniary consideration. Even when the act of the master was purely an act of benevolence, it was the practice to stipulate some such nominal consideration as five shillings,[164] one dollar,[165] or five dollars.[166] Deeds of manumission were in frequent use between 1782 and 1800 by persons of very decided antislavery views,[167] as, for example, the Quakers. Though of less frequent occurrence in the deed-books of the nineteenth century, deeds of emancipation were used by free negroes who purchased and set free their relatives and friends, or by masters who agreed with their slaves to set them free upon payment of a certain sum of money.

The most common type of deeds of emancipation is exemplified by the following instrument, taken from the court records of Henrico County:—

> To all whom these presents may come know ye, that I Peter Hawkins a free black man of the City of Richmond having purchased my wife Rose, a slave about twenty-two years of age and by her have had a child called Mary now about 18 mo. old, for the love I bear toward my wife and child have thought proper to emancipate them and for the further consideration of five shillings to me in hand paid . . . I emancipate and set free the said Rose and Mary . . . and relinquish all my right title and interest and claim whatsoever as slaves to the said Rose and Mary.
>
> PETER HAWKINS (Seal)[168]

From the standpoint of proslavery men of the nineteenth century, manumission by last will and testament was the method most likely to be abused. It was certainly the method which remained in most common use throughout the entire period of the Commonwealth. When a slaveowner recognized that he was approaching the end of life,

[164] MS. Deeds of Henrico County, no. 2, pp. 569, 574; no. 6, p. 274.

[165] Ibid., no. 7, p. 205.

[166] Ibid., no. 7, p. 454.

[167] Betsey Barlow, who from benevolent motives freed her slaves by deed in 1789, gave them not only freedom but new names: "I set free Jacob and Sarah to whom I give the names Jacob Holland and Sarah Marnick" (MS. Deeds of Northampton County, 1785–1794, p. 291). Manumitted slaves often assumed the surnames of their former owner.

[168] MS. Deeds of Henrico County, 1800, no. 6, p. 78.

he was likely to give serious consideration to his duty to his own slaves, regardless of his views respecting slavery in general. There remained to him only one appropriate way of acknowledging his debt of gratitude for the long, patient, and faithful service of the slaves of his household. Confronted with the alternative of dying ingrate or bequeathing to their servants freedom from bondage, many masters chose the latter course, and down to the Civil War the wills of slave-owners frequently contained such a clause as, "I give unto my negro her freedom on account of her faithfulness of service."[169] Giles Fitzhugh, a descendant of a long line of slave-owners, freed all his slaves by his last will in 1853.[170] A will of manumission sometimes represented a tardy effort or last resort to ease a goaded conscience. John Randolph of Roanoke wrote in his last will, "I give to my slaves their freedom to which my conscience tells me they are justly entitled."[171] Edmund Ruffin, lamenting in 1859 the abuse of testamentary manumissions by slave-owners of "sensitive or feeble minds, or morbidly tender consciences . . . especially of wealthy old men and old women," saw in the motives of such slave-owners a resemblance to the motives appealed to by priests in the dark ages "when inducing rich sinners to smooth and pay their future pass to Heaven.

[169] MS. Wills of Norfolk County, 1836–1868, p. 66. The will of J. A. Schwartz, of Nottoway County, affords a striking illustration of the way in which the reflections of slave-masters in their last illness often impelled them to acknowledge their debt of gratitude to their slaves while there was opportunity. With his slaves standing around him as he lay upon his death-bed, Schwartz questioned them separately before dictating orally what was intended for his will in respect to them.

"Bob, do you wish to be freed?"

"I am willing to serve *you*, but I had rather be freed than have another master," said Bob.

"He should be free," answered the master.

When a similar conversation had taken place between Frank and the dying man with a like result, Polly enquired: "What are you going to do for poor me?" "Polly and her children," said he, "should be free" (3 Leigh, 142).

[170] A. Crozier, Virginia County Records, vol. vii, p. 110.

[171] Garland, vol. ii, p. 150. This last act of Randolph, liberating about three hundred and eighty-five slaves, was referred to by opponents of testamentary manumission as "the shocking example of John Randolph" (Ingle, p. 266).

Such emancipations have been made in great amount and in many cases, and not only by the unquestionably benevolent and pious . . . but also by persons whose lives and actions, both as men and as masters, had indicated anything but piety, benevolence, or even a just and good treatment of their slaves."[172]

The last will and testament was naturally the legal instrument selected by a slave-owner of moderate antislavery views who wished to retain the services of his negroes during his life, but desired at the same time to guarantee them, by providing for their freedom at his death, against being sold with his estate or separated from their homes and each other. The testamentary method served equally well the master who wished to "lend" his slaves to his heirs for a fixed period during the lifetime of the heirs or until the slaves should arrive at a certain age.[173] "Manumission in futuro" was the term applied to the act of a master whose will provided for the freedom of his slaves at a specified time after his death.

Slave-owners making wills of manumission in futuro often attempted to affix conditions to the possession of freedom by their slaves. A condition precedent to the manumission was held by the courts to be valid, that is to say, a master by his will could make the freedom of a slave depend upon some act or condition of the slave or upon some event, if such act, condition, or event was to be determined before the slave's freedom began. A condition subsequent was invalid. If a master manumitted his slave upon condition that the slave serve him for hire or otherwise after acquiring freedom or that the negro's children be slaves, the manu-

---

[172] E. Ruffin, African Colonization Unveiled, p. 9.

[173] James Johnson, of Louisa County, made his will in 1785, bequeathing to his wife all his negroes during her lifetime. After her death the negroes were to be set free upon attaining the age of twenty-one years (10 Leigh, 277). John E. Taylor in his last will said: "I lend my slaves Margaret, Bridget, Ben, George, John and Sandy to my wife Keziah and my daughter Margaret during their natural lives, but in the event of the death of my said wife and daughter, I do hereby emancipate them and their issue forever" (MS. Wills of Norfolk County, 1836–1868, p. 25).

mission was valid, but the conditions stipulated were of no effect or force.[174] Any effort to control or direct the conduct of a negro after manumission or to put him in a status intermediate between slavery and freedom was futile.[175] Some wills conditioned the freedom of slaves upon the choice or election of the slaves when they arrived at certain ages or when certain conditions were fulfilled. Until 1858 such wills were treated by the courts as valid.[176] In the case of Baily et al. v. Poindexter the supreme court of appeals, contrary to the sentiment of the legal profession, ruled that slaves had no legal capacity even to choose to be free, and that allowing them such choice did not manumit them or provide for their manumission.[177]

---

[174] Minor, vol. i, p. 167. John Fitzgerald of Petersburg bequeathed freedom to a female slave with the reservation that her children should be slaves. When the instrument came for construction by appeal to the supreme court in 1827, it was held that the children of the woman set free were free and in no way under the control of their mother's former owner (Fulton v. Shaw, 4 Randall, 597). It was different in the case of children born of a slave-woman at any time before she had a right, according to the provisions of the will, to her freedom. Such children were slaves (Maria et al. v. Surbough, 2 Randall, 228).

[175] A will recorded in 1847, reading "I bequeath my negro girl Eliza to daughter Jimmey after the decease of my wife, not as a bond slave, but to be under her care and tuition" was held to be void of effect even to manumit the slave girl (2 Grattan, 227).

[176] Pleasants v. Pleasants, 2 Call, 319; Elder v Elder's Executor, 4 Leigh, 252; Dawson v. Dawson's Executor, 10 Leigh, 602.

[177] 14 Grattan, 132. See also Williamson v. Coalter's Executors, 14 Grattan, 394. Minor, vol. i, p. 160.

CHAPTER IV

THE LEGAL STATUS OF THE FREE NEGRO

The legal status of free individuals is involved in the usual two-fold relation of persons to the state,—that of receiver of protection and security from the government, and that of active participant in its affairs. Considering the status of the free negro in this double relation, the question which first demands an answer is, What protection was afforded him in rights of property and in the enjoyment of life and liberty?

The common-law right to own and to alienate property was at an early date recognized as belonging to free negroes, and it suffered fewer limitations in their possession than any other of the rights generally regarded as fundamental to a free status. In the "order-book" of the county court of Accomac for 1632–1640 is an order "that Francis the negare shall have his chist wch he clameth now being in the house of John Foster in case there be noe lawful reason shown to the contrary betwine this and the next courte alledged."[1] Contracts involving the recognition of full rights of free negroes to personal property were recorded in the county courts as early as 1645.[2] Among the early Virginia land patents are a number representing grants to negroes of from fifty to five hundred acres to be held in fee simple. The first of such grants made to a negro of which we have any record was one of two hundred and fifty acres to Anthony Johnson of Northampton County in 1651 as "head-rights" on the importation of five persons into the colony.[3] Other examples in this and other counties could be cited.[4] Among

---

[1] Transcribed copy in the Virginia State Library, p. 152.

[2] MS. Court Records of Northampton County, 1645–1651, pp. 83, 131; above, pp. 27, 28 n.

[3] MS. Land Patents of Virginia, 1643–1651, p. 326.

[4] See above, p. 38.

the deeds of York County for the year 1664 is one conveying a tract of land[5] from a white man to a negro. The county court of the same county held in 1660 that a free negro was capable of receiving property by bequest.[6]

The right of free negroes to property, personal and real, thus amply recognized in the seventeenth century, was preserved by the courts throughout the entire period under review. In the case of Parks v. Hewlett,[7] decided in 1838, the supreme court of appeals says: "He [the free negro] is at once entitled to acquire and enjoy property. His person is under the protection of the laws, and he has a right to sue for injuries done to person or to property. He may even acquire lands and hold slaves and will transmit them by inheritance to his children." In 1858, when the laws no longer allowed free negroes to acquire slaves except by descent, the courts still upheld the property rights of free negroes by holding that when a bequest of slaves was made to persons in trust for free negroes, the slaves must be sold or exchanged for a kind of property which free negroes could lawfully possess, and that the proceeds of the sale must be distributed among the free negroes according to the provisions of the will.[8]

Free negroes owning property transferred it by deed or transmitted it by will just as did white persons.[9] Courts of record and probate were open to them for recording legal evidences of sale or transfer of property,[10] and upon the

[5] MS. Court Records of York County, 1664–1672, p. 327, in Virginia State Library.

[6] "Itt is ordered yt John Negro servant to Thomas Whitehead Dec'd be and is hereby declared Free and that he have his cattle & other things belonging to him delivered (to him) according to ye Dec'd Will & Costs" (MS. Court Records of York County, 1657–1662, pp. 211, 217, in Virginia State Library).

[7] 9 Leigh, 511.

[8] 14 Grattan, 251.

[9] Hening, vol. xiii, p. 619.

[10] In 1829 William Yates, a free negro, died leaving a will by which he gave his "estate real and personal," after payment of his debts, to Henry Edloe and Robert McCandlish in trust for his wife Maria, who was his slave, to be paid over to her as soon as she could be freed and be allowed to remain in the State. The will was admitted to probate, and an administrator was appointed to carry out its provisions (3 Grattan, 330).

courts devolved the duty of seeing that estates of intestates were lawfully administered for the benefit of the rightful heirs. In the case of Hepburn v. Dundas,[11] by the authority of the highest court of the State the rights of collateral heirs to the estate of a free negro who died intestate and without children were fully asserted. The agency of the courts, either of common law or equity, was resorted to with no unusual difficulties by free negroes in the enforcement of bequests of property to them.[12]

The inviolability of the property rights of free negroes was an effective argument against the frequent proposals to remove the entire free negro population from the State. In the legislature of 1832 General Brodnax affirmed that the free negroes, in the event of deportation, could easily dispose of their small holdings. But Marshall, who opposed forcible deportation, declared that there are those "who have property which they must dispose of before leaving the country. Will you force them to bring their property into market all at once to be sacrificed by one precipitate sale?"[13] The argument prevailed against those who favored the measure, and the bill was lost.

In order that certain individuals might have time to dispose of property left them by their deceased masters, numerous private acts were passed by the legislature granting them permission to remain in the State contrary to the law of 1806.[14] In 1842 a House of Delegates bill to prohibit free negroes from acquiring real estate met with but slight consideration.[15]

The most remarkable property right possessed by free negroes was the right to acquire, own, and alienate slaves. Indeed, for more than twenty years from the time when free negroes first appear in the courts there was no legal

---

[11] 13 Grattan, 219.

[12] Dunlap v. Harrison, 14 Grattan, 251.

[13] Richmond Enquirer, February 14, 1832.

[14] Acts, 1821–1822, p. 85; 1828–1829, p. 157; 1829–1830, p. 134; 1830–1831, p. 306; 1832–1833, pp. 198, 199. The law of 1806 here referred to required slaves manumitted after May 1, 1806, to leave the State within twelve months. See above, p. 45, 45 n.

[15] House Journals, 1841–1842, pp. 66, 114, 162.

restriction upon their right to own indentured white servants. Such a reversal of the usual order may have been in a few cases actually attempted, for in 1670 a law was enacted which declared that "noe negro or Indian though baptized and enjoyned their own ffreedome shall be capable of any purchase of Christians, but yet not debarred from buying any of their owne nation."[16] There is on record in the Northampton County court-house a clear case of the ownership by a free negro of a negro servant as early as 1655.[17]

Not before 1832 were free negroes forbidden to own negro slaves. That this right was quite commonly exercised, notably in the nineteenth century, is a fact well supported by evidence. It was not unusual among the free colored people for one member of the family to hold one or more of the other members in legal bondage. The following indenture of 1795 illustrates this form of slavery:—

Know all men of these presents that I, James Radford of the county of Henrico for and in consideration of the sum of thirty-three pounds current money of Virginia to me in hand paid by George Radford (a black freeman) of the city of Richmond . . . hath bargained and sold unto George Radford one negro woman aggy, To have and to hold the said negro slave aggy unto the said George Radford his heirs and assigns forever.

JAMES RADFORD (Seal)[18]

Equally instructive is the following "Deed of sale of slaves to a freeman" of the same date:—

Know all men of these presence that I David A. Jones of Amelia County of the one part have for and in consideration of the sum of five hundred dollars granted unto Frank Gromes a black man of the other part a negro woman named Patience and two children by name Phil & Betsy to have and to hold & to hold the above

[16] Hening, vol. ii, p. 280. The act of 1748 concerning servants and slaves declared "that no negroe, mulatto, or Indian although a Christian or any Jew, Moor, Mohametan or other infidel shall at any time purchase any Christian servants nor any other except their own complexion, or such as by this act are declared slaves: and if any of the persons aforesaid shall nevertheless presume to purchase a Christian white servant, such servant shall immediately become free, and be held deemed and taken" (ibid., vol. v, p. 550).

[17] MS. Court Records of Northampton County, 1651–1654, p. 226; above, pp. 32, 33.

[18] MS. Deeds of Henrico County, no. 5, p. 585.

named negroes to the only proper use, behalf and benefit of him and his heirs forever.

DAVID JONES (Seal)[19]

Free negro men often thus purchased their slave wives, and, fearful of residence prohibitions upon manumitted negroes, held their wives and children as their bond slaves.[20] Free negro women sometimes purchased their slave husbands to subject them to a more agreeable bondage, themselves becoming in an unusual sense their mistresses and owners.[21] Daughters were sometimes the property of their mothers, as in the case of Janette Wood, of Richmond, who in the year 1795 was emancipated by her mother "for and in consideration of natural love."[22] John Sabb of Richmond in the year 1801 purchased his aged father-in-law, Julius, and manumitted him for the nominal sum of five shillings.[23]

Prior to 1806 the purchase of one member of a family by another was usually soon followed by a deed of manumission, but after an act[24] of that year had made illegal the continued residence of negroes manumitted after May 1, 1806, the relation of master and slave within free negro

[19] MS. Petitions, Amelia County, A 768.

[20] A free negro of Prince William County, Daniel Webster by name, being sixty years of age and expecting soon to die, petitioned the legislature to permit his wife and children to remain in Virginia contrary to the law of 1806, which required slaves manumitted thereafter to leave the State within twelve months. During his life he had avoided the evil consequences of this law to the members of his family by continuing to own them as his slaves; but at his death the danger of their being sold by an administrator was more threatening than the danger of removal from the State, and he wished to manumit them (MS. Petitions, Prince William County, 1812).

[21] In 1828 Phil Cooper and his wife, free people of color, petitioned the legislature for a law permitting the husband to reside in Virginia. His wife owned him as her slave, but wished to manumit him provided that he might live in the State (MS. Petitions, Gloucester County, A 6987). See also Lower Norfolk County Virginia Antiquary, vol. iv, p. 177, for statement concerning Betsy Fuller, a free negro huckstress of Norfolk, who owned her husband. Upon the approach and outbreak of the Civil War the slave husband was loud in the expression of southern views, and evidently was indifferent as to his emancipation.

[22] MS. Deeds of Henrico County, no. 4, p. 692.

[23] Ibid., no. 6, p. 274.

[24] Hening, vol. xvi, p. 252.

families became quite common. A petition of a slave woman, Ermana, to the legislature of 1839 stated that her husband had been a free man of color, that he had died intestate, and that she, her children, and her property had escheated to the literary fund. She prayed that the right of the fund to her and to her property be relinquished.[25] Sally Dabney, a slave of her husband, was bequeathed property by his will as if she had been free. The testator died without heirs. The wife, being a slave, was not competent to receive the bequest; hence the property escheated to the literary fund. The question arose as to whether the wife also should not be sold for the benefit of the fund, and an act of the legislature was passed to release the claims of the State to her.[26]

In the exercise of their legal right to own slaves black masters did not always confine themselves to the purchase of their kindred for beneficent purposes. Some negroes purchased and held slaves with the same considerations of profit in view as governed the actions of white owners of slaves. An example in the seventeenth century is that of John Casor, a negro, who was by order of a county court remanded to the service of Anthony Johnson, a negro freeholder.[27] Judith Angus, a well-to-do free negress of Petersburg, owned two slave girls as her personal servants. At her death she left a will, dated 1832, by which she disposed in regard to these two girls as follows: "My servants Jimmy and Docy shall work until they obtain money enough to enable them to leave the state and thereby secure their freedom according to the laws of Virginia. In the event of their remaining here, they shall belong to my son Moses."[28] Against a free negro who held another negro in slavery could be used only such legal remedies as could be used

[25] It is probable that all the relatives of the deceased man were slaves; hence his property escheated to the State (House Journal, 1839, p. 21).

[26] Acts, 1834–1835, p. 242.

[27] MS. Court Records of Northampton County, 1651–1654, p. 226; above, pp. 32, 33.

[28] MS. Petitions, Dinwiddie County, 1833, A 5123.

against a white master. Mary Quickley, a free black woman of Richmond, held as her slave a woman named Sarah. Suit was granted in the hustings court to Sarah against her black mistress only after appointed counsel had inquired into the claims of Sarah based upon her own free status. Suit was granted at the same time to Sarah's children, who were held by white persons.[29]

Complete as were the free negro's rights in property lawfully possessed, he was nevertheless limited in a few respects as to the kinds of property he could acquire. The limitations imposed were police regulations, and were apparently not discriminations against the free negro as such. In the ownership of slaves, dogs, firelocks, poisonous drugs, and intoxicants, free negroes were subject to limitations which did not apply to white persons.

As early as 1670 free negroes were forbidden to own white servants.[30] By an act of 1832 they were declared incapable of purchasing or otherwise acquiring permanent ownership, except by descent, of any slaves other than husband, wife, and children; contracts for any such purchase were declared void.[31] By the Code of 1849 the limitation was the same, except that parents were included among the persons whom free negroes could acquire.[32] An amendment of this section, made March 31, 1858, changed the law to read: "No free negro shall be capable of acquiring, except by descent, any slave."[33] There is evidence, however,

---

[29] "On a petition of Sarah alledging herself illegally detained in slavery by Mary Quickley a free black woman of this city . . . [and on a similar petition of Sarah's children] for leave to sue their owners for freedom in forma pauperis, Ordered that James Rind Gent. be requested to certify his opinion to this court respecting the probable claims of the petitioners . . . which he having done, It is further ordered that they be allowed to sue for their freedom" (Orders of Hustings Court of Richmond, vol. 5, p. 41).

[30] Hening, vol ii, p. 280.

[31] Acts, 1831–1832, p. 20. The vote by which this bill was passed in the Senate was 15 to 14 (Senate Journal, 1832, p. 176).

[32] Code (1849), p. 458.

[33] Acts, 1857–1858; Code (1860), p. 510. "The object of this law is probably to keep slaves as far as possible under the control of white men only, and prevent free negroes from holding persons of their own race and color in personal subjection to themselves.

that these laws prohibiting the purchase and sale of slaves by free negroes were not enforced, and that free negroes continued after 1832 to go into the market to purchase slaves for profit. Had it not been so, there would have been no occasion for the repeated propositions made and the laws passed after 1832 to prevent the practice. Moreover, there are persons living who affirm from observation that down to the Civil War some free negroes owned slaves merely in order to profit by them.[34]

Another limitation upon the right of free negroes to own property was that in respect to firearms or other weapons, with which they might themselves do injury, or, by placing them in the hands of slaves, menace the safety of society. An act of 1680 declared that "no negro or other slave" could own or carry a "club, staffe, gunn or any other weapon of defense or offense."[35] In the revision of the laws in 1705 the word "negro" was omitted, so that slaves only were forbidden to keep arms.[36] In 1723 free negroes, mulattoes, and Indians were forbidden to "keep or carry any gun, powder or shot or any club or other weapon whatsoever offensive or defensive." Free negro housekeepers and those enrolled in the militia were, however, excepted.

Perhaps also it is intended to evince the distinctive superiority of the white race" (Opinion of Judge Lee in Dunlop v. Harrison's Executors, 14 Grattan, 260).

[34] Reuben West, a free negro barber who lived in Richmond during the last three decades before the Civil War and paid taxes on real property valued at $4420 (City Tax Books, 1856, 1859), is said by William Mundin, a mulatto barber now living in Richmond, who was born free in 1837, to have purchased a slave house servant. According to the statement of Mundin, who was at that time serving an apprenticeship to Reuben West, this woman slave showed toward her black master a spirit of insubordination, and was therefore soon sold by him. James H. Hill, another colored contemporary of Reuben West, asserts that West owned two slaves, and that one of them was a mulatto barber. As far as the statements made by these men in lengthy interviews with the author could be verified in authentic records, they were found to be trustworthy. See also Lower Norfolk County Virginia Antiquary, vol. iv, pp. 174–182, for negro slave-owners enumerated in a list, prepared by the commissioners of the revenue, of all slave-owners of Princess Anne County in 1840.

[35] Hening, vol. ii, p. 481.

[36] Ibid., vol. iii, p. 459.

Such as lived on frontier plantations could upon application be granted licenses to keep and use one gun.[37]

The acts regulating the enlistment of free negroes in the militia in the eighteenth century show the distrust which was felt of negroes in possession of firearms. The militia act of 1748 declared that "all such free mulattoes, negroes or Indians, as are or shall be listed, as aforesaid, shall appear without arms."[38] The substance of this provision was repeated in 1755[39] and in 1757.[40] The provision was dropped during the Revolution, manifestly for the purpose of permitting free colored men to become soldiers.[41] With the increase of the free negro class and following the discovery of a negro plot in 1800, the feeling of danger from free negroes in possession of firearms became more intense; and a law of 1806 forbade any free negro or mulatto, housekeeper or otherwise, to "keep or carry any fire-lock of any kind, any military weapon or any powder or lead" without first obtaining a license from the county or corporation court.[42] A free negro caught with a gun or other weapon in violation of this act forfeited the weapon to the informer, and received thirty-nine lashes at the whipping-post.[43]

More rigid still was the law dealing with this subject which was passed in the first session of the legislature after the Southampton insurrection.[44] So much of former acts as permitted justices to grant licenses to free negroes or

---

[37] Hening, vol. iv, p. 131.

[38] Ibid., vol. v, p. 17.

[39] Ibid., vol. vi, p. 33.

[40] Ibid., vol. vii, p. 95.

[41] Ibid., vol. ix, p. 27 (1775); vol. ix, p. 268 (1777); see below, p. 110.

[42] A Norfolk County court in 1820 made the following order: "Upon the application of James Cuffie, a free man of colour, residing in this county, a license is granted him to keep a gun with ammunition for the protection of his property" (MS. Orders, 1819–1820, circa p. 280). Note also the following: "Ordered that the order of this court made the 9th day of August last granting permission to James Harris a free man of colour to carry and use a gun be rescinded" (MS. Minutes of Henrico County, no. 27, p. 516).

[43] Hening, vol. xvi, p. 274.

[44] Acts, 1831–1832, p. 20.

mulattoes to keep or carry a firelock or any powder or lead were by this law repealed. This absolute denial to free negroes of the use of firearms imposed a serious disability upon the farming element of this class. In 1839 Thomas Beasley, a free negro of Giles County, remonstrated to the legislature against this prohibition, saying that the mountainous frontier country where he lived was infested with wild beasts, and that the law prohibiting free negroes to use firelocks subjected him and his class to a great hardship in that they had no means of protecting their domestic animals and crops.[45] A similar petition, endorsed with the signatures of eighty white citizens, was presented in 1840 by James and Joseph Viney, free negroes of Giles County.[46] In spite of remonstrances against this law, it remained in force until the Civil War.[47] In 1839 patrols in search of arms unlawfully held were granted authority to force open the doors of such free negroes as were suspected of violating these laws.[48]

The ownership by free negroes of dogs, as of firearms, was objectionable, and for similar reasons. Prowling free negroes accompanied by dogs became a menace, particularly to the sheep-raising industry,[49] and efforts were made in several counties to prevent free negroes from keeping dogs. In 1848 an act forbade free negroes in Mathews County to own dogs.[50] In 1858 a similar law was passed for the counties of Essex, King and Queen, James City, and New Kent.[51] For passing through or going about in any of these last named counties with a dog a free negro was liable to punishment by stripes, not exceeding thirty-nine, and a fine of five dollars. A bill to make general the prohibition through-

[45] MS. Petitions, Giles County, 1839, A 6812.
[46] Ibid., 1840, A 6821.
[47] Code (1849), p. 754; Code (1860), p. 816.
[48] Acts, 1839, p. 24.
[49] See a petition to the legislature which represents that both free negroes and dogs kill sheep as they prowl through the neighborhood (MS. Petitions, Chesterfield County, 1854, A 4321).
[50] Acts, 1847–1848; House Journal, 1847–1848, p. 436.
[51] Acts, 1857–1858, p. 152.

out the State passed the House of Delegates in 1848, but failed to receive the approval of the Senate.[52]

The laws of Virginia extended their protection not only, as we have already seen, to the property of the free negro, but, as we shall now see, to his life and liberty. In any case in which the freedom of a negro was disputed the burden of proof was upon the negro to show that he was free. Unlike the recognized principle of English law which demands that every man be regarded as innocent till his guilt is established by evidence, a free negro taken up and deprived of his liberty as being a slave had, in order to procure his release, to produce evidence that he was not a slave. In 1806 George Wythe, chancellor of the State of Virginia, gave as grounds for decreeing the freedom of three persons claimed as slaves that freedom is the birthright of every human being. He laid it down as a general proposition that whenever one person claims to hold another in slavery, the onus probandi lies on the claimant. This application of the Declaration of Independence was completely repudiated by the supreme court of appeals when the case came up for final review.[53] Judge Tucker, who spoke for a unanimous court, asserted that the burden of proof is not upon the claimant, but upon the negro to show that he is free; whereas with a white man or an Indian held in slavery the burden is with the claimant.[54] Again, in Fulton's Executors v. Gracey

---

[52] House Journal, 1847–1848, p. 436. In the act incorporating the town of Manchester authority was given to the trustees to prohibit slaves, free negroes, and mulattoes from raising hogs and dogs (Acts, 1843–1844, p. 96).

Although free negroes were not forbidden to possess poisonous drugs and intoxicating liquors, the sale of these articles to them was a matter of rigid regulation or absolute prohibition (Acts, 1855–1856, p. 45; 1857–1858, p. 51). Complaint came to the legislature in 1836 that free negroes were acting as agents for slaves in purchasing ardent spirits from the venders (MS. Petitions, Northumberland County, 1836, B 4969).

[53] Hudgins v. Wright, 1 Hening and Munford, 133.

[54] In the argument Judge Tucker supposes that "three persons, a black or mulatto man or woman with a flat nose and woolly head; a copper-colored person with long jetty black or straight hair; and one with fair complexion, brown hair, not woolly, nor inclined thereto, with a prominent Roman nose, were brought together before

the court declared that "in the case of a person visibly appearing to be a white man or Indian the presumption is that he is free, but in the case of a person visibly appearing to be a negro, the presumption is that he is a slave. . . . The plaintiff in a suit for freedom must make out his title against all the world."[55]

The presumption being thus against the freedom of negroes, there was always a temptation to "divers ill-disposed persons" to force free negroes into slavery by theft, capture, or collusion, especially those free negroes whose occupations were already servile.[56] A law of 1765, designed to prevent this practice, fixed at £70 the penalty for selling as a slave a colored person who was only a servant.[57] In 1788, when the precious character and value of liberty was receiving unusual emphasis, a law was enacted which fixed upon persons guilty of stealing or selling as a slave any free negro or mulatto the extreme penalty of death without benefit of clergy.[58] By the enactments of 1792 the penalty remained the same, but in the codification of 1819 it was changed from death[59] to imprisonment in the penitentiary for at least two years.[60] An act of 1848 raised the minimum term to three years, and after that no further change was made in the penalty for this offense.[61]

Far from becoming empty verbiage in our criminal code, these laws received general and often rigorous enforcement.[62] In the opinion of the general court in Common-

---

a judge upon a suit of habeas corpus. . . . How must the Judge act in this case? . . . If the whole case be left with the judge, he must deliver the [white man and the Indian] out of custody, and permit the negro to remain in slavery, until he could produce proof of his freedom." Cf. case of Aron Jackson, in MS. Minutes of Henrico County, no. 27, p. 142.

[55] 15 Grattan, 323.

[56] For examples, see Calendar of Virginia State Papers, vol. i, p. 10; 11 Leigh, 633; MS. Minutes of Henrico County, no. 27, p. 129.

[57] Hening, vol. viii, p. 133.

[58] Ibid., vol. xii, p. 531.

[59] Ibid., vol. xiv, p. 127.

[60] 1 Revised Code, 427.

[61] Acts, 1847–1848, p. 97; Code (1860), p. 785.

[62] MS. Minutes of Henrico County, no. 27, p. 129; Commonwealth v. Nix, 11 Leigh, 636.

wealth v. Mercer they were not to be construed as a protection for a white man who might become the victim of fraud if a free negro should be sold to him as a slave, but their purpose and use was the protection of free negroes in their freedom.[63] In Davenport v. Commonwealth[64] the supreme court of appeals held that kidnapping a free negro without the actual sale constituted the crime against which the law was directed, and, further, that stealing a free negro with felonious intent to appropriate him was criminal, whether the person knew him to be free or not. The activity and interest manifested in the prosecution of violators of this law is shown by the proclamation of Governor Lee issued July 8, 1794:—

> Whereas I have received information that some wicked and evil-disposed persons . . . did on the night of the 20th of June last feloniously steal and take away two children of Peggy Howell, a free Mulatto living in the county of Charlotte, with a design as is supposed to sell them in some of the neighboring states as slaves, the name and description of which children are contained in the Hue and Cry subjoined, and whereas the rights of humanity are deeply interested in the restoration of the children to their parents, and the good order of society is involved in the punishment of the offenders, I do by and with the advice of the Council of State issue this Proclamation offering a reward of Fifty Dollars for the recovery of each of the said children and the further sum of one hundred dollars for apprehending and securing in the public jail of Charlotte County the offender or offenders.
>
> HENRY LEE.[65]

Against the easy abuse of the principle of presuming slavery from color the liberty of the free negro was further safeguarded by remedial laws of procedure and by a general liberality in the courts in consideration of all claims to freedom. A legally certified register, called by the free negroes

---

[63] Abram Hiter, a free negro, entered into an agreement with a white man named Mercer to allow himself to be sold as a slave. Hiter, it was planned, would later assert his freedom and share with Mercer the proceeds of the sale. Mercer's act of defrauding the purchaser was not punishable under the law, inasmuch as it involved no fraud upon the negro (2 Va. Cases, 144).

[64] 1 Leigh, 588.

[65] MS. Proclamation Book, p. 53; Calendar of Virginia State Papers, vol. viii, p. 231. See MS. Court Records of Charlotte County, 1794, for proceedings of a court held for the purpose of taking depositions in this case.

"free papers," was sufficient to repel the presumption and to shift the burden of proof to the person denying freedom to its possessor. "To suppose," said the court in Delacy v. Antoine, "that a free negro in possession of regular free papers may be falsely imprisoned without redress is indeed to attribute a gross and lamentable omission to the law. To confine that redress to a suit in forma pauperis to establish his freedom when he already has the conclusive proof of it in his hands would be a mockery. A free negro as well as a free white man must be entitled to the habeas corpus act."[66]

After 1793 every free negro was required to register in the county or corporation court, and for twenty-five cents was entitled to a copy of the register with the seal of the court annexed, which copy was prima facie evidence of freedom.[67] In the absence of immediate evidence of freedom, a free negro detained as a slave could bring suit in forma pauperis, in which he had the benefit of assigned counsel and which was conducted without cost to the plaintiff.[68] He was protected by the laws against intimidation in his suit from the person claiming to be his master.[69] Courts of equity were open to him.[70] Liberal rules of evidence in suits either in law or equity where freedom was involved were applied. If he had lost his free papers, he could offer evidence that he had once had them.[71] Hearsay and reputation were received as evidence of the status of one's ancestors in an effort to establish free birth.[72] An

---

[66] 7 Leigh, 438; cf. 15 Grattan, 256, 323.

[67] Hening, vol. xiv, p. 238; 1 Revised Code, 440.

[68] Hening, vol. xiv, p. 363; 1 Revised Code, 481. "On petition of Sarah [and her children] . . . It is ordered that they be allowed to sue for their freedom in this court in forma pauperis and James Rind Gent is assigned their counsel to prosecute the said suits and that their owners do not presume to remove, beat or misuse them upon this account, but suffer them to come to the Clerk's office of this court for subpoenas for their witnesses and to attend their examinations" (Orders of Hustings Court of Richmond, no. 5, p. 41).

[69] Orders of Hustings Court of Richmond, no. 5, p. 41.

[70] Sam v. Blakemore, 4 Randall, 466; 1 Hening and Munford, 133.

[71] MS. Minutes of Henrico County, no. 27, p. 503.

[72] In Pegram v. Isabell, a suit for freedom, a witness for the negro testified that he had heard a very old man say that he believed a certain ancestor of Isabell was free. The supreme court of appeals

oft repeated doctrine of the supreme court of appeals was that the laws should be construed as far as possible in favor of freedom. "I will remark," said Judge Campbell, "that this court has often declared that the same strictness as to form will not be required in actions for freedom as in other cases."[73] Judge Roane, speaking for the court in Patty v. Colin in 1807, said: "The spirit of the decisions of this court in relation to suits for freedom, while it neither abandons the rules of evidence nor the rules of law, applying to property, with a becoming liberality, respects the merit of the claim. . . . On this ground it is that parties suing for freedom are not confined to the rigid rules of proceeding and that their claims are not repudiated by the Court as long as a possible chance exists that they can meet with a successful issue."[74]

These special rules of procedure were needed, however, only in cases in which the question of freedom was being tried. "Where there is no contest about that right, but the litigation arises out of other matters it would be absurd to send the petitioner [a free negro] to sue in forma pauperis," said Judge Tucker, in a case before the court in 1836; "the remedy of habeas corpus must of course prevail."[75] A trial upon a writ of habeas corpus could not be denied a free negro if detained or deprived of his liberty by any person not claiming to be his master,[76] as, for example, by a creditor

held that such evidence was admissible (2 Hening and Munford, 210; cf. Gregory v. Baugh, 2 Leigh, 665, and Hudgins v. Wrights, 1 Hening and Munford, 134). In 15 Grattan, 314, the supreme court says: "Evidence of her having acted and been generally reputed as a free person is certainly admissible evidence of her freedom." In Fulton's Executors v. Gracey the court held that "any legal evidence tending to show that the plaintiffs are free tends to repel the presumption arising from color that they are slaves, and is, therefore, admissible" (15 Grattan, 323).

[73] McMichens v. Amos, 4 Randall, 134.

[74] 1 Hening and Munford, 519.

[75] 7 Leigh, 538.

[76] Delacy v. Antoine et al., 7 Leigh, 443 (1836); Rudler's Executors v. Ben, 10 Leigh, 467; Shue v. Turk, 15 Grattan, 256; Minor, vol. i, p. 169. In the case of Peter et al. v. Hargrave (5 Grattan, 14), tried in 1848, Judge Baldwin said concerning the rights of a free negro, "Against continued force he may invoke the high and summary remedy by writ of habeas corpus."

of himself or of his former owner; nor was he handicapped in such cases with the burden of proof or a presumption of guilt against him. Against persons doing him injury or for the enforcement of contracts he could bring suit in any court that was open to any other freeman.[77] In case the decisions of the lower courts were adverse, he could appeal even to the highest court of the State.[78] He could, and often did, petition the legislature when his grievances were such as could not be redressed by the courts.[79]

Prior to 1832, trial by jury was the method of determining the guilt or innocence of free negroes charged with crimes. They were regularly indicted or presented by a grand jury, and were entitled to a hearing upon the indictment before a petit jury.[80] Being indicted, they were allowed to go at liberty when they could furnish a satisfactory bond to secure their appearance in answer to the indictment.[81] They were entitled to counsel, could make exceptions in arrest of judgment, and the unanimous consent of

---

[77] "William Palmer appeared to answer the complaint of Peter Robinson (a free black man) against him for breach of the peace." Palmer was bound under penalty of forfeiture of one hundred dollars "to keep the peace and be of good behavior . . . and particularly toward Peter Robinson" (Orders of Hustings Court of Richmond, no. 5, p. 132). The Norfolk County court records (1718–1719, p. 1) contain the following entry: "Robert Richards and the rest of the free negroes agst. Lewis Corner Meritt in an action for debt not being prosecuted is dismissed." See also, MS. Orders of Henrico County, no. 6, p. 4, for the case of "David Cowper, a free negro, Plt. against Beltaes Dorish Deft. Suit abated by death of Deft." Also MS. Court Orders of Norfolk County, 1768–1771, p. 257: "Frank (a free negro) against Jane Miller;" and Jefferson's Reports, 90.

[78] Ex parte Morris, 11 Grattan, 292 (1854), was a case in which a free negro appealed from a corporation court to a circuit court and finally to the supreme court of appeals. Winn's Administrators v. Jones was a case taken on appeal in 1835 by a negro to the supreme court of appeals; this court sustained his challenge of free negro witnesses used against him in the lower court (6 Leigh, 74).

[79] See Calendar of Virginia State Papers, vol. i, p. 10 (1665); Journal of the House of Burgesses, 1766–1769, p. 198: "a petition of the people called mulattoes and free negroes;" MS. Petitions, Henrico County, 1838, and below, pp. 142–144, for examples of petitions of free negroes to the state legislature.

[80] John Aldridge v. the Commonwealth, 2 Va. Cases, 447; St. G. Tucker, A Dissertation on Slavery, pp. 56–58.

[81] Orders of Hustings Court of Richmond, no. 11, p. 153.

the jurymen was necessary for conviction. Prior to 1832, in the method of trial for crimes free negroes were on the same footing as white men.[82]

In the first session of the legislature following the Southampton insurrection in 1831, free negroes were denied by statute the right of trial by jury, except for offenses punishable with death. Thereafter they were tried by courts of oyer and terminer,[83] which had been in use since 1692 for the "speedy prosecution of slaves . . . without the sollemnitie of jury."[84] No fewer than five justices of the county or corporation could sit as a court, and a unanimous decision was necessary for conviction. The decisions of the court, comprehending both the law and the fact, were final.[85] The trial took place within ten days after commitment of the prisoners to jail, and conviction was followed by a speedy execution of the sentence.[86] The substitution of this summary method of trial for the former method of trial by jury is indicative of the disfavor into which the free negro had fallen, and represents no small change in his legal status.

For minor offenses and misdemeanors free negroes suffered penalties similar to those inflicted upon slaves for similar violations. Throughout the entire period whipping, "not exceeding thirty-nine lashes on the bare back, well laid on," was not an unusual penalty for free negroes as

---

[82] St. G. Tucker, A Dissertation on Slavery, pp. 56, 57; Peter v. Hargrave, 5 Grattan, 12. See Hening, vol. xv, p. 77, on "due course of law" to be pursued in convicting free negroes of conspiracy with slaves.

[83] Acts, 1831–1832, ch. 22, sec. 9; Code (1860), ch. ccxii. An amendment to strike out of the law the clause denying to free negroes jury trial was lost in the Senate by a vote of 9 to 20 (Senate Journal, 1832, p. 177). The act provided that free negroes should be tried by the slave courts "in all cases where the punishment shall be death." Disputes at once arose as to whether this meant offenses for which slaves had suffered death or offenses capital when committed by free negroes. The courts prevented the severity of the law relating to the punishment of slaves from passing to the free negroes by determining that the act changed the method of trial but not the method of punishment (4 Leigh, 652, 658, 661).

[84] Hening, vol. iii, p. 102; vol. iv, p. 127.

[85] 1 Revised Code, 428–430; Supplement to Revised Code, 248; Anderson (Free negro) v. Commonwealth, 5 Leigh, 740.

[86] 1 Revised Code, 428.

well as for slaves. Corporal chastisement was prescribed as a punishment for free negroes in many cases which, had the offender been a white man, would have merited the penalty of a fine. For instance, for importing a free negro a white man was to be imprisoned from six to twelve months and fined not less than five hundred dollars, whereas a free negro for the same offense was to receive not less than twenty nor more than thirty-nine lashes at the public whipping-post.[87] For unlawful destruction of oysters in the tidewater section a white man would under the law be fined fifty dollars, while a free negro would be fined twenty dollars and given thirty-nine lashes on the bare back.[88] For unlawfully harboring a slave a white man and a free negro alike forfeited ten dollars, but if the negro was unable to pay the fine, he was given thirty-nine lashes instead.[89] In many such instances the law openly discriminated against the free negro, making his punishments more severe than those inflicted upon white freemen, while the shield given to slaves in their misdemeanors by the disciplinary authority of the master rendered the liability to public punishments of the slave less than that of the free negro. The free negro was the individual for whom the laws seem to have been intended, and to him they were applied with peculiar rigor.

For the more serious offenses, that is, for grand larceny and other felonies, the punishments to be administered to free negroes and whites were for the most part the same. A notable discrimination was introduced in 1823 when crime among the free negroes was believed to be rapidly increasing, and the penitentiary system was receiving blame for a lack of restraint on and moral improvement of this class of the population.[90] The legislature enacted that free negroes previously punishable with imprisonment in the

---

[87] Acts, 1833–1834, p. 78.

[88] Ibid., 1836–1837, p. 56.

[89] Hening, vol. xv, p. 77. "They are subjected to restraints and surveillance in points beyond number" (Howison, vol. ii, p. 460).

[90] Report of the Superintendent of Penitentiary, in Documents of the House of Delegates, 1848–1849, no. 15, cited as House Documents.

penitentiary for terms of more than two years were thereafter to be whipped, transported, and sold into slavery beyond the limits of the United States.[91] This act was construed to mean that any free negro found guilty of a crime for which the maximum penalty prescribed was more than two years, even though the minimum might be only six months, should be whipped and sold as a slave. Thus construed, the act included within its scope almost every crime, except petty larceny, committed by free negroes. Public sentiment disapproved of this inhuman law, and forced its repeal, although thirty-five negroes were transported and sold into slavery during the four years that it remained in force.[92] In 1828 imprisonment in the penitentiary was again resorted to as a punishment for free negroes, but five years was made the shortest term for which a free negro could be sentenced, whereas two years was the minimum for white persons.[93] In 1833 proposals to make more severe the penalties upon free negroes were voted down in the House of Delegates as inexpedient.[94] The penal code of 1848 made uniform for all free persons the penalties for most criminal offences.[95] A final discrimination was introduced in 1860 by an act which provided that free negroes convicted of crimes punishable by sentence to the penitentiary could at the discretion of the court be sold into perpetual slavery.[96]

The right to go from place to place without hindrance might well be regarded as a right fundamental to real freedom, yet in few other respects was the liberty of free ne-

---

[91] Acts, 1822–1823, p. 36. The constitutionality of this act was passed upon and maintained by the general court of the State in the case of John Aldridge (free negro) v. the Commonwealth, 2 Va. Cases, 447.

[92] Reports of the Superintendent of Penitentiary, in House Documents, no. 15, 1848–1849, and no. 4, 1853–1854, p. 45; W. B. Giles, comp., Political Miscellanies: Letters to La Fayette; opinions of Dade and Parker in John Aldridge v. Commonwealth, 2 Va. Cases, 452, 457.

[93] Acts, 1827–1828, p. 29.

[94] House Journal, 1832–1833, p. 208.

[95] Acts, 1847–1848, p. 99; Code (1849), p. 728 et seq.

[96] Acts, 1859–1860, p. 163.

groes restricted so much as in this. In the colonial period there was little regulation of their movements; but from the time that their number reached several thousand on to the Civil War their liberty to move about in the State and to go out and return was very much restricted. In 1793 free negroes were forbidden to come into the State from any source to take up permanent residence.[97] The penalty upon a "master of a vessel or other person" for bringing in any free negro or mulatto was £100. A free negro living within the State could not go from one town or county to another to seek employment without a copy of his register, which was kept in the court of his county or corporation. Violators of this law were often committed to jail until they made proof of their freedom and paid the jailer's fee. If they were unable to pay this fee, they were hired out to the highest bidder for a time sufficient to pay the charges.[98] By an act of 1801 any free negro who, even though in possession of "free papers," removed into another county or corporation was declared an intruder, and made liable to arrest as a vagrant.[99] By a later act they were denied the right to change their residence from one county or town to another without permission from the court of the county or corporation to which they wished to go.[100] After 1848 no free negro could leave the State for the purpose of education, or go for any purpose to a non-slave-holding State and re-

[97] Hening, vol. xiv, p. 239. Free negroes travelling as servants to white persons or working on vessels were excepted; but if such negro servant got away from his master or from the ship, the burden of proof was upon him to show why he should not be whipped as an unlawful emigrant (Acts, 1833–1834, p. 79).

[98] Hening, vol. xiv, p. 238; 1 Revised Code, 441; Code of Va. (1849), 467. "Ordered that the Jailor discharge from his custody Aron Jackson and Johnson who were committed to Jail for want of free papers (it appearing to the satisfaction of the court that they are free) upon their paying the Jailor's fees and the costs of this order" (MS. Minutes of Henrico County, no. 27, 1830).

[99] Hening, vol. xv, p. 301; 1 Revised Code, 441. By the vagrancy laws of this time, "persons within the true description of a vagrant" were committed to a public workhouse for a term not exceeding three months, or were hired out by the overseers of the poor (2 Revised Code, 275, 276).

[100] House Journal, 1815–1816, p. 94, for grant of a petition to remove from one county to another; Code (1849), 468, (1860) 522.

turn.[101] Although these laws restricting the movements of the free negro were not enforced with equal thoroughness throughout the State, they were nevertheless enforced sufficiently to render precarious the condition of any violator.

Possibly the most extraordinary legal right possessed by free negroes at any time during the continuation of slavery was the right to choose a master and to go into voluntary bondage. Liberty to become a slave was one variety of liberty which a white man could not have exercised had he wished to do so. One might surmise that this right possessed for a while by free negroes was of a higher class of rights than the fundamental, inherent rights spoken of by the constitutional fathers; for a free negress who exercised it deprived and divested her posterity of liberty, and subjected both herself and it to perpetual tyranny.

Regardless of what may be said of the nature of this very unusual right, it is a fact that free negroes did not possess it until near the end of the slavery regime. Before 1856 a special act was deemed necessary to render legal the slavery of a free negro who of his own will selected a master. A number of such private acts, making it lawful for certain free negroes, whose names were mentioned in the acts, "to select a master or mistress," were passed in the first half of the decade of the fifties.[102] In 1856 a general act was passed making it lawful for any free colored man over twenty-one and any free colored woman over eighteen years of age to select a master or a mistress.[103] A free negro desiring so to alter his status could file a signed petition with the circuit judge stating the name of the proposed master or mistress. The petition would be posted for one month at the door of the court-house; if the judge was satisfied that there was no fraud, he would grant the request and fix a value on the petitioner. When one half of the designated price was paid into the public treasury, the petitioner became as much the

[101] Acts, 1847–1848, p. 119.
[102] Ibid., 1853–1854, p. 131; 1855–1856, p. 278.
[103] Ibid., 1855–1856, p. 37 et seq.

absolute property of his chosen master as if he had been born a slave. The rule that the status of a child followed the status of the mother at the time of the birth of the child was applicable to the offspring of free colored females who elected to be slaves.

Hard as was the lot of some free negroes in Virginia between 1856 and 1861, the courts had not many petitioners seeking the refuge of slavery. The reports of the auditor who took account of the receipts of the treasury from this source show that not more than a score of free negroes took advantage of their opportunities under the act of 1856. For the year ending September 30, 1859, $2308.91 was received into the treasury as receipts of the sale by the local courts of four free negroes.[104] The report for the fiscal year ending September 30, 1860, shows that three negroes went into voluntary bondage, and that $902.50 was received by the State from their purchasers.[105]

Thus far in this chapter attention has been confined to the question of the extent and degree of protection over property and liberty enjoyed by the free negro under the laws of Virginia. A question no less essential to a full treatment of the free negro's legal status is the extent of his participation in the affairs of the government. In what capacities could he, and did he, lend support to that government which afforded him the measure of benefits already described?

From a very early date in the history of the colony up to the close of the Civil War military service was required of the free negro. As early as 1723 there were some free negroes enlisted in the state militia, and they were, for that reason, permitted to keep one gun, powder, and shot.[106] During the last war between the English and the French for supremacy in America free negroes were employed in the Virginia service as "drummers, trumpeters, or pioneers or

[104] House Documents, 1859–1860, no. 5, p. 423.
[105] Ibid., 1861, no. 5, p. 652.
[106] Hening, vol. iv, p. 131.

in such other servile labour as they shall be directed to perform."[107]

In the War of Independence the free negro in Virginia performed a worthy and useful service.[108] The recruiting laws made eligible for service "all male persons, hired servants and apprentices above the age of sixteen and under fifty,"[109] but did not permit the enlistment of slaves or of servants bound to serve till thirty-one years of age.[110] That free negroes were enlisted under these laws there is no room for doubt. A letter written April 24, 1783, to the governor by William Reynolds, commissary of military stores, states that James Day had been accused of "transgressing in defrauding a black soldier and through a hasty & rather unfair hearing was ordered to prison where he now lies punishing."[111] In 1777 an act of Assembly designated drumming, fifing, and pioneering for the employment of the free mulattoes of the company.[112] Runaway slaves pre-

[107] Hening, vol. v, p. 17 (1748); vol. vi, p. 533 (1755); vol. vii, p. 95 (1757).

[108] Cf. G. H. Moore, Historical Notes on the Employment of Negroes in the American Army of the Revolution, p. 16.

[109] Proceedings of Convention of Delegates for the Counties and Corporations of the Colony of Virginia, 1775, p. 36.

[110] Hening, vol. ix, pp. 81, 346, 592; MS. Petitions, Prince William County. The enforcement of this act excluding servants gave rise to the following statement of certain officials in a petition to the legislature: "Jesse Kelly, a mulatto man bound agreeably to act of assembly to Lewis Lee until the said Kelly should arrive at the age of thirty-one years . . . was enlisted as your petitioners believe they had a right to do by act of May session, 1777." By the act referred to, "Apprentices and servants could be enlisted" (Hening, vol. ix, p. 275). Strictness was shown also in enforcing the law against the enlistment of slaves. A court martial was held in Goochland County, March 19, 1781, to try Colonel Jolly Parrish on the accusation of having "enlisted a slave as a substitute for his division knowing him to be so." Parrish pleaded that he believed the negro to be a free man; but the evidence showed the contrary, and Parrish was cashiered (Calendar of Virginia State Papers, vol. i, p. 582).

[111] Calendar of Virginia State Papers, vol. iii, p. 472.

The following advertisement appeared in the Virginia Gazette for March 7, 1775: "Deserted the following recruits from King William County: Copeland a white man & William Holmes a mulatto about 45 yrs of age is about 6 ft high. A Guinea reward for the white man as a Pistole for Holmes." (A bound volume of the Virginia Gazette in the Library of the Johns Hopkins University.)

[112] Hening, vol. ix, p. 268.

man." His complaint was received, and the court, "seriously considering & weighing ye premises," rendered the following verdict, than which there are none stranger on record: "The court . . . doe fynd that ye sd Mr. Robert Parker most unrightly keepeth ye sd Negro John Casor from his r[igh]t Mayster Anthony Johnson & . . . Be it therefore ye Judgment of ye court & ordered that ye sd Jno. Casor negro shall forthwith return into ye service of his sd Mayster Anthony Johnson and that the sd Mr. Robert Parker make payment of all charges in the suite and execution."

This record is quoted at length because in itself it supports a number of important propositions: (1) Before the middle of the seventeenth century some negroes in the colony were servants by indenture under the laws of servitude. (2) Some negro servants who had become freemen owned indented negro servants. The act of 1670 forbidding free negroes to own Christian servants but conceding them the right to own servants of their own race[62] is thus given a concrete explanation. (3) By the middle of the century it was with difficulty that an African immigrant escaped being reduced to slavery. If by the aid of a county court one negro could reduce to slavery another who unfortunately was unable to produce his indenture, this proceeding taking place prior to any statute supporting slavery, it can readily be seen how difficult it had become for negroes to escape being made slaves for life by white masters into whose hands they came.

It is noteworthy that all the records after the middle of the century indicate that slavery was fast becoming the rule. An entry upon the minutes of the general court in 1656 shows that a "Mulatto was held to be a slave and appeal taken."[63] Negro servants were sometimes compelled by threats and browbeating to sign indentures for long terms after they had served out their original terms. In 1675

[62] Hening, vol. ii, p. 280.

[63] General Court Records. Printed in Virginia Magazine of History, vol. viii, p. 163.

complaint was made by Philip Cowen, a negro, that Charles Lucas, "not being willing that he should enjoy his freedom, did with threats and a high hand and by confederacy with some other persons" compel him to set his hand to a writing which Lucas claimed was an indenture for twenty years, and to acknowledge it in the county court of Warwick.[64]

Fifteen years before the passage of the first act in the Virginia slave code, white persons were making assignments of negroes as slaves, and county courts were recording and recognizing the validity of contracts involving the service of negroes for life, and, in the case of female negroes, the service of the female and her offspring. In 1646 Francis Pott, preparing to return to England, sold to Stephen Charlton a negro woman called Marchant and a negro boy called Will, to be "to ye use of him . . . his heyers etc. forever."[65] A contract was made and recorded in Northampton County in 1652 according to the terms of which William Whittington "bargained & sold unto Jno. Pott . . . his heyers, Exors. Adms. or Assigns one negro girle named Jowan, aged about ten years, with her Issue and produce . . . and their services forever."[66]

---

[64] MS. in Virginia State Archives, at one time on exhibition in a glass case; compare Calendar of Virginia State Papers, vol. i, p. 10. The petitioner says that at the expiration of his term of service he was entitled to "enjoy his freedom & be paid three barrels of corn and a suit of clothes." This illustrates the statement of P. A. Bruce that upon the close of the negro servant's term he was entitled to the same quantity of clothing and corn as the white servant (Economic History of Virginia, vol. ii, p. 53). The practice is clearly stated in a petition made by a servant to the governor and council in 1660: "yor petins lately servid Henry Sprat of ye County of Lower Norff. who 1efuseth to pay him Corn and Cloths according to custome for wh ye petins obtained order of ye aforesaid Court against ye sd Mr. Sprat & C" (Calendar of Virginia State Papers, vol. i, p. 4. See also Hening, vol. iii, p. 451).

[65] MS. Court Records of Northampton County, 1651–1654, p. 28. Six years later the woman was living with Charlton, although during the six years since her sale by Francis Pott she had run away from her new master to go and live with John Pott, and later left his service to return to Charlton. She apparently exercised some liberty in the choice of her master (MS. Court Records of Northampton County, 1651–1654, p. 81).

[66] MS. Court Records of Northampton County, 1651–1654, p. 124. See also MS. Records of Lower Norfolk County, 1646–1651, p. 23,

paid £25 sterling, but from whom he had had only twenty-one years of service. Hence it would seem that £25 was regarded as a price too high for servants except those whose terms were for life.

In the inventory of the estate of William Burdett, recorded in 1643, Nehemia Freenton, aged twenty-two years, having eight years to serve, was rated at a thousand pounds of tobacco, while "Caine the negro boy, very Obedient," was rated at three thousand pounds of tobacco. Edward Southers, "a little Boy having seaven years to serve," was valued at seven hundred pounds of tobacco, while "one negro girle about 8 years old" was put down at two thousand pounds.[69] The inventory of Major Peter Walker's estate, recorded in 1655, shows that two good men servants having four years to serve were worth thirteen hundred pounds of tobacco each, and that a woman servant having two years to serve was worth eight hundred pounds of tobacco. Two negro boys with no term limit specified were rated at forty-one hundred pounds of tobacco each, and a negro girl was rated at fifty-five hundred pounds.[70] The valuation put upon the servants of Thomas Ludlowe of York County in 1660 reveals the fact that a white boy, a "seasoned hand," with six years to serve, was worth less than an old negro man and just half as much as Jugg, a negro woman.[71] The only reasonable explanation of the wide difference in the valuation of white servants having long terms of service and negroes whose terms of service were not specified is that the negroes were servants to whose service no limit was set, that is, slaves.

Thus it appears that before legislation affected in any way the development of slavery the institution had grown up, and without doubt included within its scope a large part of the African immigrants who arrived after 1640. Be it remembered, however, that the legislative recognition and

[69] MS. Court Records of Northampton County, 1640–1645, p. 225.
[70] Ibid., 1654–1655, p. 110.
[71] MS. Court Records of York County, 1657–1662, pp. 275, 278, in Virginia State Library.

Some time before 1660 Jane Rookins and Henry Randolph jointly purchased a negro woman called Maria, with the understanding that she and her children should belong to William Rookins and William Randolph and their heirs. William Randolph died, and his father, Henry Randolph, by deed gave to William Rookins all his right and title to the negro woman and her children. A creditor of William Randolph obtained an order against the estate of the deceased, and the Surry County court adjudged one half of the negroes, the negroes being Maria and her children, to belong to the estate of William Randolph.[67]

If further evidence is required to show that some negroes were regarded and held as slaves between 1640 and the date of the statutory sanction of slavery, it may be found in inventories of estates of some persons who held negroes. From the records of various counties it appears that negroes for whose service no limit is mentioned are valued in inventories at £20 to £30 sterling, while white servants of the longest terms of service receive a valuation of not more than £15 sterling.[68] In the journal of the House of Burgesses is recorded a petition of William Whittaker, an ex-member of the House, that he might be reimbursed from the public treasury for a loss incurred by an act of the House which set free a negro for whom the petitioner had

---

for the deposition of Cornelius Loyd concerning "a little black negro boy" and his mother. The boy was given as a present to Thomas Silsey. See also Records of Northampton County, 1654–1655, April, 1654, for record of sale "unto Henry Armsteadinger one negro girle named patience to him . . . and his heyers . . . forever with all her increase both male and female."

[67] Petitions to the Governor and Council, in Virginia State Archives; also printed in Calendar of Virginia State Papers, vol. i, pp. 2, 3.

[68] MS. Court Records of York County, 1657–1662, p. 195, in Virginia State Library. In 1668 two servants, one having four and a half and the other three years to serve, were valued at £12 each, but a negro woman whose term was not specified was valued at £27 (ibid., 1664–1672, p. 291, in Virginia State Library). In an inventory of the latter part of the century an Indian woman was valued as follows: "1 Indian Woman, if a slave for life £25" (MS. Court Records of Elizabeth City County, 1684–1699, p. 223, in Virginia State Library). Compare P. A. Bruce, Economic History, vol. ii, pp. 51, 52.

tending to be free were accepted for enlistment to an extent that demanded in 1777 an act which required of every negro a certificate from a justice of the peace that he was a free man before he could be admitted into the army.[113] Some white slave-owners preferred to offer their slaves as substitutes rather than render personal service in the army. In order to induce the negroes to enlist and to get them accepted they were presented for substitutes as if they were free. When the war was over, a law was passed to make good the promise of such masters by declaring free all negroes who had served in the war, and by further providing that any such negro held as a slave could recover damages by a suit at no expense to himself.[114]

There were some free negroes in Virginia who took part in the War of 1812. For example, Lewis Bowlagh, a Virginia free negro, served for a time in the United States army, and was transferred to the squadron of Commodore John Shaw, where he served until the close of the war.[115] A good many were drafted into the Confederate service in the War of Secession. All male free negroes between the ages of eighteen and fifty years were held "liable to per-

---

[113] Hening, vol. ix, p. 280. The Virginia Gazette for April 14, 1783, contained an advertisement over the name of Henry Skipwith which offered a "handsome reward" for the apprehension of a mulatto slave who had run away from his master and had been received as a substitute in the continental army. He "reenlisted for the war last fall," says the notice, "went with the troops to Winchester from whence he deserted. . . . Since his desertion he has cut off his forefinger of his right hand in order to marry a free woman near Pine Creek Mill in Powhatan County, who had determined never to have a husband in the continental army, and supposed this mutilation would procure him a discharge."

[114] Hening, vol. xi, p. 308 (1783). It should be observed that the law held these negroes to be free from the time they enlisted, and that it was passed to protect them in their right to freedom and not in any sense to confer freedom upon them. The few slaves that, contrary to law, were enlisted as slaves were unaffected by this act. To receive freedom for their services in the cause of independence, slaves had to obtain the passage of special acts (ibid., vol. xiii, pp. 103, 619; Virginia Historical Collections, vol. iv, p. 309). See the petition of Saul, a slave who served in the American army both as a soldier and as a spy among the British (MS. Petitions, Norfolk County, B 4314). Compare also Petition B 4051, New Kent County; B 314, Norfolk County.

[115] MS. Petitions, Henrico County, 1816, A 9353.

form any labor or discharge any duties with the army or in any connection with the military defenses, producing and preparing materials for war, building roads, etc."[116] Such free negroes as were engaged in the public service were subject to the military rules, which were explained especially for their benefit by the officers of the army. In both the Confederate and the United States navies service was performed by Virginia free negroes.[117] The positions they filled were doubtless of the lowest rank, and the services performed of a menial or routine nature, as indeed was most of their military service throughout the entire period under consideration.

In the matter of taxation, also, the free negro stood in relation to the government as its supporter. Far from being exempt from taxation, he was usually required to pay a higher poll-tax than the free white man. As early as 1668 a question arose as to whether free negro women should be exempted from capitation taxes as English women were. The legislature declared in an act that they ought not "in all respects to be admitted to full fruition of the exemptions of the English," and that they were still liable to payment of taxes.[118] In 1769 a petition signed by free negroes and

[116] Acts, 1861–1862; Senate Bill no. 129, among pamphlets relating to the Confederate government, in Virginia State Library.

Joseph Tinsley, a freeborn negro of Hanover County, was drafted into the Confederate service, and was at first assigned to the duty of keeping the telegraph lines in repair. He was later put to driving a government wagon. An aged antebellum free negro living (1910) at 208 Broad Street, Richmond, says that his father was drafted for service in the Confederacy.

[117] MS. Petitions, A 9353; cf. Hening, vol. xiii, p. 103. John Miller, at one time a colored statesman of the reconstruction period, and in 1910 overseer of laborers in the United States Navy-yard at Portsmouth, gave the following account of his life: Born of free parents in Portsmouth, Virginia, August 15, 1839; worked on a farm when a boy; served for one year W. W. Davis, a groceryman; went into the service of the United States Navy in 1858; was on board the Cumberland when it was attacked by the Merrimac; was discharged at the expiration of his time; went to Boston, reenlisted, and served to the close of the war. He soon got a position in the navy-yard, where he has since remained in the service of the United States Government.

[118] Hening, vol. ii, p. 267; vol. iv, p. 133. Only white women and children under sixteen years of age were exempted from the pay-

mulattoes was presented to the legislature praying that the wives and daughters of the petitioners might be exempt from taxation.[119] It met with a ready response in the law-making body, and an act was passed which, after declaring that the former law was very burdensome to such negroes, mulattoes, and Indians and derogatory to the rights of free-born subjects, exempted "from the payment of any public, county, or parish levies all free negro, mulatto, and Indian women and all wives other than slaves of free negroes, mulattoes and Indians."[120]

Male free negroes were of course still subject to the payment of taxes on the same basis as were white males. It appears that collecting from them offered unusual difficulties, which the legislature endeavored to meet in 1782 by a law providing that any free negro who failed to pay the levies should be hired out by the sheriff upon the order of a county court for a time sufficient to pay all back taxes, provided he had not sufficient property upon which distress could be made for the amount.[121] In 1787 capitation taxes were abolished.[122] The burden of the revenue was placed upon property, and this burden was borne by free negroes just in proportion as they were property owners. It does not appear that there was ever any legal discrimination against free negroes in the taxation of their property. They paid the same rate on their possessions as did white property owners.[123]

---

ment of poll-taxes, with the exception of a few individuals who were exempted by special act (ibid., vol. ii, p. 84; vol. iii, p. 259). In the seventeenth century the taxes were principally polls assessed upon "every master of a family and every freeman." The taxes upon servants were paid by the master or owner (ibid., vol. i, p. 143).

In 1666, when the entire colored population in Virginia was between one and two thousand, there were as many as nine negroes in Northampton County who paid their own taxes (Virginia Magazine of History, vol. x, pp. 194, 254).

[119] Journal of the House of Burgesses, vol. v, p. 198.

[120] Hening, vol. viii, p. 393.

[121] Ibid., vol. xi, p. 40.

[122] Ibid., vol. xii, p. 431.

[123] Land books of the various counties of Virginia, in the keeping of the state auditor of public accounts, Richmond. For the year 1856 Reuben West, a free colored man of Richmond, paid $17.62 on

In 1813, however, discriminations in capitation taxes were again renewed by laying a special poll-tax of $1.50 upon all male free negroes above sixteen years of age, except such as were bound as apprentices.[124] This rate was continued till 1815, when it was raised to $2.50 per poll and applied to all male free negroes between the ages of sixteen and forty-five.[125] The occasion for levying this poll-tax was the need for an increased revenue brought about by the War of 1812. The reason for levying it upon free negroes only may have been a widespread desire and purpose, strong at this time, to get rid of them. A tax of $2.50 assessed upon the most active, and therefore the most objectionable, free negroes was supposed to operate to induce some to leave the State, and to reduce others, who refused to pay, to a state of servitude.[126] Rigid enforcement provisions were made which authorized the sheriff to hire out any free colored tax delinquent till the required amount plus five per cent commission should be raised.[127] Although some free negroes allowed unpaid assessments to reduce them to servitude, these capitation taxes were collected with remarkable success. In 1814 $8322 was paid into the treasury by 5547 free negroes, or about ninety per cent of the male free negroes within the taxable age. In 1815, when the rate was $2.50 instead of $1.50, as in the two preceding years, and only such as were between the ages of sixteen and forty-five were taxable, 4023 free negroes paid their assessments, which amounted to $10,057.50,—or a sum

---

real estate, the assessed valuation of which was $4420. Scott Clemenze, free colored, paid $22.72 on property valued at $5680. The free colored population of Richmond paid in this year $286.81 on property assessed at $71,702.50.

[124] Acts, 1812–1813, p. 20.

[125] Ibid., 1814–1815, p. 8.

[126] House Journal, 1816–1817, p. 90; Alexander, p. 63; House Journal, 1804, December 3.

[127] Acts, 1814–1815, p. 61. If the free negro failing to pay the tax had property, distress was made upon that before hiring him out (1 Revised Code, 431). By the Code of 1860 the minimum price per day at which a free negro could be hired to raise back taxes was fixed at ten cents, and five years was made the limit of time for their collection (p. 522).

which was equal to the amount received into the treasury from lawyers' licenses or from the tax on carriages, and was one and a half per cent of the total revenue of the State.[128] During the three years when free colored men were paying a high poll-tax the white inhabitants were paying none.

The capitation tax on free negroes was dropped in 1816, after which for twenty years the assessments made on their small property holdings were the sum of their contributions to the public revenue.[129] In 1850 a tax of one dollar was levied annually upon all male free negroes between the ages of twenty-one and fifty-five.[130] According to the provisions of this law and one of 1853, this tax was to have been used for colonizing free negroes in Liberia, but it seems that only small amounts were ever paid out for that purpose. The disbursements of the treasury for the fiscal year ending October, 1858, show that $2100 was the amount spent in colonization. Between 1850 and 1853 less than $2000 per annum was expended for the purpose. The balance of the funds arising from the taxation of free negroes remained in the treasury for public purposes.[131] This levy continued in force for ten years, and was regularly collected from the free colored taxables with about the same success that similar assessments were collected from white taxpayers.[132]

In 1860 a capitation tax of eighty cents was levied upon all free male persons, white and colored, above the age of twenty-one years. The former levy of one dollar per head on free negroes had not been repealed, and when a question

---

[128] Auditor's Report for 1815–1816; Acts, 1815–1816, p. 88.

[129] In the constitutional convention of 1829–1830 Leigh remarked that free negroes were included as taxpayers, "though it is well known that they contribute little or nothing to the treasury. They should be excluded from the lists of taxpayers" (Proceedings and Debates, 1829–1830, p. 152). Joynes, of Accomac County, said "Instead of contributing to the revenue they are a perfect nuisance" (ibid., p. 211).

[130] Acts, 1849–1850, p. 7.

[131] Auditor's Report for 1859–1860, p. 407; Message of Governor Johnson, in House Documents, 1853–1854, no. 1.

[132] The average amount contributed to the public treasury from 1850 to 1860 by free negroes varied between $9000 and $13,000 (Auditor's Report for 1854–1855, p. 6; for 1861, no. 5, pp. 653, 669; for 1859–1860, p. 401 et seq.).

arose as to whether one or the other or both of these taxes should be collected, it was decided in favor of collecting both assessments. The collections at $1.80 per head on free negroes for 1860 amounted to $13,065.22.[133] The revenue act of 1861 declared that no more collections should be made under the law of 1853, thus leaving the tax on male free negroes over twenty-one years of age at eighty cents per poll.[134] The war revenue acts raised the rate rapidly. In 1862 adult male free negroes were paying $1.25 per capita, and the following year $2. At the latter rate they contributed in 1863 $11,554 to the public treasury.[135] After 1860 the poll-tax assessments were uniform for whites and free blacks.

The services of the free negro in official capacities were not demanded or accepted in Virginia. In the seventeenth century a few seem to have been entrusted with minor offices. The justices of Lancaster County appointed as beadle a negro whose duty it was to inflict punishment by stripes upon those whom the court adjudged deserving of corporal punishment.[136] In 1660 a testator nominated as executor of his will and as guardian of his foster daughter a negro whose freedom was stipulated in the will.[137] The court, however, did not confirm the nomination. In at least one instance in the last decade of the seventeenth century a negro acted as surety.[138] All office-holding by free negroes was stopped by an act of Assembly of 1705 declaring that "no negro, mulatto or Indian shall presume to take upon him, act in or exercise any office, ecclesiastic, civil or military."[139] The penalty for violation was £500. Even the ability of a free negro to become a legal witness was lim-

[133] Auditor's Report for 1861, no. 5; Code (1860), p. 243 n.

[134] Acts, 1861, p. 4.

[135] Auditor's Report for 1863; Acts, 1862–1863.

[136] MS. Court Records of Lancaster County, 1652–1657, p. 213, cited in P. A. Bruce, Economic History, vol. ii, p. 128.

[137] MS. Court Records of York County, 1657–1662, pp. 211, 217, in Virginia State Library.

[138] Ibid., 1689–1698, p. 58; P. A. Bruce, Economic History, vol. ii, p. 127.

[139] Hening, vol. iii, p. 251.

ited.[140] By this law of 1705, negroes were forbidden to be witnesses in any case whatsoever; but it was found that this disability afforded a shield for dishonest free negroes who avoided the payment of their just debts for the reason that other free negroes were not admitted as witnesses. Therefore, in 1744 the law was amended so that "any free negro, mulatto or Indian being a Christian" should be admitted as a witness in both civil and criminal suits against any negro, mulatto, or Indian, slave or free.[141] But to allow free negroes to be witnesses even in civil suits to which a white man was plaintiff against a negro defendant was discontinued in 1785; after that time they were competent witnesses in pleas of the Commonwealth for or against negroes or in civil pleas where free negroes alone were parties, and in no other cases whatsoever.[142]

Before any negro could become a witness in any case he had to receive the following extraordinary charge: "You are brought hither as a witness, and by the direction of the law I am to tell you, before you give your evidence, that you must tell the truth, the whole truth, and nothing but the truth; and that, if it be found hereafter that you tell a lie, and give false testimony in this matter, you must for so doing have both your ears nailed to the pillory and cut off, and receive thirty-nine lashes on the bare back well laid on at the common whipping-post."[143] Some time before 1849 this special injunction against lying was dropped.

Prior to 1723 there were no legal discriminations against free negroes in the limitation or extension of the suffrage.

---

[140] Andrew Burnaby mentions the exclusion of the evidence of negroes as one of the laws "which make it almost impossible to convict a planter or white man of the death of a negro or Indian" (p. 54 n.).

[141] Hening, vol. v, p. 245.

[142] Ibid., vol. xii, p. 182; 1 Revised Code, 422; Code (1849), 663. An interesting case arose in the circuit court of King William County in 1835 in which a white man in an action for debt against J. Winn, a free negro, used as witnesses two free negroes. Winn appealed to the supreme court of appeals on the ground that free negroes were not competent witnesses in the suit. The court sustained the negro's claim (6 Leigh, 74).

[143] Hening, vol. vi, p. 107; 1 Revised Code, 431.

Elections in Virginia in the seventeenth century were conducted in a very democratic fashion, in this respect resembling mass-meetings more than modern elections in which tickets and ballot-boxes figure so conspicuously. The sheriff presided over or governed the voters assembled at a voting precinct, and determined the choice of the electorate either "by view" or by subscribing the names of the voters under the name of the candidate for whom they openly declared their preference.[144] It was the general feeling in Virginia well up to the close of the seventeenth century that it was "something hard and unagreeable to reason that any persons shall pay equal taxes and yet have no votes in elections."[145] Hence all freemen, and servants "having served their tyme," were permitted to take part in elections provided they would "fairly give their votes by subscription and not in a tumultuous way."[146] There is no reason or evidence which would lead to a belief that the free negroes in the colony were excluded from these "free elections"[147] to which freed servants were admitted.

In 1670, in accordance with the wishes of the representatives of the restored English monarch, but contrary to the feelings of the masses, the principle and practice of universal suffrage were abandoned. Voting privileges were restricted to freeholders and housekeepers of certain qualifications, with the avowed purpose of disfranchising persons recently freed from servitude; these were thought to have little interest in the country, and "oftener make tumults at the election to the disturbance of his majesty's peace than provide for the conservation thereof by making choyce of persons fitly qualified for the discharge of soe great a trust."[148] The disfranchisement of a part of the rabble was a cause of popular discontent, a fact evidenced by the repeal of the restrictions by the Assembly, which was under the

[144] Hening, vol. iii, p. 172.
[145] Ibid., vol. i, p. 403.
[146] Ibid., vol. i, p. 403; vol. ii, p. 280.
[147] "Description of the Province of New Albion," in Force Tracts, vol. ii, p. 30.
[148] Hening, vol. ii, p. 280.

influence or domination of the liberal leader, Nathaniel Bacon.[149] When the conservative government regained control, Bacon's laws were repealed, and a statute was enacted which restricted the suffrage further than it had ever been restricted.[150] Previously, freeholders and housekeepers could vote, but now only freeholders could exercise that right.

From the date of this act, 1676, to 1723 the possession of a freehold was a prerequisite to the exercise of the elective franchise. Although the laws specifically stated that "no woman, sole or covert, infants under the age of twenty-one years, or recusant convicts, being freeholders," should be allowed to vote, no discrimination was made against freeholders of color.[151] The restrictions would not have eliminated all free negroes, for some at that time were freeholders. A freeholder was defined as a person who had "an estate real for his own life or the life of another, or any estate of any great dignity,"[152] which meant that the possession of almost any property entitled a man to voting privileges.

It is almost certain that some free negroes exercised the suffrage rights under these provisions, for in 1723 a law was enacted which specifically denied to free negroes the right to vote. The act declared that "no negro, mulatto, or Indian shall hereafter have any vote at the elections of burgesses or any election whatsoever."[153] When this act was referred by the Board of Trade to Richard West for the consideration of its legal aspects, he remarked: "I cannot see why one freeman should be used worse than another merely because of his complexion. . . . It cannot be right to strip all free persons of black complexion from those

---

[149] Hening, vol. ii, p. 356.

[150] Ibid., vol. ii, p. 425.

[151] Ibid., vol. iii, p. 172.

[152] Ibid., vol. iii, p. 240.

[153] Ibid., vol. iv, p. 133. As revised in 1762, the law provided that any free negro or mulatto or other person not having the right to vote, who should "presume to vote or poll at any such election, shall forfeit and pay 500 pounds of tobacco" (ibid., vol. vii, p. 519).

rights which are so justly valuable to freemen."[154] His protest was overruled; but an order was passed by the Board of Trade and Plantations directing "that a letter be wrote to the Governor to know what effect the act . . . by which free negroes are deprived of voting in all elections had."[155] A draft of such a letter was presented to the board and agreed to on December 10, 1735. Evidence is wanting as to what effect the act had, but it marked the close of the period prior to the adoption of the Fifteenth Amendment to the Constitution of the United States when negroes could vote. By the first three constitutions of the Commonwealth of Virginia voting privileges were restricted to white males of certain qualifications.[156]

The question whether the free negro in Virginia was a citizen either of the Commonwealth or of the United States is one that can be answered only when it has been made clear what is connoted by the word "citizen." The free negro was always a person in the eyes of the law, and could maintain at law certain rights of personal liberty and property. He was undoubtedly a national, a subject of Virginia and of the United States. If by the word "citizen" is meant a subject having full civil and political rights, the free negro was not a citizen of the Commonwealth of Virginia, for after 1723 he could not bear witness except in cases in which negroes alone were parties; he could not be a juror or a judge; he could not bear arms without special permission, and even though he owned property and paid taxes he could not vote or hold office.

If we attempt to answer the question by reference to the statutes and constitutions, we are confronted by the use of the word "citizen" in a variety of senses. In an act of 1779 it was declared that "all white persons born within this

---

[154] E. D. Neill, Virginia Carolorum, p. 330; see S. B. Weeks, "The History of Negro Suffrage in the South," in Political Science Quarterly, vol. ix, p. 671.

[155] Sainsbury Transcripts from the British Public Record Office, vol. i, p. 158.

[156] Constitution of 1776, art. 7; constitution of 1830; constitution of 1850.

Commonwealth and all who have resided therein two years . . . shall be citizens of this Commonwealth."[157] This act was repealed and supplanted by an act of 1783 which declared that "all free persons born within the territory of this commonwealth shall be deemed citizens of this commonwealth."[158] George Bancroft says that the treaty of peace between the American Commonwealths and Great Britain "as interpreted alike in America and England . . . included free negroes among the citizens."[159] In 1785 the General Assembly used the word in a sense which included free negroes in the citizen body. A bill being before the Assembly defining the part of the citizen body which should have the right to vote, and attention being called to the necessity of excepting free negroes and mulattoes, the words "every male citizen" were changed to read "every male citizen other than free negroes or mulattoes."[160] Judge Tucker observed in 1796 that "emancipation does not confer the rights of citizenship on the person emancipated; on the contrary, both he and his posterity of the same complexion with himself must always labor under many civil incapacities."[161]

If free negroes in Virginia were citizens in the meaning of the clause of the Federal Constitution which provides that "citizens of each State shall be entitled to all privileges and immunities of citizens of the several States," the constitutional guaranty was of no practical value to the Virginia free negroes against discriminatory action of state governments in whose domains they might attempt to travel or reside. "Citizens of the United States," said Chief Justice Taney in the Passenger Cases,[162] "must have the right to pass and repass through every part of it without interruption as freely as in [their] own States." In Crandall v.

---

[157] Hening, vol. x, p. 129.
[158] Ibid., vol. xi, p. 323; vol. xii, p. 263.
[159] History of United States, author's last version, vol. v, p. 579.
[160] House Journal, 1785, p. 96.
[161] St. G. Tucker, A Dissertation on Slavery, p. 75.
[162] 7 Howard, 492.

Nevada[163] the Court sustained this view, holding that the right to pass through a State by a citizen of the United States is one guaranteed to him by the Constitution. But throughout the first sixty-five years of the nineteenth century every branch of the government of Virginia participated in making or enforcing restrictions upon the liberty of free negroes to move from place to place or to go from the State and return. When a bill was introduced in the Virginia legislature providing for the deportation of free negroes without their consent, the argument that it was unconstitutional was feebly made, but General Brodnax, a leading member of the House, scoffing at the idea, asserted that the Constitution was about to be worn threadbare. "In truth," said he, "free negroes have many *legal* rights but no constitutional ones." There is no doubt that the opinion of the tribunals before whom the legal rights of free negroes were to be tested and applied was in agreement with this assertion.

[163] 6 Wallace, 35.

CHAPTER V

The Social Status of the Free Negro

The three principal elements in the population of Virginia to which the free negro had to adjust himself were the whites, the native Indians, and the negro slaves. A discussion of the social relations of the free negro class with each of these three other elements of the population of the State in the order named may well occupy a place of first consideration in this chapter.

If prejudices did not exist in the minds of the white inhabitants of Virginia against persons of the black race before the coming of the negro, they were not long in springing up after the two races met on Virginia soil. From the very first mention by whites of Africans in Virginia special care was taken, in writing or in speaking of them, to designate their race or color. In the earliest records of the courts and the parishes they were carefully distinguished from other persons by such words and phrases as "negroes," "negro servants," and "a negro belonging to" such a one. As early as 1630 the conduct of a white man who had violated a rule of strict separation of the white and black races was denounced as an "abuse to the dishonor of God and shame of Christians," and in atonement for such conduct the white man received a sound whipping and was required to make a public apology.[1] In the case of a similar violation of decency and standards of race purity in 1640 the guilty white man was compelled to "do penance" in the church, and the negro woman was whipped.[2] So prominent and uncouth were the physiological characteristics and so

[1] Hening, vol. i, p. 146.
[2] Ibid., vol. i, p. 552.

rude were the manners of the African emigrants that before the end of the seventeenth century many of the white colonists came to regard them as not of the human kind.[3]

This prejudice against the negro was not the result of his servile station; for in that respect he was on a par with a large part of the white population. Freedom, therefore, was not sufficient to make a negro servant or a negro slave the social equal of the whites. By the middle of the seventeenth century there were negroes who were free from all forms of legal servitude or slavery, but they were not absorbed into the mass of free population. Their color adhered to them in freedom as in servitude, and the indelible marks and characteristics of their race remained unchanged.[4] In 1668 the law-making body of the colony gave unmistakable sanction to the exclusion of the free negroes from social equality in a declaration that "negro women set free, . . . although permitted to enjoy their freedom, yet ought not in all respects to be admitted to full fruition of the exemptions and impunities of the English."[5]

Yet, in spite of strong racial antipathies, there were some illicit relations between shameless white persons and negroes, by reason of which it was deemed necessary as early as 1662 to enact legislation concerning the status of mulatto children. In 1691 a law prescribed for "any white woman marrying a negro or mulatto, bond or free," the extreme penalty of perpetual banishment.[6] The strength of public sentiment was soon tested in the matter of enforcing this law in the case of Ann Wall, an English woman, who was arraigned in the county court of Elizabeth City on the charge of "keeping company with a negro under pretense of marriage."[7] Upon conviction, she and two of her mulatto chil-

[3] M. Godwyn, Negro's and Indian's Advocate, suing for their Admission into the Church, p. 23 et seq.

[4] Compare G. Bancroft, History of the United States, ed. 1843, vol. iii, p. 410.

[5] Hening, vol. ii, p. 267.

[6] Ibid., vol. iii, p. 87.

[7] MS. Court Records of Elizabeth City County, 1684–1699, p. 27, in Virginia State Library. In 1737 a negro who attempted to assault a white girl was compelled to stand in a pillory for an hour, was

dren were bound for terms of service to a man living in Norfolk County, and a court order was recorded to the effect that in case she ever returned to Elizabeth City County she should be banished to the Barbadoes.[8] Whether the "abominable mixture or spurious issue," as the mulatto was called, was of slave or free negro parentage, it was equally detested by respectable white persons.

In the seventeenth century there were a few free negroes of exceptional merit who were accorded, in all relations not involving or leading to a blending of the races, social privileges about equal to those accorded to freed white servants. A few were prosperous owners of personal and real property, respected by white persons, dealt with by white men in business relations, and permitted to participate in elections,—facts which seem to indicate that for a while the prejudices of the white inhabitants against the negroes went only to the extent of preserving the Teutonic blood from contamination, and did not at first deny to the African freedom of opportunity to take such station in other relations as his individual merit enabled him to assume. At that time the theory that the negro was fit for nothing but slavery or some servile capacity had not been so carefully elaborated nor so generally applied as it was in the eighteenth and nineteenth centuries. Although precluded from the possibility of intermarrying with white persons, the negro freed from servitude or slavery had about the same industrial or economic opportunities as the free white servant. But as slavery advanced toward a more complete inclusion and subjection of the negro race in Virginia, the social and industrial privileges of the free negro were gradually curtailed. The denial to him, by laws passed in 1723, of the right to vote, the right to bear arms, and the right to bear witness is proof of the fact that prejudice had extended beyond a demand for race separation and race purity to an imposition upon the negro of a low and servile station.

"pelted by the populace, and afterwards smartly whipped" (Virginia Gazette, August 19–26, 1737; quoted in Virginia Magazine of History, vol. xi, p. 424).

[8] MS. Court Records of Elizabeth City County, 1684–1699, p. 83.

From 1723 to the end of the colonial period the number of the free negroes was, both absolutely and relative to the other populations, so small that the social status of the class would have been unimportant except for the fact that prejudices accumulating in this period were handed down to the time when the free colored class became numerically important. Except for natural procreation, the principal additions or recruits to this class throughout this period were the result of illegitimacy. There was no tendency to attribute to a few free negroes and mulattoes of such low origin any higher social standing than that occupied by more than ninety-nine per cent of their race and color. Too small and of too low an origin to preserve for itself, by the formation of an exclusive caste, higher social rights than slaves, the free colored class was nevertheless sufficiently large to pass on to the larger free negro class of the period of the Commonwealth all the disabilities and social disadvantages that it had gathered to itself for a hundred years. The freedom which masters were to be allowed to confer upon their slaves under the act of 1782 was the freedom of the colonial free negro and no more. Even those persons who professed a desire to apply to the slaves the principles of natural and equal rights had no intention or desire to exalt the manumitted slave to social equality with the whites. Chastellux, travelling through Virginia in the early eighties of the eighteenth century, noticed the inferior social status of the free negroes, and wrote: "In the present case it is not only the slave who is beneath his master, it is the negro who is beneath the white man. No act of enfranchisement can efface this unfortunate distinction."[9]

The free negro population which came to be numbered by tens of thousands in the nineteenth century was as remote from a social plane upon which intermingling or intermarriage with the white race was possible as were the slaves. "A companion to slaves . . . forbidden to intermarry with whites or to bear testimony against them; forbidden to learn

[9] Vol. ii, p. 99.

to read or to write, or to preach the word of God even to his fellows, to bear arms or to resist assault—in every relation from the cradle to the grave he was never allowed to forget that he was an inferior being."[10] Illegal marriages or associations of whites with free negroes were so disreputable and disgraceful that they were entered into by the vilest white persons at the peril of chastisement by privately organized bands of white persons supported by community sentiment.[11] The free mulatto class, which numbered 23,500 by 1860, was of course the result of illegal relations of white persons with negroes; but, excepting those born of mulatto parents, most persons of the class were not born of free negro or free white mothers, but of slave mothers, and were set free because of their kinship to their master and owner.[12]

When we come to consider the social contact and affiliation of the free negro with the native Indian, the barriers to social affinity and intermixing of races on terms of equality are seen to be less important than those between free negroes and whites. No law forbade the intermarriage of free negroes and Indians, and there existed between them some fundamental grounds of sympathy and mutual appreciation. Both bore the marks of a savage race and had a colored skin; hence they shared the racial antipathy of the whites, although possibly to a different degree. Both were wanting in experience and acquaintance with the manners of civilized life, to which they were being introduced through the agency of an alien race. Both enjoyed liberty to go and come at will; but, unlike slaves, they were dependent upon their own resources for subsistence. Both were, in a way, misfits and discordant elements in a society organized as was that of Virginia, on a basis of slavery,—a society economically and politically complete, with a governing white aristocracy and a class of colored toilers living in a condition of com-

[10] Message of Governor Smith, 1848–1849, in House Journal, p. 21.

[11] MS. Petitions, Amelia County, 1821, A 781.

[12] MS. Petitions, King William County, 1825, B 1191; Essex County, 1825, A 5396; Halifax County, 1857, A 7724.

plete subjection. While there existed dissimilarities between free negroes and Indians, there was certainly a common bond of union; and it is significant that in the massacre of 1622 not an African perished at the hands of the Indians, although there were at the time of the massacre more than twenty negroes scattered throughout the little colony.[13]

Before 1724 there were in the colony some persons of mixed blood, part negro and part Indian, called mustees or mustizos.[14] A number of reservations of land, containing from a few hundred to many thousand acres, were set apart in the eastern section of Virginia in the seventeenth and eighteenth centuries for the use and enjoyment of the Indians.[15] After a time, these reservations became the common homes of free negroes and the tribesmen for whom they were intended, who associated on terms of social equality. It was said in 1787 of the inhabitants of the Gingaskin reservation[16] that those who were not entirely black had at least "half black blood in them."[17] The place was called Indian Town, but many of the squaws had negroes for husbands, and Indian braves lived with black wives. As a means of improving the social order in Indian Town, the white people thereabouts proposed that no negroes, except the husbands of female Indians, be allowed to remain in the tribe. The town, they said, afforded "a Harbour and convenient asylum to an idle set of free negroes," and was a great nuisance to the public.[18]

In 1744 the Nottaway and kindred tribes possessed about

---

[13] McDonald Transcripts from the British Public Record Office, vol. i, p. 46; Hotten, pp. 218–258; Colonial Records of Virginia, Senate Document, 1874, Extra, p. 61.

[14] "Such as are born of an Indian and negro are called Mustees" (H. Jones, The Present State of Virginia, p. 37).

[15] Hening, vol. ii, p. 290; P. A. Bruce, Economic History, vol. i, p. 492 et seq.; vol. ii, p. 115.

[16] See Hening, vol. viii, p. 414, for facts concerning this reservation in Northampton County. In 1769 it contained six hundred acres. The legislature then passed an ordinance providing for the sale of two hundred acres of this land, the proceeds to be used by the parish to provide for such of the tribe as should become public charges. Compare Hening, vol. ii, p. 13; vol. iii, p. 85.

[17] MS. Petitions, Norfolk County, 1787, B 4865.

[18] Ibid., 1782, B 4865; 1782, B 4845.

20,000 acres of land which they could not, according to law, alienate.[19] In 1821 they still occupied 3370 acres. White persons in the vicinity of this reservation affirmed in 1821 that "their [the Indians'] wives and husbands are free negroes,"[20] and that they had neither prudence nor economy.

As late as 1843 the Pamunkeys possessed sixteen hundred acres of land in King William County. One hundred and forty-three citizens of the county petitioned the legislature to have the lands divided, saying that all but a small remnant of the old Indian tribe was extinct, and that in its place were free mulattoes, all of whom were believed to have one fourth negro blood,—an amount sufficient under the provisions of the code of 1819 to class them as mulattoes.[21] "They are so mingled with the negro race as to have obliterated all striking features of Indian extraction. It is the general resort of free negroes from all parts of the country."[22]

The association and intermarriage of free negroes with Indians was not confined to areas given up to Indians. From an early date mustees were a small constituent element of the population, intermingling with the other inhabitants of the colony.[23] John Dungie, an Indian of King William County, was in 1824 legally married to Anne Littlepage, a mulatto daughter of Edmund Littlepage, esq., a man of considerable wealth. "The husband was a sailor . . . constantly employed in the navigation of the Chesapeake Bay and Rivers of Virginia." His free mulatto wife was heir to a considerable annuity.[24] In a case before the supreme

---

[19] Hening, vol v, p. 270.
[20] MS. Petitions, York County, 1821.
[21] Hening, vol. xiv, p. 123; 1 Revised Code, 423.
[22] MS. Petitions, King William County, 1843, B 1207. Petition B 1208 is a counter-petition from the chief men of the tribe, who wish to retain their lands. They admit that some persons not of their tribe are within their boundaries, but claim that the inhabitants generally are of at least half Indian extraction. That members of the Pamunkey tribe to this day (1912) bear in their features evidences of a mixture of the tribe with negroes may be stated on the authority of a prominent citizen of Richmond who has observed them.
[23] Jones, p. 37.
[24] MS. Petitions, King William County, 1825, B 1191.

court of appeals in 1831 we find an attorney making the assertion as an historical fact that Indians had intermarried with negroes.[25]

The names "mustizo" or "mustee" and "mulatto" were not always applied with discrimination, the latter being often used where the former should have been applied.[26] In the censuses no separate enumeration is made of the mustees, but there is no doubt that a considerable element in the free colored population of the nineteenth century was of Indian extraction.

The most congenial companion of the free negro outside of his own class was found among his kinsmen in bondage. The larger part of the free negro class met and mingled with negro slaves on a plane of almost perfect social equality.[27] Prior to 1782 the fact that the free colored persons were few in number would have been sufficient to prevent the formation of an exclusive caste had there been differences between free and slave negroes so radical as to render conditions favorable for such a development. Even when their numbers became sufficiently large for the formation of an exclusive caste, there were absent those differences in economic and political station to make it desirable either for the free negro or the slave class to exclude the other from its social life, the freedom of the free negro being in most lines of activity only nominal. There were lacking to the free negro the better education, the higher standard of wants, and the better opportunities for acquiring wealth and position necessary to supply an actual basis of superiority and to give him higher social rank than that occupied by the slave.

[25] Gregory v. Baugh, 2 Leigh, 665; cf. also Jenkins v. Tom, 1 Hening and Munford, 123; T. Jefferson, Notes on the State of Virginia, ed. 1801, p. 182.

[26] Virginia Gazette, December 1, 1782. A reward is offered for a runaway slave who, according to the description, was the offspring of an Indian and a negress; but he is called a mulatto.

[27] "The free negroes continue to live with the negro slaves, and never with the white man" (Chastellux, vol. ii, p. 199).

Had it been possible for the free negro to hold himself aloof from the slaves, he might have borne a better reputation among slave owners; for, as will appear later, his connection and his relation with slaves rendered him the object of much undeserved suspicion and criticism. To the slaves themselves the free negro was a welcome visitor; at feasts, barbacues, dances, and negro meetings of every kind he was present to participate on a plane of equality with his slave neighbors. While very few would have exchanged this condition for that of the slave, they rarely ever regarded slavery as the badge of a rank inferior to their own.

It was very common in the nineteenth century and the twenty years immediately preceding for free negroes to marry slaves. Numerous instances can be cited of marriages of free negro women with slave men. A case occurred in Brock County in 1826.[28] A free negress by the name of Rachel married a slave in Alleghany County in 1828.[29] Dilly, a free negro woman of Giles County, was married to a slave husband by whom she had two children.[30] Similar examples may be found in almost any county.[31]

Since the status of the mother became the status of the offspring, it might be supposed that free colored women would have had less aversion to choosing slave husbands than free colored men would have had to marrying slave wives, but that does not appear to have been the case. Numerous examples might be cited to show that the prospect of having children who would be slaves did not deter free negro men from marrying slave wives. Rice Stephens, a freeborn negro, was living in Northampton County in 1843 with a slave wife and three children.[32] Samuel Johnson, a

[28] MS. Petitions, Brock County, A 2684.

[29] MS. Petitions, Alleghany County, A 651.

[30] MS. Petitions, Giles County, 1829, A 6784.

[31] MS. Petitions, Goochland County, 1840, A 7109. According to the story of Mary Winston, a free negro woman of Hanover County still living (1909), her grandmother and great-grandmother married slaves.

[32] MS. Petitions, Northampton County, B 4905.

free negro of Fauquier County, had a slave daughter who became the wife of a free negro.[33]

Indeed, it is apparent that there were not a few free negroes who preferred a slave to a free wife. Certainly there was less responsibility upon a husband whose wife and children were slaves and were therefore supported by their white owners than upon one whose wife and children had to be provided for by himself. "A freeman," says a proslavery editor in 1802, "as soon as he is his own master, marries the female slave of some farmer. He cannot well be prevented from residing with his wife. She feeds him *gratis.*"[34] This was the opinion also of a later pamphlet writer who wrote under the pseudonym of "Calx." "Every male free negro," he wrote, "prefers to have a slave wife, and will be so provided, if permitted by too careless indulgence. In this manner he will not only have his wife and children supported by the owner, and a lodging provided for himself, but much of his own food will be obtained from his wife and, directly or indirectly, to the loss of her master."[35]

In addition to the temptation to free colored men to select wives who were sure of support, and who might even partly support their husbands, there was after 1806 another reason why some free negroes might have considered themselves fortunate to be connected by marriage with a slave woman. Such a family connection often prevented a free negro manumitted after 1806 from having to leave the State, according to law, within twelve months from the date of his manumission. If such a free negro husband comported himself well and made a useful laborer in the community, he was sure to have the good will of his wife's master, to whose interest it was to keep his slaves contented in their place. If the free husband stayed in the community, his presence would not only be a guaranty against his slave family making trouble for their master by becoming runaways, but he himself might also become a useful employee of his wife's

[33] MS. Petitions, Fauquier County, 1837, A 5859.
[34] Richmond Recorder, November 10, 1802.
[35] "Calx," p. 5 et seq.

master. If he was forced to leave, he immediately endangered the interest of the master by establishing himself in a border State and inducing his wife and children to join him. Many a free negro petitioning the legislature for permission to remain in the State made a special point of the fact that his wife and children were slaves.[36] Many slave-owners endorsed their petitions, and joined in asking the legislature to grant the privilege asked for. Particularly was it true in counties bordering on Maryland, Pennsylvania, Ohio, and Kentucky that the slave-owners realized and were frank to admit that a free negro, though not desirable on his own part, was more desirable in Virginia than in a border county of an adjoining State.[37]

There is, however, nothing in the facts above stated, nor in truth in any authentic evidence thus far examined, to give support to the contention frequently made by slavery apologists in the nineteenth century, and to this day not infrequently repeated, that slaves generally regarded free negroes as of inferior social rank. The negro "aristocracy," if such there was, was not based on the superiority of slaves over the free negroes, but on the superiority of the wealthy planter's "servants" over the "poor man's nigger."[38] Thomas Bruce, writing in 1891 concerning the happy state of slavery, said: "As a class, happier beings never existed, and they had a most unbounded contempt for a free negro . . . and shunned him as they would a leper, and even to this day that prejudice still exists in the minds of the negro who can recall the days of slavery."[39] Ellen Glasgow, in her novel entitled "The Battle-Ground," depicts Free Levi as a free

[36] House Journal, 1832–1833, p. 201.

[37] Writing to the legislature to ask that a certain free negro be permitted to remain in the State, fifty-five slave-owners of Harrison County say: "He will take up his residence in the nearest point in Pennsylvania or Ohio and of course will make occasional visits to his family, and from the clamor which is going on in those states upon the subject of abolition we judge that we should have more to fear from that source than from his being permitted to remain among us" (MS. Petitions, Harrison County, 1839, A 8677; see also MS. Petitions, Cumberland County, 1815, A 4728).

[38] A. Bagby, King and Queen County, p. 283.

[39] T. Bruce, Southwest Virginia and the Shenandoah Valley, p. 46.

colored man "who shares alike the pity of his white neighbors and the withering contempt of his black ones."[40] If there is a basis of truth which gave rise to this mistaken belief here and elsewhere expressed, it is in the fact that slave-owners disapproved of the association of their slaves with free negroes, whom they suspected of scattering seeds of discontent in slave quarters. The master of slaves did indeed have a withering contempt for free negroes, but one of the reasons for such a feeling was the realization that his slaves might readily emulate the superior privileges of freedom as exemplified in the free negro. The slaves, being generally of a docile, tractable disposition, may have pretended to regard free negroes as their inferiors, but their "unbounded contempt" was merely an echo.[41]

From one source, however, there sprang up in slaves a certain dislike of free negroes with whom they were required to work, but the feeling was quite different from contempt. When free negroes were employed to work for wages with slaves, as they often were,[42] and to do no harder work than the slaves, the slaves were sometimes envious of the free negroes because of the superior privileges of the latter in the way of recompense. Such dislike for the free negroes on the part of slaves was envious dislike for a superior rather than contemptuous dislike for an inferior.[43]

---

[40] P. 148.

[41] William Dunston, slave of John R. Dunston, of Accomac County, married a free negress whose name was Jane Jubilee. In this instance it required not a little determination and self-will for the slave to follow his suit to victory; for he was constantly met by his master's reproachful queries: "Bill, would you marry into that family of Jubilees? They are *free* negroes." This incident, related to the author by C. C. James, of Northampton County, illustrates the way in which masters tried to create in their slaves a dislike for free negroes.

[42] "They [free negroes] are sometimes hired for field labour in times of harvest and on other particular occasions" (Madison's Writings, vol. iii, pp. 310–315).

[43] William E. Waddy, esq., of Eastville, Virginia, born in 1827, and familiar with the facts concerning the relation of free negroes and slaves from his boyhood to the close of the Civil War, vividly recalls that a distaste for working with free negro hired laborers was often manifested by slaves. He was unaware, however, of the existence among slaves owned or observed by him of a feeling of social superiority over free negroes.

The acknowledgment repeatedly made by the enemies of the free negro is alone sufficient to controvert the traditional belief that slaves considered themselves in a superior station or social rank to that of the free negroes. The latter were spoken of as "possible chieftains of formidable conspiracies," and "leaders" in servile outbreaks.[44] Mr. Moore, in the slavery debate of 1832, said, "I lay it down as a maxim not to be disputed, that our slaves, like all the rest of the human race, are now and will continue to be actuated by a desire of liberty."[45] This assumption was constantly made by both antislavery and proslavery advocates, and particularly by that portion of the latter class who regarded the presence of the free negroes as a source of danger to the institution of slavery as well as a menace to the discipline and control of slaves. Antebellum free negroes and their descendants still living are very proud to relate facts concerning their free ancestry; and while the most reliable of the survivors of this class admit that many free negroes were on no higher plane than slaves, they hold to the view that many of the better class of free negroes considered themselves socially superior to any slave. This must indeed have been true of the free negroes who owned considerable property, or owned or hired negro slaves and servants, as did a few in the seventeenth century and many in the nineteenth. It was certainly true of some free mulattoes who because of their white connections had received special opportunities for education and an independent support.[46]

Whether a free negro was to be married to a free person or to a slave, who was legally incapable of making a con-

[44] Richmond Enquirer, January 18, 1805.

[45] Ibid., January 19, 1832.

[46] In 1857 eight quadroon children belonging to Craddock Vaughn of Halifax County made petition to the legislature for permission to reside in the State notwithstanding the law of 1806, which applied to them. The petitioners affirmed that they had had every care in bringing up, and that they were "beyond the sphere of the free negro class so degraded" (MS. Petitions, Halifax County, 1857, A 7724). See also MS. Petitions, King William County, 1825, B 1191; Alleghany County, 1828, A 651; Halifax County, 1783, A 7551.

tract,[47] legal forms were adhered to, and the nuptial ceremonies observed by white persons were imitated. White ministers officiated at weddings of all classes of colored persons. Free colored candidates for matrimony obtained licenses just as did white persons, and often procured the parlor of a white family as a place for the ceremony. A glance at the records of marriages by the ministers of Henrico parish from 1823 to 1860 will reveal numerous instances of marriages of free colored persons and a few of marriages of free negroes with slaves.[48] Of six marriages solemnized by Rev. Edward Peet in 1831 one was the union of free colored persons; and of sixteen persons married by the same minister in 1832, four were free colored. In 1829 Rev. W. F. Lee married eight white and two free colored persons; in 1833 the record was the same as in 1829; in 1834 he married ten white and two free colored couples; and in 1846, four white couples and one free colored couple.[49]

In the seventeenth century and the part of the eighteenth when the free negro class was so small as to be numbered in hundreds there were to be found examples of well regulated, orderly families, appreciative of the sanctity of the family relations, in which both parents were free colored. The Northampton County records show a few examples as early as 1655.[50] The parish registers of the eighteenth century contain numerous examples of free colored parents

[47] "It is agreed that slaves have no power [of contract]. Hence the marriages of slaves are void" (Minor, vol. i, p. 168).

[48] L. W. Burton, Annals of Henrico Parish, pp. 236–248. For instances of marriages of free with slave negroes, see p. 247: "Morris Harris a free colored man, to Patience, a servant to Mrs. Mary E. Robinson, by Rev. H. S. Kepler, 1855." "Servant" in this register was a euphonious designation for "slave." The entries concerning the marriage of a free colored man with a free colored woman uniformly stated that both were free, as: "Ned lightfoot and Sophy Buck, both free people of color. License bearing date as above." By Rev. W. M. Hart: "Aug. 16, 1825, John Jarvis, a free man of color, and Lucy Marble, a free woman of color. License bearing date Henrico Court, Aug. 1825." For another example, see p. 248.

[49] Burton, pp. 236–244.

[50] MS. Court Records of Northampton County, 1651–1654, pp. 28, 161.

whose children were regularly baptized into the church.[51] When toward the latter part of the eighteenth century and on to the end of the antebellum period the free colored population came to be numbered by tens of thousands, numerous examples of respectable free colored families are to be found. On a petition signed by ninety free colored persons of Richmond in 1823 there were nineteen families represented by the names of both husband and wife.[52] It was thought that a rather large proportion of free colored females, particularly free mulattoes, were unchaste.[53] However this may have been, there is ample documentary evidence to show that in the nineteenth century there was a certain large class of the free colored population the members of which were respectable and observant of decency and regularity in their family relations.[54]

Throughout the period of the colony when the number of free negroes was comparatively small, and even in the nineteenth century before the time of the active propagation of antislavery doctrines, there existed little if any prejudice against the education of free colored persons. In the third quarter of the seventeenth century there was opposition to offering baptism to negro slaves until it was determined by law that the administration of the baptismal rite did not bestow freedom.[55] This objection did not apply, however, to the religious instruction of free negroes or negro apprentices. Before the middle of the seventeenth century provision was made by certain white persons for guaranteeing religious instruction and education to negro servants who would eventually become free.[56] In 1654, when Richard

[51] Bruton Parish Register, p. 57 ff. Original copy, Bruton Church, Williamsburg.

[52] MS. Petitions, Henrico County, 1823, A 9335.

[53] "Calx," pp. 5–11.

[54] Cf. MS. Petitions, Accomac County, A 42.

[55] Hening, vol. ii, p. 260; Godwyn, p. 11 ff.

[56] General Court Records, printed in Virginia Magazine of History, vol. xi, p. 281; MS. Court Records of Northampton County, 1645–1651, p. 82.

Vaughan freed his negroes, he provided in his will that they should be taught to read and to make their own clothes, and that they should be brought up in the fear of God.[57]

In colonial times the Anglican church did a great deal to provide for the religious instruction and baptism of the free colored class. The reports made in 1724 to the English bishop by the Virginia parish ministers are evidence that the few free negroes in the parishes were permitted to be baptized, and were received into the church when they had been taught the catechism.[58] It had been a practice of the seventeenth century to stipulate in the indenture or contract by which a free negro was apprenticed to a master that the master, in return for the negro's service, must provide instruction in the Christian religion in addition to sufficient food, apparel, and lodging.[59] In 1691 the church became the agency through which the laws of negro apprenticeship were carried out.[60] Free mulatto children born of white mothers and any free colored boy or girl without visible means of support were bound by the churchwardens to serve white men for a certain term of years. The custom of the churchwardens of requiring these masters to provide some degree of education for the colored apprentices remained in vogue throughout the colonial period, as is shown by numerous orders of the vestry meetings and orders of the county courts for binding out free colored children. For example, in 1727 it was ordered that David James, a free negro boy, be bound to Mr. James Isdel, "who is to teach him to read ye bible distinctly also ye trade of a gunsmith that he carry

[57] MS. Court Records of Northampton County, 1654–1655, pp. 102, 103.

[58] Papers Relating to the History of the Church: Westminster parish, p. 261; Lawn's Creek parish, p. 289.

"The church is open to them all" (Report of the minister in Isle of Wight County, in Papers Relating to the History of the Church, p. 274). As a means of encouraging baptism of negro children, a proposition was made to exempt from taxation for four years any negro or mulatto child baptized (ibid., p. 344).

[59] See an indenture to this effect executed by Francis Pott in 1646, in MS. Court Records of Northampton County, 1645–1651, p. 82.

[60] Hening, vol. iii, p. 87.

him to ye Clark's office & take Indenture to that purpose."[61] By the Warwick County court it was "ordered that Malacai, a mulatto boy, son of mulatto Betty be, by the church wardens of this Parish, bound to Thomas Hobday to learn the art of a planter according to law."[62] By the order of the Norfolk County court, about 1770, a free negro was bound out "to learn the trade of a tanner."[63] After 1785 the duty of binding out free colored children was placed upon the overseers of the poor, who required of the masters, according to the laws and the custom, an agreement to teach the apprentice reading, writing, and arithmetic.[64]

In the period between the Revolutionary War and the beginning of the nineteenth century there were two religious societies that were very active in teaching and offering religious instruction to the free negroes, namely, the Quakers and the Methodists.[65] The Quakers set free no inconsiderable part of the slaves manumitted in this period, and the various meetings took official action to see that negroes set free by their members were taught and Christianized.[66] It was in accordance with the advice of the yearly and quarterly meetings of Friends that the monthly meetings extended "a watchful care over those negroes . . . set free within the verge of the monthly meeting, administering counsel and advice particularly to those in their minority" and rendering them temporal and spiritual assistance.[67] In 1781 a

[61] From the court records of Princess Anne County, cited in Virginia Magazine of History, vol. ii, p. 429. See also MS. Minutes of Northampton County, 1754–1757, p. 100.

[62] MS. Minutes of Warwick County, 1748–1762, p. 30, in Virginia State Library.

[63] MS. Orders of Norfolk County, 1768–1771, pp. 232–233. See also ibid., pp. 11, 91; Vestry Book of Saint Peter's Parish, p. 135: an order, 1771; Register of St. Peter's Parish, p. 117.

[64] Hening, vol. viii, pp. 376–377; vol. xii, pp. 28, 29; vol. xvi, p. 124.

[65] The friendship of the Quakers and the Methodists for the negro was mentioned by Randolph in the Federal Convention at Philadelphia, 1787 (Papers of James Madison, ed. by Gilpin, vol. iii, p. 1396).

[66] MS. Minutes of the Hopewell Monthly Meeting, 1777–1791, p. 190.

[67] MS. Minutes of the Fairfax Monthly Meeting, 1776–1802, p. 105 (1776), pp. 110, 243 (1782); MS. Minutes and Proceedings of Goose Creek Monthly Meeting, 1785–1818, p. 533.

committee of Friends appointed by the Warrenton and Fairfax Quarterly Meeting "to have under their Care and labour to promote the Education and religious Instruction of such negroes as have been set free" reported that "a good degree of care and labor had been extended, and that there still remained other work along the same line that must be done."[68] The Methodists were likewise mindful of the spiritual welfare of the negroes, whether free or slave, and were so active in the advocacy of the cause of freedom that they were denied by many slave-owners the opportunity of instructing slaves;[69] but they continued to offer private instruction to free negroes, and to slaves when opportunity was afforded.[70] Besides Quakers and Methodists, there were smaller religious societies, such as Moravians, Harmonites, and Shakers, who, besides giving the negroes religious instruction, taught them many useful industries, and even worked with them in creating a common property.[71]

After the fears of the slave-owners were aroused by the Gabriel insurrection in 1800 and by rumors of a general outbreak, it was thought desirable to curtail the opportunities of the free negroes for acquiring a knowledge of books which might render them propagators of seditious anti-slavery doctrines among the slaves; hence the overseers of the poor were commanded by legislative authority to cease requiring the master or mistress to whom a free negro or mulatto child was apprenticed to teach the child reading, writing, and arithmetic, as had hitherto been the custom.[72]

---

[68] MS. Minutes of Warrenton and Fairfax Quarterly Meeting, 1776–1787, p. 123.

[69] Journal of the Rev. Francis Asbury, vol. ii, p. 71; vol. iii, pp. 253, 257; Bennett, p. 547.

[70] "What directions shall we give for the promotion of the spiritual welfare of the colored people?

"We conjure all our ministers and preachers . . . to leave nothing undone for the spiritual benefit and salvation of them . . . and to unite in Society those who appear to have a real desire of fleeing from the wrath to come; to meet such in class and to exercise the whole Methodist discipline among them" (Annual Minutes, 1787, quoted from H. N. McTyeire, History of Methodism, p. 381).

[71] Madison's Writings, vol. iii, pp. 495, 497.

[72] Hening, vol. xvi, p. 124.

A more rigorous enforcement of the laws against unlawful assemblages of slaves further discouraged efforts to give instruction to negroes, bond or free. Quakers were prosecuted in court for assembling negroes for instruction in their meeting-houses.[73] Probably owing to discouragement thus received and to some relaxation of their former zeal due to other causes, the Friends were not so active in behalf of the negro in Virginia as they had been in the eighteenth century, although they continued to hold a prominent place among his sympathizers and helpers. In 1816 a committee appointed by the Goose Creek Monthly Meeting to inquire into the opportunities for education afforded African children in the homes of Friends reported that "only two instances were found of colored children suitably provided for, and opportunity afforded them of acquiring useful school learning."[74]

In the nineteenth century the Baptist Church, by a less bold assertion of views in opposition to slavery than those advanced by Methodists, avoided the hostility of the slave-owners which fell to the share of the Methodists, and thus gained the larger share of negro evangelization.[75] Even when the laws discouraged negro education, the Baptists did much toward instructing free negroes privately and in Sunday schools,[76] and received them into their churches.[77] In churches where colored persons attended in considerable numbers a section of the pews was set aside for their use, and at all times a strict observance of the color line seems to have prevailed. The condition of the free colored people before 1831 as regards religious and educational advantages is so well shown by a petition to the legislature in 1823 of

---

[73] See E. Woods, Albemarle County, in Virginia, p. 111, for instances of indictments of Friends for unlawfully assembling slaves.

[74] MS. Minutes of Goose Creek Monthly Meeting, 1785–1818, p. 534.

[75] In 1835 Professor E. A. Andrews wrote a letter from Fredericksburg saying that the "religious instruction [of the free negroes] has fallen, in a great measure into the hands of the Baptists, as in Baltimore it is conducted by the Methodists" (Slavery and the Domestic Slave Trade in the United States, p. 162).

[76] Cf. The Liberator, July 4, 1845.

[77] MS. Petitions, Floyd County, 1836, A 6081.

ninety-one free negroes of Richmond that the document is worth reproducing in full:—

The petition of a number of persons of colour residing in the City of Richmond, respectfully represents: that from the rapid increase of population in the City, the number of free persons of colour and slaves has become very considerable and although few of them can boast any knowledge of letters, yet that they are always desirous of receiving such instruction from public and divine worship as may be given by sensible and prudent Teachers of religion.

It has been the misfortune of your petitioners to be excluded from the churches, meeting-houses and other places of public devotion which are used by white persons in consequence of no appropriate places being assigned for them, except in a few Houses, and they have been compelled to look to private Houses, where they are much crowded and where a portion of their Brothers are unable to hear or to partake of the worship which is going on. Your Petitioners consisting of free persons and slaves, have been for some time associated with the Baptist church. A list of their members consisting of about 700 persons has been submitted for his inspection to the Head of Police of this City and no objection has been by him made to their moral characters.

Your Petitioners for these reasons humbly pray that your honourable body will pass a law authorizing them to cause to be erected within this city a house of public worship which may be called the Baptist African Church. To such restrictions and restraints as are consistent with the laws now existing or which may hereafter be passed for the proper restraint of persons of colour and for the preservation of the peace and good order of society . . . your petitioners are prepared most cheerfully to submit, and although it would be pleasing to them to have a voice in the choice of their Teachers yet would they be quite satisfied that any choice made by them should be approved or rejected by the Mayor of this city, they ask not for the privilege of continuing in office any preacher who shall in any manner have rendered himself obnoxious to the Mayor, nor can they reasonably expect to hold night meetings or assemblages for Baptizing but with the consent of that officer. And your Petitioners as in duty bound will ever pray. . . .[78]

---

[78] MS. Petitions, Henrico County, 1823, A 9335. Affixed to this petition were the following names of free colored persons of Richmond and the mayor's certificate, as follows:—

"I hereby certify that I have examined the list of signatures of free persons of colour hereunto attached and believe them to be respectable.

"I am of opinion that the prayers of their petition, if granted, may be productive of benefit to themselves as well as to the white population of Richmond and most sincerely wish them success.

John Adams,
Mayor of the City of Richmond.

Free persons of colour of the City of Richmond of the Baptist denomination:

Richard Dye,
Teanah Dye,
Hembrey Tompkins,
Mary Tompkins,

Although it appears that the bill introduced in the House of Delegates granting the privileges asked for in this petition was lost, the negroes were enabled by some means to erect church houses for their use. There were three African Baptist churches and two African Methodist churches in Richmond in the decade before the Civil War.[79]

When the agitation for the abolition of slavery became acute and antislavery tracts and pamphlets were in wide circulation in the State, the friends of the institution of slavery became apprehensive of the evil which might result from the reading of such literature by free negroes, and in consequence brought about legislation to prevent free negroes from acquiring a knowledge of books.[79a] The proximate cause of legislative action was probably the discovery in 1830 by the mayor of Richmond of a copy of Walker's Appeal to the Colored Citizens of the World in the house of a free negro after his death.[80] By an act of April 7, 1831, "all

William Caswell,	Nancy Ellis,
Robert Dandridge,	Phillip Robenson,
Martha Dandridge,	Richard Vaughan,
Thomas Mondowney,	Agness Vaughan,
Catherine Mondowney,	John Harper,
Exland Henderson,	Caesar Hawkins,
P. Wm. Reynolds,	Fanny Hawkins,
Sarah Reynolds,	James Greenhow,
Isaac Vines,	Alice Greenhow,
Nicholaus Scott,	Minis Hill,
Betsy Scott,	Cas Hill,
Mary Barges,	Isaac Reynals,
David Bowles,	Billy Swann,
Susan Bowles,	Aley Swann,
Joseph Bell,	Edwd. Lightford,
John Peters,	Edward Casey,
Agness Peters,	Nanney Casey,
Douglass Tinsley,	Wilson Morris,
John Green,	Fanney Drummond,
Isham Ellis,	Pleasants Price.

and 47 others, with certificates and endorsements by Joseph Price, master of police, and seven other prominent white men of the city.

[79] Richmond Directory, 1852, p. 165; 1856 passim.

[79a] In his message to the legislature Governor Floyd asserted that the free negroes had helped to stir up revolt, and had "opened more enlarged views," and that inasmuch as they were allowed to go at liberty they could "distribute incendiary pamphlets and papers" (House Journal, 1831–1832, p. 10).

[80] Richmond Enquirer, January 28, 1830. Cf. J. B. McMaster, History of the People of the United States, vol. vi, p. 70.

meetings of free negroes or mulattoes at any school-house or other place for teaching them reading or writing, either in the day or night, under whatever pretext," were declared to be unlawful assemblies. Any justice either of his own knowledge or on information of others could issue his warrant to an officer authorizing him to enter the house and arrest or disperse the offending free negroes and to inflict upon them, at the discretion of a justice of the peace, corporal punishment not exceeding thirty-nine lashes. If a white person attempted to teach free negroes for pay, he was liable to a fine of fifty dollars and imprisonment.[81] After "Brother" Nat Turner's insurrection the ban was put upon negro preachers and teachers by an act declaring it unlawful for negroes, whether ordained or licensed or otherwise, to preach, exhort, or conduct any meeting for religious or other purposes.[82] In the revision of this law in 1842 it was declared that "every assemblage of negroes for the purpose of religious worship, when such worship is conducted by a negro, and every assemblage of negroes for the purpose of instruction in reading and writing, or in the night time for any purpose, shall be deemed an unlawful assembly."[83] Some free colored persons who possessed sufficient means began sending their children to the North to be educated; but in 1838 all such efforts were forestalled by an act declaring that any free person of color who should go beyond the State for education should be considered to have emigrated.[84] This was equivalent to a declaration that no free negro going out of the State for education should return. It was apparently in anticipation of this act forbidding Virginia free negroes to seek education in the North that sixteen free negroes of Fredericksburg, all of whom possessed considerable property, petitioned the Virginia leg-

---

[81] Acts, 1830–1831, p. 107; Supplement to Revised Code, 244–245.

[82] Acts, 1831–1832, p. 20; Supplement to Revised Code, 246–247. In 1834 ten free negroes of Richmond complained in a petition to the legislature that the consequence of this law was that many colored human beings were interred like brutes, their friends and relatives being unable to procure the usual ceremony in the burial of the dead (MS. Petitions, Henrico County, 1834, A 9483).

[83] Acts, 1840–1842, p. 21; 1847–1848, p. 120; Code (1860), 810–811.

[84] Acts, 1838, p. 76; Hurd, vol. ii, p. 10; Acts, 1847–1848, p. 119.

islature in 1838 for the privilege of establishing a school for free colored children in their city.[85] They complained of the inconvenience of sending their children to the North for education, and very tactfully added that they preferred not to send them where "they imbibe bad doctrines." The legislature refused them the right to establish the school,[86] and attended in its own way to the danger of imbibing bad doctrines by withdrawing from free negroes even the privilege of educating their children beyond the limits of the State. From 1838 to the close of the Civil War the only educational advantage that could lawfully be given to the free negroes was strictly private instruction. Rarely and with difficulty did some free colored families procure white persons to teach their children privately.[87]

In view of the difficulties to be met by free colored persons in the pursuit of learning, the discovery of a high percentage of illiteracy in that class of the population occasions no surprise. "Calx," writing in the later fifties, observed that "the free negroes, as a class, are ignorant."[88] There were, however, in 1850 a little above one free negro in six who could read and write. In the white population of the State a little more than eleven out of twelve were literate. In other words, about eighty per cent of the free colored population throughout the State was illiterate, as compared with eight per cent in the white population.[89] Quite generally throughout the entire period of two and a half centuries under review free negroes and mulattoes could merely make their marks in affixing their signatures to records of legal or business transactions.

In the fifty years before 1861 it was the practice of persons

[85] MS. Petitions, Spottsylvania County, 1838.

[86] House Journal, 1837–1838, p. 248.

[87] Upon the authority of elderly men who are able to recall events of the last two decades before the Civil War, it may safely be stated that white persons sometimes taught free negro children in the homes of the negroes.

[88] "Calx," p. 4.

[89] Census of 1850, Population, vol. vii, p. 271.

opposed to the residence of free negroes in Virginia, particularly the promoters of societies for colonizing them in Africa, to condemn them almost indiscriminately as being not only morally depraved but economically worthless.[90] Fortunately there are other and less biased witnesses from whose evidence may be formed an estimate of the value and merits of the free colored class as an economic factor. It should be remembered that all efforts to remove the free negroes from Virginia failed utterly, and with truth it may be said that one of the chief obstacles in the way of those efforts was, then as at the present time, the demand for their labor. Between 1790 and 1860 the free negro class, numbering from twelve thousand to sixty thousand, was far from being a negligible factor in the labor supply of that half of the State in which they resided and to which their labor was accessible. Any conception that the free negro was crushed in the scramble for employment between the slave and the white laborer may at the outset be banished from mind. Let us see in a general way what were the conditions affecting the economic opportunities of the free negro from 1782 to the Civil War as regards the character of employment and employers.

The agricultural and especially the plantation work was done principally by slaves. But there was a large element in the white population, even in the eastern part of the State, which was non-slaveholding and not devoted to agriculture, except in an avocational and subsidiary manner. To this element belonged the larger part of town and city populations. Whatever employment was furnished to laborers by the non-slaveholding class of whites was open to competition by the free negro; and his competitors were white laborers and persons who had slaves to hire.[91] But many non-slave-

[90] Compare what William Jay had to say in 1835 on the character and tendency of the American colonization societies, in a little book entitled Slavery in America, chapters i–v. He quotes C. L. Moseby's address before the Virginia Colonization Society, as follows: "This class of persons is a curse and a contagion wherever they reside" (p. 12; African Repository, vol. iii, p. 203).

[91] Local newspaper advertisement, City Point, 1800: "Encourage-

holding employers preferred free labor to slave labor because of conscientious scruples as to the moral justification of slavery,[92] and hired slaves were not well suited to do small irregular jobs. Hence there was a certain amount of employment for which the free negro had no competitor, except the white laborer, or white hireling, as he was sometimes called.

Within this field of demand for free laborers, where the only handicap upon the free negro in his contest with the free white workman was race prejudice, he was easily the winner. In the first place, white men of pride, disdaining to enter into competition with the free negro for employment open to them, emigrated to the West. "While he [the free negro] remained here," asserted citizens of Henrico County in 1825, "no white laborer will seek employment near him. Hence, it is that in some of the richest counties east of the Blue Ridge the white population is stationary and in many others it is retrograde."[93] Governor Smith in his message of 1847 to the legislature said, "I venture the opinion that a larger emigration of our white laborers is produced by our free negroes than by the institution of slavery."[94]

Such white laborers as remained to seek employment in the State fared badly where the free negroes were at all numerous. There were at least two important reasons for the free negro's supremacy over the white laborer: First, his standard of living and mode of living permitted him to accept smaller wages than the whites could accept and live. Governor Smith protested in 1848 that in the kind of work

---

ment offered to free negroes or to persons having negroes to hire.—William Heth." The work to be done was ditching and draining. (Taken from a fragment of a newspaper accompanying a legislative petition, in Virginia State Library.)

[92] MS. Petitions, Loudoun Co., 1843, B 1900; F. L. Olmstead, A Journey in the Seaboard Slave States, p. 94; see statement of Randolph in the National Federal Convention, 1787, in Madison Papers, vol. iii, p. 1396.

[93] MS. Petitions, Henrico County, 1825, A 9358, A 9359.

[94] House Journal, 1847–1848, p. 20. Governor Smith reaffirmed this belief in his message of 1848 (ibid., 1848–1849, p. 22).

required in cities and in odd jobs the free negroes "wholly supersede by the smallness and nature of their compensation the employment of white men."[95] Secondly, the free negro, being naturally of an obedient, tractable disposition and respectful of personal authority, and being hedged about by numerous legal incapacities and perils, was more easily commanded and directed, and was therefore a more desirable servant. Again, we have Governor Smith to testify, not in praise, but in blame, of the free negroes that "they perform a thousand little menial services to the exclusion of the white man, preferred by their employers because of the authority and control which they can exercise and frequently because of the ease and facility with which they can remunerate such services."[96]

The extent of the white employer's power to command a free negro workman or servant was even greater than that of a master over a slave; for by nature the free negro was quite as docile and as amenable to supervision as the slave, and unlike the slave he could be driven from the job and thus deprived of his means of support. Hence, as a matter of practice, the free negro was not infrequently a better "slave" than his kinsman in bondage. Between 1806 and 1860 large numbers of free negroes, when found beyond the limits of the counties or towns where they were known to have legal residence rights, were hired out by law as vagrants. Upon an occasion of a number of arrests, or when such prisoners arrested at various times had accumulated, the sheriff held a public auction, and cried off to the highest bidder the services of these freemen for a definite term of months or years, their labor selling from a few cents up to twenty-five cents per day.[97] Certainly with this system of hiring out free negroes under the vagrancy laws nothing but "poor white trash" could compete. The feelings of the white

---

[95] Message, in House Journal, 1848–1849, p. 22.

[96] Message, in House Journal, 1847–1848, p. 20.

[97] Hiring out free negroes who were willing to be engaged by enterprising white agents became such a prosperous business that in 1852 a license tax of twenty-five dollars was exacted of such agents (Acts, 1852–1853, p. 15; 1855–1856, p. 45).

laborer in view of the conditions were correctly voiced by a white citizen writing in the Richmond Whig, December 11, 1845: "Those whose hearts are now sickened when they look into the carpenters' shops, the blacksmiths' shops and the shops of all the different trades in Richmond and see them crowded with negro apprentices and negro workmen, are ready to quit in disgust." Laws imposing direct restriction upon the economic activities and competition of the free negro were repeatedly asked for, but were refused by the legislature.[98]

Further light may be thrown upon the character and scope of the economic need served by the free negro by summarizing from many concrete cases the occupations in which he prospered. From the list may be eliminated lawyers, doctors, and, after 1832, teachers and preachers. Free negroes were forbidden by law to act in an official capacity, to administer medicine, and to teach or preach to persons assembled.[99] By reason of a prejudicial interpretation of the laws, if not in open violation of them, free negroes were not allowed to pursue unmolested the business of an innkeeper or proprietor.[100] A small part of the free colored class were landowners and farmers, having come into possession of land usually by bequest from their former owner.

[98] House Journal, 1830–1831. Citizens of Culpeper County petitioned the legislature in 1831 to pass a law "for encouraging white mechanics by forbidding any slave free negro or mulatto to be bound apprentice to learn any trade or art" (House Journal, 1831–1832, pp. 2, 84). Certain limitations were placed by law upon the economic freedom of the free negro; but they were ostensibly for police purposes, and only incidentally affected his freedom in getting employment.

[99] See above, pp. 116, 144.

[100] In 1844 Jacob Sampson, a free mulatto, was ordered to show why his license of the court of Goochland County for keeping an inn or ordinary should not be revoked, and with no charges against him his license was revoked without any portion of the tax being refunded to him. By way of appeal to the legislature, he procured testimonials from a number of white citizens showing that he was honest, sober, and of good character; that in an orderly house which he had kept for fifteen years on the "three chopped" road he had entertained persons generally, and stock drivers especially, in a satisfactory manner. But his appeals were rejected by the legislature (MS. Petitions, Goochland County, 1844, A 7113; House Journal, 1844–1845, p. 37).

But the free negro was in general a toiler. Tucker observed that "the occupations of persons of this class are nearly the same as those of slaves."[101] Among those petitioning the legislature between 1776 and 1860 were the following, enumerated by trades and occupations: barbers, coopers, carpenters, mechanics, cabinet-makers, wheelwrights, chair-makers, bricklayers, plasterers, painters, tanners, shoemakers, blacksmiths, millers, sawyers, wood-dealers, draymen, hucksters, gardeners, confectioners, bakers, fishermen, fishmongers, oysterers, commanders of boats, lead miners, day laborers at all work, body servants and attendants, household servants, and washerwomen. There were known also to be a few merchants or dealers,[102] a few musicians,[103] and a few undertakers.[104]

A glance at this list will reveal the reason why free negroes flocked to the cities and towns. The employment in urban districts was in the nature of job work and service in unskilled trades to which the free negroes were adaptable. "Bad as they are," admitted an unfriendly critic in 1859, "the free negroes [in cities and towns] serve best in many menial and low stations."[105] Furthermore, as between occupations on the water and on the land, the free negro showed an inclination to choose the former. Tucker thought that one reason why the number of adult free colored females

---

[101] G. Tucker, Progress of the United States in Population and Wealth in Fifty Years, p. 139. In the census enumeration made in Virginia in 1782 some free negroes appear as appurtenances of the estates of white persons (Heads of Families, First Census of United States, 1790, Virginia, pp. 112–118).

[102] Law and sentiment were not favorable toward free negro dealers, especially hawkers and pedlars (2 Revised Code, 43). See Richmond Daily Dispatch, February 18, 1858, on the whipping of a free negro poultry dealer for stealing.

[103] At one time before the Civil War the colored band of the Richmond Blues was composed of free negroes.

[104] A free negro undertaker of Charlestown, West Virginia, makes the assertion that before the Civil War he buried the dead of the better classes of whites.

[105] "Calx," p. 15. See petition from Norfolk to the legislature, which, while pleading the cause of a free negro who was about to be forced to quit the city, pleaded also in behalf of "female families" of the city whom the free negro had been supplying with fuel (MS. Petitions, Norfolk County, 1834, B 4566).

exceeded the number of adult males of this class, while the reverse was true of other classes of the population, was that the male free negroes sought a seafaring life.[106] Bagby hints that the negro's preference for the Baptist Church may possibly find some explanation in his love for the water.[107] Fishing, oyster-dredging, and working on ships or boats as servants, cooks, stewards, stevedores, or navigators were all enticing employments for the free negro. Many of the best patronized boats on the rivers and bays were owned by free persons of color.

Probably the most prosperous and useful class of free negroes were the barbers. Many of the towns and cities, for example Lynchburg and Richmond, were at times almost wholly dependent upon free colored barbers.[108] Reuben West, a Richmond free negro following the trade of a barber, acquired a fortune of several thousand dollars.[109] In his shop on Main Street he ran from one to four chairs, and had as apprentice a free mulatto, William Mundin, who learned, and for a number of years followed, the trade as an apprentice to this free black man. If an assertion may be based wholly upon the declaration of a freeborn and very respectable negro yet living[110] who knew Reuben West, the latter owned for a few years two slaves whom he employed at his trade in his shop.

In some trades there were free negro entrepreneurs, who used and directed the labor of hired free negroes and slaves. A. E. Andrews, writing from Fredericksburg in 1835, asserted that "some of the best mechanics of the city are coloured men, and among them are several master workmen,

[106] G. Tucker, Progress of the United States, p. 60.

[107] P. 278.

[108] A distinguished gentleman of Richmond, who in 1912 was eighty-four years of age, asserts that in all his life he never had a barber who was not colored to cut his hair or shave him. This was told the author to illustrate the extent to which the free negro was relied upon in the barber's trade.

[109] Tax-books, 1856, 1857, 1859. City Hall, Richmond.

[110] James H. Hill, 227 V Street, N. W., Washington, D. C., instructor in wood-work in the public schools, owns property in Richmond which belonged to the Hill family of free negroes long before the Civil War.

who employ a considerable number of coloured laborers."[111] It was no uncommon practice for free negroes to hire slaves to labor for them. The legislature considered repeatedly the expediency of denying to free negroes the right to hire slaves,[112] the ground of objection probably being the tendency of such employment to cause the slave, commanded by one not socially his superior, to despise his slavery, or the opportunity in such employ to acquire a knowledge of antislavery doctrines and propaganda.

How largely the failure of all attempts to remove the free negro from the State was due to a fairer appreciation of his economic worth when the value of an individual was to be considered than when the class as a whole was under review is shown by the protests forthcoming from the white inhabitants wherever and whenever an effort was made to enforce the law requiring negroes set free after 1806 to quit the State.[113] The protests are hardly less significant because they attempt to have only individuals excepted from the operation of the law than if they aimed at saving the entire class. In 1810 sixty persons prayed the legislature to allow a free negro wheelwright, "who will benefit the whole country," to remain in the State and the county;[114] and in the same year citizens of Petersburg declared to the Assembly that the town could not spare without loss one Uriah Tyner.[115] In 1812 a large number of citizens of Berkeley and Frederick counties told the legislature that "there is not a human being in this part of the country where they [Jerry and Susanna, free colored] reside who is

---

[111] P. 162.

[112] The matter was before the legislature of 1841–1842 (House Journal, p. 16); a bill was introduced to prevent the practice in 1843 (ibid., 1842–1843, p. 182); the expediency of similar legislation was considered in 1844 (ibid., 1844–1845, p. 66), but the committee asked to be discharged.

[113] "The harsh measures often proposed in the legislature by those who feel the evil of their increasing numbers, have not been carried into laws" because of "the examples of intelligence, honesty and worth among them" (Message of Governor Smith, in House Journal, 1850–1851, p. 30).

[114] MS. Petitions, Henrico County, 1810, A 9180.

[115] MS. Petitions, Dinwiddie County, 1810, A 4946.

opposed to their remaining in Virginia."[116] The plea of the inhabitants of Lynchburg for Pleasant Rowan, a free colored carpenter and mechanic, was that "his loss would be felt in the community;"[116a] for Frederick Williams that he was a much needed barber;[116b] and for Ned Adams, that he was an almost indispensable cooper.[117] The people of Henrico County, petitioning for John Hopes, a free negro, said that he was a cooper "who would be useful in any community."[118] The same thing was said of Daniel Warner, a free negro barber of Warrenton, by one hundred and twenty white petitioners.[119] Ninety-five citizens of Accomac County declared to the legislature in 1838 that the services of John, a free negro sawyer, "are much required in his neighborhood."[120] Henry Parker of Loudoun County was considered by his white neighbors as "a good and useful man," desirable in the community as a day laborer.[121] No better example of the economic value placed upon the free negro could be found than the following petition from thirty-eight citizens of Essex County: "We would be glad if he [Ben, a free negro] could be permitted to remain with us and have his freedom as he is a well disposed person and a very useful man in many respects, he is a good carpenter, a good cooper, a coarse shoemaker, a good hand at almost everything that is useful to us farmers."[122]

In behalf of Harriet Cook, free colored, nearly one hundred white persons, among whom were seven justices of the peace, five ex-justices, sixteen merchants, six lawyers, and one postmaster, made to the legislature this petition: "It

[116] MS. Petitions, Berkeley County, 1812, A 1980. Cf. a petition in behalf of Thomas Richard, of Lee County, who, it was asserted, could have got every man who knew him to consent to his remaining (MS. Petitions, Lee County, 1820, B 1315).

[116a] MS. Petitions, Campbell County, 1826, A 3482.

[116b] Ibid., 1834, A 3546, one hundred and seventy-five white petitioners.

[117] Ibid., 1834, A 3544, one hundred and sixty names.

[118] MS. Petitions, Henrico County, 1836, A 9531.

[119] MS. Petitions, Fauquier County, 1836, A 5848.

[120] MS. Petitions, Accomac County, 1838, A 88.

[121] MS. Petitions, Loudoun County, 1848, B 1961; 1849, B 1971.

[122] MS. Petitions, Essex County, 1842, A 5413.

would be a serious inconvenience to a number of the citizens of Leesburg to be deprived of her services as a washerwoman and in other capacities in which, in consequence of her gentility, trust-worthiness, and skill she is exceedingly useful."[123] In a similar manner Fortune Thomas, free colored, had rendered her services indispensable to the town of Halifax by baking cakes and tarts and making candies. "In fact," say the petitioners in her behalf, "she has been earnestly assured by the ladies that they can in no measure dispense with her assistance and that no party or wedding can well be given without great inconvenience should her shop be broken up and discontinued."[124] But rarely were protests uttered against favorable legislation in aid of a free negro who sought permission to remain in a community.[125]

After many years of futile effort to put into operation laws for the purpose of removing the free negro from the State it gradually dawned upon some white persons that the inhumanity of such laws was not the only great obstacle to their enforcement, but that the unwillingness of his neighbors to part with his services was the freedman's constant shield and protection. In 1838 certain fishermen in Westmoreland and Prince William counties complained of the scarcity of hands that could be hired in those counties because of the emigration of white and slave laborers, and sought from the legislature the privilege of using free negroes and mulattoes from the District of Columbia and Maryland,[126] contrary to the laws forbidding the migration of free negroes into the State.[127] In 1852 citizens of Accomac County frankly admitted that they wished the free negroes to remain among them, and prayed "the Honorable Assembly to privilege them to remain and pass a law binding all male negroes under 45 years who are not mechanics or sailors

[123] MS. Petitions, Loudoun County, 1850, B 1988.

[124] MS. Petitions, Halifax County, 1850, A 7722.

[125] See MS. Petitions, Accomac County, 1850, A 403a.

[126] MS. Petitions, Westmoreland County, 1838; Prince William County, 1839.

[127] The petitions were rejected (House Journal, 1839, pp. 84, 180, 246, 249).

or who are not able to carry on a farm, to hire themselves out by the year."[128] With reference to female free negroes a similar plan for utilizing their services was suggested. In the same year certain citizens of Culpeper County expressed to the legislature their desire that a law be passed to make binding any contract by which a free negro obligated himself to a permanent or lifelong servitude.[129] Governor Henry A. Wise, in a message to the General Assembly in 1857, asserted that one objection to a wholesale removal of the free negroes has been and is "that their labor is needed in many parts of the state where they are most numerous and that to get clear of them in any way is considerably to reduce *pro tanto* our population."[130]

In the foregoing paragraphs setting forth the position of the free negro population with reference to industry the aim has not been to convey an impression that opportunities to find useful, remunerative employment were abundant for all persons of this class. While it is true that of free laborers of all kinds the free negro was best fitted to survive under the adverse conditions confronting them, and that he appropriated for himself the better share of employment open to free laborers, the fact remains that a proportionately large class of free negroes were without any settled employment. Aside from every consideration of the character or natural propensities of the free negroes, that a portion of this population should have become vagabonds was the inevitable result of legislation made applicable to the free negro only. Two laws deserve particular mention in this connection. By an elaborate act passed in 1801 free negroes and mulattoes were forbidden to go beyond the county or town in which they were registered in order to seek employment or for any other purpose. A violator was made liable to arrest as a vagrant.[131] It is unimportant in this connection that the law was not consistently or generally enforced;

[128] MS. Petitions, Accomac County, 1852, A 137.
[129] MS. Petitions, Culpeper County, 1852, A 4630.
[130] House Documents, no. 1, 1857, p. 151.
[131] Hening, vol. xv, p. 301; 1 Revised Code, 441.

the terms of the act placed a penalty upon white persons employing a free colored person not known to be a resident of the county or town in which the employer lived, thus narrowly limiting the scope of industrial activity of every free negro to his home town or county unless he ventured abroad to face conditions of employment doubly hazardous.

Five years later an act made unlawful the permanent residence in Virginia of any slave set free after May 1, 1806. For a number of years there was almost no effort made to punish violators of this law; consequently there accumulated a considerable number of free colored persons who were not by law entitled to reside in the State. By and by spasmodic efforts began to be made to give the act life. The efforts were not such as to prevent the increase of this expatriated class by means of manumission, but were sufficient to incite many of them to leave a community in which they were threatened or molested, and to seek safety and a means of subsistence elsewhere in the State. Some who were forced to move by the operation of this law were kept from settling by the above-mentioned prohibitions upon white employers to furnish them work. By 1860 probably from one fourth to one third of the free colored population in Virginia were unlawful residents under the provisions of the act of 1806. How little wonder it is that a colored population, facing the adverse industrial conditions which produced the "poor whites," and contending furthermore with every obstruction to economic freedom that laws could provide short of slavery, furnished many recruits for a class of negroes that were idle, vagrant, and parasitical in their method of obtaining a living.

In passing now to a discussion of the moral character of the free negro, we must avoid the error of his unfriendly contemporary critics who judged him solely by that portion of his class which was wandering through or living in the State without employment. If we have in mind only this idle set of vagabond free negroes, it would indeed be difficult to exaggerate the moral degradation into which they fell. It is well worth while to take notice of some of the many adverse criticisms of the Virginia free negro by persons and societies unfriendly to him, because such characterizations may be justly applied to the worst element of the free colored population.

A petition of the Virginia Colonization Society for legislation in aid of efforts to remove the free negroes declared in 1833 that "the free negro is degraded, vicious and criminal."[132] In 1846 Governor Smith asserted that "our criminal statistics . . . demonstrate the moral degradation of the free negro, the hopelessness of his reform, the mischievous influence of his associations."[133] Again, in 1847 Governor Smith characterized the free negro class as "a race of idlers, thriftless and unproductive; they labor only from necessity, are content to put up with only a meagre supply of wants, prowl at dead of night and filch the labor of others."[134] Olmstead found a Virginia slave-owner who contended with him that the free negroes were "a miserable set of vagabonds, drunken, vicious, worse than those who are retained in slavery."[135] C. L. Moseby, in a speech before the Virginia Colonization Society, characterized the free colored class as "a large mass of human beings who hang as a vile excrescence upon society."[136] General Mercer, vice-president of the society, described the class as "a horde of miserable people—the objects of universal suspicion—subsisting by plunder."[137]

---

[132] MS. Petitions, Henrico County, 1833, A 9456.

[133] House Journal, 1846–1847, p. 9.

[134] Ibid., 1847–1848, p. 20. But Governor Smith's generalizations were not expressed in words which conceal his prejudiced point of view. Having declared that the free negro was "a moral leper," he added: "That he will prove the ready instrument of those to be found in certain sections of our Union, who would kindle into flame our social edifice, cannot be doubted," thus revealing a strong motive for finding fault with the free negro character (ibid., 1846–1847, p. 9.)

[135] P. 44.

[136] Address before the Virginia Colonization Society, quoted from Jay, Slavery in America, p. 12; African Repository, vol. iii, p. 203.

[137] African Repository, vol. ii, p. 189.

A few of the free negro's critics were more discriminating, and by carefully confining their criticisms to the lowest stratum of the free negro class they afford additional proof that persons or societies who indiscriminately condemned all free negroes were judging the whole in view of only its worst part. For an example of the more conservative opinion of the degradation of the free negroes we may note the petition of the county court of Loudoun County to the legislature in 1836: "It is a curious fact that this unfortunate and degraded population, unwilling to leave the state; and placing itself in a condition to elude the officers of justice by flying from neighborhood to neighborhood and from county to county, is restrained from making permanent settlements; and is thus actually legislated into poverty, vagrancy, and crime."[138]

In the debate of 1832 Thomas Marshall with truth and with a discernment not usual with those who attempted to solve the free negro problem declared that in proportion as they were idle they were mischievous.[139] Professor Thomas R. Dew saw the close relation which the crimes and moral degradation of free negroes bore to their poverty and want, and explained it thus: "Idleness generates want, want gives rise to temptation, and strong temptation makes the criminal."[140] The wisdom of these observations is abundantly verified when we turn to the record of free negroes who were able to find remunerative employment in a tolerant community. In the place of such descriptive words as "degraded," "idle," "vicious," "drunken," "dishonest," which filled the memorials of the colonizers, there appear such phrases as "a man of integrity and honesty,"[141] "honest and prosperous man,"[142] "gentility, trustworthiness and skill."[143] In 1810 some of the most prominent citizens of Accomac County certified to the legislature that Jingo, a free negro,

[138] MS. Petitions, Loudoun County,, 1836, B 1849.
[139] Richmond Enquirer, February 14, 1832.
[140] P. 83.
[141] MS. Petitions, Campbell County, 1822, A 3460.
[142] Ibid., 1851, A 3684.
[143] MS. Petitions, Loudoun County, 1850, B 1988.

"hath uniformly supported an excellent character for sobriety, honesty and industry and that he hath a wife and five children. . . . His wife is a woman of good character. . . . The husband and wife have provided well for their children and bring them up in a moral way."[144] Even among the class of whites who were hostile to the continued existence of the free negroes in Virginia there was an occasional witness to the fact that "examples of intelligence, honesty and worth are not lacking among them,"[145] and that "there are many of better habits—and a few who are industrious, provident and even worthy and useful;"[146] and a traveller from a Northern State expressed the opinion that "the free blacks are more moral and respectable than many among the lowest class of whites."[147] In view of the various conflicting assertions we are led to give credit to the recollections of respectable free negroes still living, who insist on dividing the free negroes, on a moral and social basis, into two classes, the upper one of which was thoroughly respectable, law-abiding, and prosperous, while to the lower element properly belongs the reputation for being evil associates and corruptors of slaves, and parasites on the community in which they lived.[148] Persons of the former class were designated by the respectful name of "men of color;" individuals of the latter class were called "free niggers."[149]

The foregoing remarks on the moral character of the free

---

[144] MS. Petitions, Accomac County, 1810, A 42.

[145] Governor Floyd's message, in House Journal, 1850–1851, p. 30.

[146] "Calx," p. 5. In his essay, written about 1859, Calx proposed a scheme for reducing the number of free negroes by making a lack of employment evidence of guilt sufficient to authorize sale into slavery as a punishment. He opposed any indiscriminate sale or removal of both good and bad.

[147] Andrews, p. 162.

[148] This is the testimony of William Mundin, born 1839, now living (1911) in Richmond.

[149] Interview with Richard A. Tucker, 13 Suffolk Street, Norfolk, Virginia. Judge Crothers, of Portsmouth, recalled that when he was a boy going to school four miles from his home in Isle of Wight County he passed on the way five families of free negroes. "They were respectable, respected, and fairly well-to-do." As far as he knew, there was no desire on the part of the white persons of the community to be rid of them (interview, Portsmouth, January 4, 1911).

negro have been made touching his deportment in general. To be able to determine what measure of justification there was for a vast deal of legislation imposing special limitations and restrictions upon his conduct inquiry must be made specifically into the truth of a few of the oft-repeated charges and indictments upon which discriminatory legislation was based. The four charges which were made with most telling effect were: (1) that he was a thief and a receiver of stolen goods; (2) that he was criminally disposed in an unusual degree; (3) that he was insurrectionary; and (4) that he was lazy and improvident.

First, then, as to his propensity to steal. That the free negro class produced a rather disproportionate number of thieves should not be doubted, but that the free negroes were worse in this respect than the slaves, or that they were worse than so many white persons would have become if placed in their circumstances and forced to remain there, is by no means proved. Jefferson observed with truth that "a man's moral sense must be unusually strong if slavery does not make him a thief."[150] While many of the free negroes of the period between 1782 and 1865 received their training in slavery, the possession of such qualities as trustworthiness, honesty, and faithfulness to duty was a prerequisite to the attainment of freedom. A bad slave, like an unruly horse, was more likely to go on the market, and was less likely to have the commiseration of his master, than one of better qualities. The fact is that the free negroes, as far as they had employment, were less inclined to steal than were slaves; but in this regard the less fortunate free negroes were subject to greater temptation, if possible, than slaves, and the evidence is conclusive that they were surpassed by no other inhabitants of the Commonwealth in the number and variety of their depredations. Mr. Archer, addressing the Virginia Colonization Society, said: "The free blacks are destined by an insurmountable barrier—to the want of occupation, thence to the want of food—thence to the distresses

[150] Writings of Jefferson, vol. v, p. 66 (1789).

which ensue that want—thence to the settled deprivation which grows out of those distresses and is nursed in their bosoms."[151] "Since they are idle," observed ninety citizens of Culpeper County, "they either steal or perish."[152]

It should, however, be kept in mind in a comparison of the free negro with the slave in regard to all such misdemeanors as thievery that the free negro was severely brought to account and universally criticised for his offenses, whereas the slave was often shielded from prosecution and criticism by reason of the dignity and authority of his master. Slave-owners were sometimes reluctant to admit that their slaves were as bad as or worse than the slaves of their neighbors, and by way of self-defense and self-protection from criticism condoned the misdemeanors of their slaves or punished them in private. But there was no cloak for the "free nigger." The old warning "Be sure your sin will find you out" had abundant sanction as applied to him.

The economic activities of the roguish free negroes and slaves were thoroughly complementary and harmonious. The free negro, unlike the slave, could market products, the presumption being that he lawfully possessed them. The slave possessed first-hand information as to the location of many articles of produce. Hence the problem of production was managed by the slave; the burden of transportation was borne by the free negro; and the method of distribution was determined by mutual agreement. As early as 1691 the free negro was charged with being a receiver and conveyer

---

[151] Quoted from Dew, p. 83.

[152] MS. Petitions, Culpeper County, 1846, A 4611. County and hustings court records of the nineteenth century contain numerous examples of theft by free negroes. See, for example, case of Bob Green, a free negro, who in a single night stole seven hams of bacon (Orders of the Richmond Hustings Court, no. 11, 1814, p. 153). Newspaper notes of their larcenies were sometimes tinged with a sarcasm that is indicative of their frequent repetition, as for instance the following: "The Poultry Trade—A negro engaged in the poultry business was detected a few nights ago in the act of robbing a hen house on the premises of a citizen of Manchester. A magistrate ordered '39' for his benefit the next day" (Richmond Daily Dispatch, February 18, 1858).

of stolen goods,[153] and upon this and other accusations was based the legal restriction upon manumission. Soon after the act removing these restrictions went into effect, in 1782, complaints were heard from different quarters that "free negroes are agents, factors, and carriers to the neighboring towns for slaves, of property by them stolen from their masters and others."[154]

In the neighborhood of almost every gristmill in certain parts of eastern Virginia there were located squads of free negroes who were suspected by their white neighbors of procuring a large part of their sustenance by concert with roguish slave millers. In 1831 a number of citizens of Charles City and New Kent counties, seeking from the legislature relief from such conditions, asserted that it was a custom almost universal with owners of mills in their counties and in fact in the whole lower part of the State to employ slaves to attend the mills, and that the millers "are a sort of communication between slaves and the free persons of color" in the neighborhood.[155] The legislature, however, took no action in relief of the persons aggrieved.[156]

A complaint of a similar kind was received by the legislature in 1836 from Loudoun County. According to the petitioners, free negroes who owned "trading carts" and operated them between Washington or Georgetown and the rural communities of Virginia near the District of Columbia line were in the habit of receiving stolen goods from free negroes and slaves.[157] Complaints were heard at the same time from other quarters of the State, and, although the legislature refused to grant the specified request of the Loudoun County petitioners,[158] a bill of general application was introduced which was designed to prevent free negroes from trading

[153] Hening, vol. iii, p. 87.

[154] MS. Petitions, Hanover County, 1784, A 8124; Henrico County, 1784, A 8971.

[155] MS. Petitions, Charles City County, 1831, A 3962.

[156] House Journal, 1831–1832, pp. 56, 84.

[157] MS. Petitions, Loudoun County, 1836, B 1840.

[158] House Journal, 1835–1836, p. 262.

beyond the town in which they resided. The measure met with defeat.[159]

There was a manifest reluctance on the part of the legislature to interfere by law with the right of the free negroes to trade freely, and, although complaints were becoming ominous,[160] proposed legislation for prohibiting them from selling grain without a certificate or evidence that they were the lawful possessors of it was in 1840 declared inexpedient.[161] In some counties, however, the white citizens were determined not to take further denial from the legislature. In 1843 one hundred and twenty-seven citizens of Accomac County signed a petition for a law imposing a penalty upon all white persons who made purchases of grain from free negroes without requiring from them the certificate of two respectable housekeepers showing that the grain was lawfully possessed. "Country stores are in the habit," reads the petition, "of receiving grain from free negroes who are not the producers of a single bushel of grain of any kind. The grain they sell is either stolen by the negroes who sell it or more frequently received by them of slaves who steal it from their masters and others and by this means exerts a most pernicious influence upon our slaves."[162] In response to the appeal there was introduced in the House of Delegates a bill containing provisions similar to those asked for by the Accomac petition and applicable to the entire State. It was later narrowed in application to the counties of Accomac and Richmond and enacted into law.[163]

---

[159] Ibid., p. 244.

[160] In 1836 the following petition was made to the legislature by citizens of Northumberland County: "This class of people, as is well known to your honorable body, is everything that is the very opposite of honesty and industry. . . . The law to prevent dealing with slaves is a dead letter . . . for the slave has nothing to do but to pass over the plundered property of his owner to the free negroes who can openly carry it to market and make sale of it as the production of his own labor."

Since 1785 it had been unlawful for free persons to trade with a slave without leave from the slave's master and to trade with slaves, free negroes, or mulattoes on Sunday (1 Revised Code, 426).

[161] House Journal, 1840–1841, p. 59.

[162] MS. Petitions, Accomac County, 1843, A 98.

[163] House Journal, 1842–1843, pp. 213, 269; Acts, 1842–1845.

The second charge or accusation, as above enumerated, which was repeatedly made against the free negro was that he was unusually criminal. Upon the assumption of the truth of this indictment were based the criminal laws of the second quarter of the nineteenth century applicable to the free negro. Before the beginning of the nineteenth century the free negro class was not so large as to attract special attention to its criminal record. Statistics relative to the inmates of the penitentiary made and published during the first quarter of the nineteenth century brought to the attention of the public the fact that the free negroes were committing from two to twelve times as many of the crimes of the State for which punishment was meted out as an equal number of average white persons. According to criminal statistics in 1804, the free negroes committed in proportion to the population twice as many crimes as the free whites. In 1808 in proportion to the population they committed twelve crimes punished in the penitentiary to one among the whites; in 1810, three to one; in 1812, eight to one; and in 1824, twelve to one. The conclusions drawn from these statistics created a very general belief that the free negro was fast becoming more criminal, and that existing criminal laws were wholly inadequate for a class so vicious as the free Africans. Consequently, in 1823 a law was passed which substituted for confinement in the penitentiary, transportation and sale as a method of punishing the crimes of free negroes. For four years this law was effective, during which time thirty-five free negroes were convicted, transported, and sold into slavery.[164] During this period the number of free negro convicts in proportion to the whites was no less than it had been under the penitentiary system. It is to the credit of Governor William B. Giles that the law was repealed in 1828. He realized the absurdity of taking the number of free negro convicts and comparing it with the number of white convicts in judging the relative criminal capacities and tendencies of the free negroes and the whites.

---

[164] House Documents, no. 15, 1848–1849; no. 4, 1853–1854.

The injustice to the negro of such a method consisted, first, in an erroneous assumption that the laws were administered as severely against white persons as against free negroes,[165] and, secondly, in a comparison of the record of the free negroes with the whole white population instead of with an equal number of whites similarly situated as to means of earning a living. So pertinent in this connection are the remarks of Governor Giles that they may be quoted at some length:—

> I am far from yielding to the opinion expressed by the intelligent committee of the House of Delegates of Virginia and the enthusiastic memorialists of Powhatan respecting the degraded and demoralized condition of this *caste*—at least in degree and extent. It will be admitted that this *caste* of colored population attracted but little of the public sympathy and commiseration,—in fact, that the public feeling and sentiment are opposed to it. It is also admitted that the penal laws against it have been marked with peculiar severity;[166] so much so, as to form a characteristic exception to our whole penal code. When I first came into the office of Governor, such was the severity of the penal laws against this *caste,* that for all capital offences short of punishment by death and for many offences not capital, slavery, sale and transportation formed the wretched doom denounced by the laws against this unfavored, despised *caste* of colored population. . . . I have also reason to fear, that under the influence of general prejudices, the laws, in some instances, have been administered against this class more in rigour than in justice. Yet, notwithstanding all these deprecated circumstances, the proportion of convicts to the whole population has been small.

He points out the fact that only about one out of every thousand free negroes was a criminal, and concludes that

---

[165] It was made a penitentiary offense for a free person "to advise any slave to abscond from his master or aid such slave to abscond by procuring for or delivering to him a pass, register or other writing or furnish him money, clothes, etc." (Acts, 1855–1856, p. 42).

In 1848 ten out of eighty-one free negroes in the penitentiary were there for aiding or abetting slaves to escape from their masters. This is only one example of the many more chances for a free negro to be sent to the penitentiary than for a white person (House Journal, 1847–1848, pp. 20, 22; MS. Petitions, Henrico County, 1844, A 9654). Two thirds of the offenses for which free negroes were arraigned before the hustings court of Richmond were defined by laws which did not apply to white persons,—such, for instance, as that which made it a criminal offense for a free negro to remain in a city or county without proper registration (Richmond Daily Dispatch, February 8, 1859).

[166] Compare Howison, vol. ii, pp. 458–459, for similar expressions. For example, he says: "They are subject to restraints and surveillance in points beyond number."

"these facts prove, first, that this class of population is by no means so vicious, degraded and demoralized as represented by their prejudiced friends and voluntary benefactors. And, second, that evils attributed to this class are vastly magnified and exaggerated."[167]

From 1828, the date of the repeal of the law fixing transportation and sale as a penalty in the case of free colored convicts, to 1861 the free colored class furnished from one tenth to one fifth of the inmates of the penitentiary. The apparent disproportion of the crimes of this class was often pointed out in argument for a general deportation or colonization.[168] Governors Smith, Floyd, Johnson, and Wise brought the fact repeatedly to the attention of the legislature.[169] Governor Smith, however, attributed much of the disparity to circumstances which, for the free negro, were unavoidable. "If there be," said he, "in his natural character the elements to make him a great and good man, it is hopeless to expect that they will ever be developed under our policy."[170] Governor Wise, in stating in 1857 some possible arguments in defense of the free negro, observed that "if many of them are corrupted and degenerated . . . it is owing not only to their own improvidence, but to evil communication with bad white men who associate and deal with them and abuse their weakness and who are not restrained by penal laws."[171]

It should be said that the penal record of the Virginia free negro was not worse than that of the negro in some northern free States,—for instance, Massachusetts. Between 1840 and 1850 the number of colored convicts to one white convict, in proportion to the population, was in Massachusetts,

---

[167] P. 20.

[168] "An ominous disparity! which was constantly pressed upon the attention of the reflecting men of the state" (Howison, vol. ii, p. 458).

[169] Messages of the Governors, in House Journal, 1846–1847; 1847–1848, p. 20; 1850–1851, p. 30; 1853–1854, doc. no. 1, p. 14; House Documents, no. 1, 1857–1858, p. 151.

[170] House Journal, 1847–1848, p. 20.

[171] House Documents, no. 1, 1857, p. 151.

9.6; in Virginia, 7.2. For the first two years of the decade of the fifties it was in Massachusetts, 13; in Virginia, 6.3.[172]

If a comparison is made of the criminal record of the negroes of Virginia at the present time on the basis of the relative number of white and black convicts in the penitentiary, the disparity will appear as great today as at almost any time prior to the Civil War.[173] The conclusion seems irresistible that the criminal capacities and tendencies of the antebellum free negro were not so great as they were quite generally believed to be.

Thirdly, was the free negro insurrectionary and turbulent? No criticism of the free negro was more general and more undeserved than that he contrived, or was disposed to contrive, insurrections, and that he induced the slaves to rebel against their masters. He was referred to on the floor of the legislature in 1805 as a possible leader of a rebellion or an "active chieftain of a formidable conspiracy."[174]

The insurrection in Santo Domingo, headed by the free blacks of the island, for a long time furnished the starting-point of arguments advanced to show that free negroes might at any time head a slave rebellion. In 1823 Lafayette asked Madison whether it was considered that the increase in the proportion of free blacks to slaves tended to increase or diminish the dangers of insurrection. Madison's answer was, "Rather increases," and that in case of a slave insurrection the free blacks would be more likely to side with the slaves than with the whites. Madison certainly gave a correct expression of the general feeling or belief of the white population, but there is really little evidence to show that the impression was correct. There are no instances on record of insurrections in Virginia initiated by or carried out under the leadership of free negroes. Not a free negro was proved to have had any criminal relation to the Gabriel plot in 1800, and only two free negro men

[172] House Documents, no. 14, 1853–1854, pp. 38, 54.

[173] Reports of Virginia Penitentiary, October, 1909, September 30, 1910.

[174] Richmond Enquirer, January 15, 1805.

whose wives were slaves were implicated in the Nat Turner insurrection; neither of the two seems to have been a leading spirit among the seventy or more slaves who participated in the affair.[175]

An insurrection always brought out expressions of fear of the free negro, first, because he was presumed to have kindred and sympathetic feelings for the slave and to share with him prejudices against the whites; and secondly, because he was known to have intimate relations with the slaves and an increased capacity for organization by reason of his freedom to go from place to place. Expressed opinions of the danger of free negro insurrections were very numerous for a while after the Southampton affair,[176] but occasionally some writer or speaker who thought twice before venturing a remedy for the ills of society pointed out the fact, which now seems plain enough, that the free negroes who had a legal right to remain and those who, despite the law, were tolerated in Virginia were too well satisfied to create insurrection.[177] Thomas Marshall observed with truth in the legislature of 1832, "There is no evidence of a disposition to join in revolt or disturb the public tranquility."[178] Professsor Dew observed that the Virginia free negro had been taught to understand his place and to occupy it humbly.[179] The antebellum free negro did not demand social or political equality, but rather felt that any right that he possessed was so much for which he should be thankful. The slave set free because of meritorious conduct or faithfulness of service, far from being insurrectionary, was an example of politeness, humility, and respect for superiors and for authority such as is rarely if ever seen at the present

[175] Richmond Enquirer, November 18, 1831; W. S. Drewry, The Southampton Insurrection, appendix.

[176] "We are not unmindful of the aid slaves would get from this source [the free negroes] in case of a servile insurrection" (Petition of 200 citizens of Northampton, in MS. Petitions, December, 1831, A 4884).

[177] See article contributed to the Richmond Enquirer, November 18, 1831.

[178] Richmond Enquirer, February 14, 1832.

[179] Pp. 85, 87.

among either the white or the black population.[180] The infusion of this, the best type of African in America, among the free negro class was sufficient in itself to influence the class toward submissiveness.

Thomas Marshall believed with not a few thoughtful men that the free negro constituted "no inconsiderable barrier to a future insurrection of slaves."[181] A similar opinion was expressed on the floor of the legislature in 1805.[182] In truth, there are numerous instances of the forestalling of insurrections and the preventing of plots of slaves through the agency of free negroes. Moses, a free negro of Goochland County, revealed a conspiracy of slaves in 1822.[183] In 1810 two hundred citizens of Petersburg declared to the legislature through a petition that a free negro, Emanuel, had saved the town from conflagration by reporting and aiding in the capture of incendiary, plotting slaves.[184] Lewis Bowlagh presented certificates to the legislature to show that he had given information to the whites in time to prevent bloodshed plotted by slaves.[185] A petition in behalf of Isaac, of Rockbridge County, was based on the ground that he had been a useful man in detecting and bringing negroes to account for their wrongdoing.[186] Daniel Brady's father, a man of good character, even surrendered up his own son to stand his trial and suffer punishment.[187] It was certainly not the disposition of the free negro, knowingly and with design, to increase the prejudices of the whites against him by creating insurrection. Far from being of "a turbulent and discontented" disposition, as those in favor of coloniza-

---

[180] "They are peaceable, orderly in their deportment, humble to those whom the law has made their superiors and polite to those who are considered their equals." Said by fifty-nine white persons of Caroline County of nine free negroes—Joseph Tyree, his wife, and seven children (MS. Petitions, Caroline County, 1821, A 3804).

[181] Richmond Enquirer, February 14, 1832.

[182] Ibid., January 15, 1805.

[183] MS. Petitions, Goochland County, 1822, A 7085.

[184] MS. Petitions, Dinwiddie County, 1810, A 5196.

[185] MS. Petitions, Henrico County, 1824, A 9353.

[186] MS. Petitions, Rockbridge County, uncatalogued.

[187] Pardons issued by Governor Wise, in House Documents, no. 1, 1857–1858, p. clxx.

tion declared him to be, he longed to be left alone in the place of his birth, free from fears of molestation and annoyance, to enjoy perfect contentment. Without question the free negro population in Virginia was in general meek and submissive and not inclined to rebellion.[188]

Fourthly, the charge often made that the free negro was lazy and improvident must not be accepted without some qualification. It is reasonable to believe that the free negroes, like the slaves, were naturally lazy; but it is really remarkable what examples of thrift and economy this class produced. Within the space of four years Rose Hailstock purchased with her saved earnings her own freedom and, one by one, the freedom of her three children, paying altogether £125 sterling.[189] Samuel Jackson saved enough to purchase in 1815 the freedom of his wife and two children.[190] Arthur Lee, of Alleghany County, displayed a perseverance and an ability to economize that is not often surpassed by laboring men of any race or condition. For sixteen years he was the slave of a man named Brown, who lived in North Carolina, but he was permitted to remain in Virginia on the condition that he pay his owner one hundred dollars per annum. Having paid, at this rate, sixteen hundred dollars by 1835, he purchased his freedom, paying his owner five hundred dollars for his future liberty. Not satisfied, he immediately set to work to earn three hundred and fifty dollars with which to purchase his wife's freedom. This done, he procured the signatures of one hundred and seventy-six citizens of Alleghany County to his humble petition to the legislature for a law granting to him and his wife a legal right to reside in the Commonwealth, that he might continue to ply the honorable trade of a blacksmith.[191] As to the character for industry of Billy Williams, forty-seven

[188] Professor Dew admitted, or, we might say, contended that the Virginia free negro was more orderly and well behaved than the free negro of the Northern States. In the North, he said, the negro was taught arrogance and equality. In the South he was made to understand his place and to occupy it humbly (pp. 85, 87).

[189] Hening, vol. xiii, p. 618.

[190] MS. Petitions, Fauquier County, 1815, A 5760.

[191] MS. Petitions, Alleghany County, 1835, A 666.

citizens of Campbell County said: "We are his neighbors and are willing and indeed desirous that the legislature pass the law permitting him to remain in the state, as he is not only an honest, prosperous man, but in truth a most useful and accommodating man to his neighbors and all with whom he has anything to do. A farmer by occupation and owns 100 acres of land."[192] Examples could be multiplied indefinitely in contradiction of indiscriminating indictments, such, for instance, as that made by Governor Smith when he characterized the free colored population as a "race of idlers, thriftless and unproductive."[193] The exaggerated and often self-contradictory character of the statements of colonization zealots will best appear by a quotation from a widely circulated memorial[194] to the legislature:—

> Their idleness is proverbial; they live, few know in what way and fewer where. . . . Whatever energy can be spared from annoying both classes [slave and white] is expended in multiplying their own numbers.
>
> And yet this same individual, the pest of the land which gives him only birth, when transported to a seat where his industry may have excitement and object becomes the active, thriving, and happy citizen of Liberia.[195]

Rigorous and discriminatory as were the laws of Virginia enacted for the purpose of controlling that presumably law-

---

[192] MS. Petitions, Campbell County, 1851, A 3684.

[193] House Journal, 1847–1848, p. 20.

[194] MS. Petitions, Henrico County, 1831, A 9431. See also memorial of the Auxiliary Colonization Society of Buckingham County, in MS. Petitions, Buckingham County, 1832, A 3080. A memorial of the Fairfax Colonization Society read: "Pursuing no course of regular business and negligent of everything like economy and husbandry they are a part of the community supported by the industry of others" (MS. Petitions, Fairfax County, 1832, A 5578).

[195] With this picture of what the Virginia colonizers professed to think the free negro would become in Liberia may be compared what citizens of Somerset County, Maryland, thought of the Virginia free negroes who had come into Maryland from Virginia after the law of 1806 made the residence of certain ones illegal in Virginia: "We reap not the rewards or fruits of our labor . . . all is snatched from us by that curse of God's Creation, the degraded free negro . . . he toils not neither does he spin, yet like Dives he fares sumptuously and is arrayed in purple and fine linen and well he may, for he appropriates to his own use the labors of the entire white population" (MS. Petitions to Maryland Legislature, in Maryland Historical Society, portfolio 7, no. 28).

less, disorderly and vicious member of society, the free negro, they fail in some respects to reveal the extent to which he was subjected to surveillance and discipline, while in other respects they represent a harsher treatment than he actually received. In the nineteenth century there existed a law for keeping watch over and controlling the conduct of free negroes not found among the statutes or supported by legal precedents. Its sanction was in community sentiment, and its name was lynch-law. The practice before the Civil War of policing the free negroes by self-appointed bailiffs was the historical antecedent of the Ku Klux Klan of reconstruction days, although there was not the same degree of organization and not so wide a gap between local sentiment and legal administration before as during that time.

Prostitution and vice among the free colored population were frequently dealt with by methods not approved by law. For example, in Amelia County in 1821 the inmates of houses of ill repute were visited and chastized by a party of disguised white men.[196] Although a fine was imposed upon at least one of the persons connected with this raid, the state of sentiment favorable to the method of procedure is seen in the effort made by half a hundred of the local residents to have the convicted man released from his fine. General Brodnax, speaking from the floor of the legislature in 1832, was not challenged upon the assertion that such methods of getting rid of undesirable free negroes were of common occurrence. "Who does not know," said he, "that when a free negro, by crime or otherwise, has rendered himself obnoxious to a neighborhood, how easy it is for a party to visit him one night, take him from his bed and family, and apply to him the gentle admonition of a severe flagellation, to induce him to go away. In a few nights the dose can be repeated, perhaps increased, until, in the language of the physicians, *quantum suff* has been administered . . .

[196] MS. Petitions, Amelia County, 1821, A 781.

and the fellow becomes perfectly willing to go away."[197] So commonly was lynch-law of this character resorted to by the whites in prevailing upon free negroes to yield to their wishes that one argument strongly urged in 1832 in favor of a law authorizing the use of force in carrying out a colonization scheme was the necessity of shielding the negroes from the cruelty of private intimidation and compulsion.[198] William Miles Cuffee, a free negro born in 1839, now living at Hickory Ground, Virginia, tells how in 1859, upon a rumor of insurrection, whites assembled in bands to intimidate and frighten the free negroes in the community. According to his report, he remained hidden in the woods for about three days and nights while the raids were being conducted against persons of his class.

While local sentiment often permitted the authority of the law to be exceeded or ignored by individuals self-appointed to discipline and punish free negroes, it no less frequently permitted laws to remain unenforced. Speaking of the laws which forbade free negroes to move from one town or locality to another and to assemble in considerable numbers and of those which compelled them to submit to search of their houses and persons by patrols, a writer in the Richmond Enquirer declared that "these provisions and many other laws on this subject are so much at variance with the feelings of our citizens that in many parts of the state they are merely a dead letter. . . . So long as our humanity preponderates over our fears, so long will those laws be very partially and feebly executed."[199]

The same writer clearly discerns and explains the reason why legislation dealing with the free negroes outran execution: "As legislators, impressed with the jeopardy that threatens the public safety, men readily give their assent to

---

[197] Richmond Enquirer, February 14, 1832. Compare Jay, Slavery in America, p. 45.

[198] Speech of Mr. Chandler, in the Richmond Enquirer, February 14, 1832. General Brodnax said that he understood that the consent of the emigrants in a cargo which had recently set sail for Africa was obtained by private compulsion.

[199] Richmond Enquirer, October 8, 1805.

any measure that seems calculated to protect it, but when they return to the bosom of their families and are surrounded by those among whom they were born and nursed and from whose labor they obtain the means of comfort and independence the sentiments of the legislator are frequently lost in the feelings of humanity and affection in the private man."

An illustration of this fact is seen in the operation of that law which directed emancipated slaves to leave the State within twelve months from the date of their emancipation. Henry Howe said in 1845 that "these laws, and every other having the appearance of rigor . . . are nearly dead letters upon our statute books, unless during times of excitement, or since the efforts of the abolitionists have reanimated them. I have, until lately, scarcely known an instance in which they have been enforced."[200] Petitions were continually being sent to the legislature by white persons complaining "that the law requiring the removal [of ex-slaves] is in its operation perfectly nugatory."[201]

In certain localities, however, and at certain times the law was rendered in some measure effective. The act was a penal statute, depending upon local officials for its execution; hence enforcement was not uniform as to times and places. The appearance of the successive census reports showing the rapid increase and accumulation of the free negroes in the State usually gave rise to some zeal for proceeding against free negroes who remained in violation of the law.[202] The number and the deportment of these negroes in a community went far toward determining the length to which the local officials would go in prosecuting them. In the counties of western Virginia, where but few negroes resided, almost no use was made of this law. In

[200] Historical Collections of Virginia, p. 157.

[201] MS. Petitions, Hampshire County, 1836, A 7904; Loudoun County, 1836, B 1849; Loudoun and Fauquier Counties, 1847, B 1952.

[202] "The excitement which now prevails will in a little while entirely subside and you will see things move on just as they have done until the next census, when we shall again begin to stir and flutter for awhile" (Richmond Whig, December 11, 1845).

most of the eastern counties the prescribed penalty—sale into slavery—was so much at variance with sentiment that grand juries usually refused to indict, or attorneys refused to prosecute, violators of the law.[203] When indictments were made, the cases were continued from time to time or finally dismissed.[204]

When arrests, prosecutions, and sales of free negroes were made, the object was usually to make examples of some that all others might take warning and leave the community. The overseers of the poor of Accomac County held a meeting in 1825, and determined to make an example of one negro, thinking that they would by this means be spared the necessity of selling as slaves the free negroes who had become unlawful residents under the act of 1806.[205] A negro named Jack Bagwell was the unlucky victim; but a single example was not sufficient to induce all other free negroes liable to sale to quit the community, and at a meeting held the following year the Board of Overseers ordered that notice be posted throughout the county "that the Overseers of the Poor . . . will sell one free negro in each district of this county for every month from this date."[206]

In pursuance of the order, seven negroes were sold into slavery on June 5, 1826. The maximum price received for any one of the seven freemen was thirty-six dollars and fifty cents. The fact that some of them brought so low a price as one dollar creates a doubt as to whether the purchasers expected to force them into bondage or whether they did not intend to allow them to escape from the neighborhood. In 1839 Richard Rew purchased at the price of five hundred and thirty dollars a free negro who had lived in Virginia contrary to law since his manumission in 1819.

---

[203] MS. Orders of Northampton County, 1831–1836, pp. 136, 147, 505; MS. Petitions, Loudoun and Fauquier Counties, 1847, B 1952; Frederick County, 1828, A 6495.

[204] "By this mode, they were annually before the court, their cases called and continued and in this evasive way, they spent the remainder of their days in their old communities" (T. K. Cartmell, Shenandoah Valley Pioneers and Their Descendants, p. 521).

[205] MS. Petitions, Accomac County, 1825, A 91.

[206] Ibid., 1826, A 80.

The negro made good his escape to New York, and Rew, who had paid a high price for him, expecting to subject him to actual bondage, appealed earnestly but in vain to the legislature for a refunding of the purchase money.[207]

Even such a timid and spasmodic enforcement of this law as these instances represent rendered the condition of a great number of free negroes anomalous and insecure. Not only those negroes emancipated after 1806, but also their posterity were liable to be sold as slaves, and many deserving negroes were forced to appeal to the humanity of their white neighbors to save them from banishment or sale. In 1834 Titus Brown, whose hair was white with age, related how he and his wife, childless and almost as old as he, had been "ordered to depart from the Commonwealth."[208] It was not often that a free negro of fair character was unable, even in times of excitement, to get his white neighbors to intercede in his behalf. These could usually bring about a relaxation of energy in the prosecution, or, as in the case of Archy Carey, they might "agree that so long as his conduct comports with his recommendation they will not enforce the law against him."[209] If in this way they could not render secure a negro threatened with sale or banishment, his white sympathizers would often draft earnest appeals to the humanity of the legislators, and procure to these petitions hundreds of white subscribers. Very frequently the legislature was moved to pass acts excepting certain free negroes from the operation of the law.[210] In some such way were tolerated nearly all ex-slaves who ventured to assume the risk of losing their freedom. It was asked in the House of Delegates in 1832 why the laws providing for the banishment or sale of certain free negroes had not been carried out. The answer was: "Because its provisions were in violation of the feelings of the people. A thousand such laws would

[207] House Journal, 1839–1840, p. 205.
[208] MS. Petitions, Loudoun County, 1834, B 1830.
[209] MS. Petitions, Campbell County, 1830, A 1013.
[210] For examples, see Acts, 1821–1822, p. 84; 1833–1834, p. 316; 1834–1835, p. 240; or Acts of any year from 1812 to 1848.

fall to the ground and be inoperative for lack of public sentiment."[211] The same explanation was given by Governor Wise in his message to the legislature in 1857. "It would be more humane and more just," he said, "to sell them wholesale into slavery" than to force upon them dispersion and extinction in the cold climate of the free States; "but the moral sense of our people would revolt at a violation of individual and personal rights like this and no such usurpation would be tolerated by public sentiment."[212]

---

[211] Richmond Enquirer, February 14, 1832.
[212] House Documents, no. 1, 1857, p. 151.

BIBLIOGRAPHY

Lack of space necessitates the omission from this list of a large number of secondary authorities having bearing upon, but not contemporary with, some portion of the period treated in this monograph. Footnote references to the most useful of the works of postbellum writers touching the subject herein treated must suffice to show the extent of the author's indebtedness to authorities. With the exception of a few county or local histories having special value because of their limited territorial scope, only primary sources are here enumerated.

MANUSCRIPT

A. County Court Records,—Orders, Deeds, Wills, Inventories, and so forth; certified copies transcribed from the original records in pursuance of an act of the Virginia State Legislature and preserved in the Virginia State Library in Richmond, Virginia. 19 vols., folio:

1. Accomac County, 1632–1640, 1676–1690.
2. Elizabeth City County, 1684–1699.
3. Essex County, 1695–1699.
4. Henrico County, 1677–1692, 1682–1701.
5. Warwick County, 1748–1762.
6. York County, 1633–1694, 1638–1648, 1657–1662, 1664–1672, 1675–1684, 1677–1692, 1677–1699, 1684–1687, 1687–1691, 1690–1694, 1694–1702, 1694–1697.

B. County Court Records,—Orders, Deeds, Wills, and so forth; original records:

1. Henrico County, various volumes, 1776–1860, in County Court House, Richmond, Virginia.
2. Lower Norfolk and Norfolk County, 1637–1646, 1646–1651, 1686–1695, and various volumes, 1700–1860, in Norfolk County Court House, Portsmouth, Virginia.

   In this county free negroes and mulattoes were registered in volumes kept for that purpose only: vol. 1, 1802–1852; vol. 2, 1852–1861. Concerning each free negro registered by the county court clerk there was recorded the answer to the following queries: Name, How free, Age, Height, Complexion, Marks or Scars. Each negro was numbered and the date of his registration recorded.
3. Northampton County, 1632–1640, 1640–1645, 1645–1651, 1651–1654, 1654–1655, 1655–1658, 1657–1664, 1683–1689, 1689–1698, 1710–1720, and various volumes, 1720–1860.

Records of the Hustings Court, Richmond, Virginia, various volumes, 1782–1860.

Ordinances of the City of Richmond, 3 vols., 1804–1860.

C. PARISH RECORDS.

At Episcopal Theological Seminary, Alexandria, Virginia:

1. Register of Christ's Church, Middlesex County, Virginia, 1653–1812.
2. Register of Kingston Parish, Mathews County, Virginia, 1674–18—.
3. Vestry Book of Charles Parish, York County, Virginia, 1670–1800.

At Bruton Church, Williamsburg, Virginia:

4. Register of Middletown and Bruton Parishes, 1662–1797.

At Library of William and Mary College, Williamsburg:

5. Register of Abingdon Parish, transcribed by Lyon G. Tyler.
6. Register of Charles Parish, 1648–1800, transcribed for Library of William and Mary College.

D. RECORDS OF FRIENDS' MEETINGS, at Park Avenue Meeting House, Baltimore, Maryland.

1. Minutes of the Baltimore Yearly Meeting held at West River and Third Haven, 3 vols., 1677–1758, 1754–1764, 1798–1821.
2. Condensed record of the action of yearly meetings on questions relating to slavery and the slave trade, 1760–1819.
3. Minutes of the Warrenton and Fairfax Quarterly Meeting, 1776–1787.
4. Minutes of the Warrenton and Fairfax Quarterly Meeting of Women Friends, 1775–1787.
5. Minutes of the Warrenton Quarterly Meeting, 1787–1801.
6. Minutes of the Fairfax Quarterly Meeting, 1787–1850.
7. Minutes of Crooked Run Monthly Meeting, 1782–1789.
8. Minutes of Fairfax Monthly Meeting: vol. A, 1745–1776; vol. B, 1776–1802; vol. C, 1802–1845.
9. Minutes of Hopewell Monthly Meeting: bk. 1, 1759–1777; bk. 2, 1777–1791; bk. 3, 1791–1811; bk. 4, 1811–1851.
10. Minutes and Proceedings of Goose Creek Monthly Meeting, 1785–1818; 1818–18—.

E. Records of the General Court of Virginia, transcribed by Conway Robinson, 1640–1661, 1670–1676. Virginia Historical Society.

F. Legislative Petitions of Virginia, 1776–1860.

This collection of original manuscript documents, one of the most important sources of this monograph, is preserved in the archives of the State and is divided into as many groups as there were counties from which the petitions or memorials originated. The arrangement within the county groups is with reference to chronology. Fifteen thousand five hundred documents are catalogued and arranged in the archives in upright filing cases, each document being assigned to a stiff folder, folio size, having upon it a letter and a number which distinguishes it from every other document in the files. The numbers run in two series, A and B. Series A runs from 1 to 10,000. Series B is complete from 1 to 5500; and the two series combined cover the counties from Accomac to Orange. The county groups from P to Y inclusive are wrapped separately in bundles, awaiting the systematic arrangement of the other county groups. In most instances double reference by date and by number has been made in the footnotes of this monograph to the petitions that are filed in the cases. Little if any use has been made, up to this time, of this, one of the richest sources for Virginia history during the period of the Commonwealth. The documents contain invaluable information about almost every subject that was of interest to the people of the various localities of the State within the period covered.

G. Virginia Land Patents, folio, vols. 1 and 2, 1623–1643; vol. 3, 1643–1651; vol. 4, 1652–1655; vol. 5, 1655–1664; vol. 6, 1666–1679. Land Office, Richmond.

H. Tax Books (for various counties), 1856–60. Auditor's Office, Richmond.

I. Transcripts made from original papers in the British Public Record Office, London. By Angus W. MacDonald, 7 vols., 1619–1695; containing abstracts or complete transcripts of 581 documents relating to the settlement and early history of Virginia. By William Noel Sainsbury, 20 vols., 1606–1740; containing abstracts of 5108 documents relating to early Virginia history. Virginia State Library.

J. Letter Book of the Executive of Virginia, 1844–1848, folio. Virginia State Library.

K. Proclamation Book; containing the proclamations of the Governors of Virginia from 1786 to Aug. 31, 1801. Virginia State Library.

L. Land Books of the City of Richmond, 1856–1860. City Hall, Richmond.

LAWS AND COURT DECISIONS

1. Statutes at Large of Virginia, 13 vols., 1619–1792. By William Waller Hening. Richmond, 1819–1820.
2. Statutes at Large of Virginia, 3 vols., 1792–1807. By Samuel Sheppard. Richmond, 1835–1836.

   Being an addition to Hening's Statutes, these three volumes are referred to in this monograph as vols. xiv, xv, and xvi of Hening.
3. Acts of the General Assembly of Virginia, 1807–1865.
4. Statutes at large of the Confederate States of America, 1861–1864, including both public and private acts and resolutions. Edited by James M. Mathews. Richmond, 1864.
5. Revised Code of Laws of Virginia, 2 vols. Richmond, 1819.
6. Supplement to the Revised Code of the Laws of Virginia. Richmond, 1833.
7. Code of Virginia. Richmond, 1849.
8. Code of Virginia. Richmond, 1860.
9. Constitutions of Virginia, 1776, 1830, 1851.
10. Reports of Cases Determined in the General Court and the Supreme Court of Appeals of Virginia:
    (*a*) By Thomas Jefferson, 1 vol., 1730–1740 and 1768–1772.
    (*b*) By Bushrod Washington, 2 vols., 1790–1796.
    (*c*) By Daniel Call, 6 vols., 1790–1825.
    (*d*) By William W. Hening and William Munford, 4 vols., 1806–1810.

(*e*) By William Munford, 6 vols., 1809–1820.
(*f*) By Francis W. Gilmer, 1 vol., 1820–1821.
(*g*) By Peyton Randolph, 6 vols., 1821–1828.
(*h*) By Benjamin Watkins Leigh, 12 vols., 1829–1842.
(*i*) By Conway Robinson, 2 vols., 1842–1844.
(*j*) By Peachy R. Grattan, 16 vols., 1844–1865.
(*k*) Virginia Colonial Decisions. The Reports by Sir John Randolph and Edward Barradall of Decisions of the General Court of Virginia, 2 vols., 1728–1741. Edited by R. T. Barton. Boston, 1909.

PUBLIC DOCUMENTS

1. Journals of the House of Burgesses, 1727–1776, 8 vols. Edited by H. R. McIlwaine, 1905–1910.
2. Journals of the House of Delegates of the Commonwealth of Virginia, 1776–1865. [Journals for May session of 1782 and session of 1796 are missing.] Richmond.
3. Journals of the Senate of the Commonwealth of Virginia, 1778–1865. [Missing Journals: 1780–1784, 1791–1799, 1802–1828, 1836–1838, 1854–1855, 1856–1860.] Richmond.
4. Proceedings of the Convention of Delegates for the Counties and Corporations of the Colony of Virginia, held at Richmond Town, in the County of Henrico, 1775. Richmond, 1816.
5. Proceedings and Debates of the Virginia State Convention of 1829–1830. Edited by Ritchie and Cook. Richmond, 1830.
6. Journal, Acts, and Proceedings of a General Convention of the State of Virginia, 1850. Richmond.
7. Journal of the Congress of the Confederate States of America, 1861–1865. In 7 vols. Issued as Senate Document No. 234, 58th Congress, 2nd Session. Washington, 1904.
8. Documents of the House of Delegates, containing the messages of the Governors to the General Assemblies and annual reports of the public officers of the State, and of boards of directors, visitors, superintendents, and other supervisors of public institutions of Virginia, 1814–1865.
9. Documents of the Senate, containing bills introduced and passed by the Senate, reports of commissions and various other state papers, 1831–1865.
10. Colonial Records of Virginia (1619–1680). Issued as State Senate Document, Extra, 1874. Richmond.
11. A Collection of the Official Publications of the Confederate States Government. Virginia State Library.
12. The Federal Censuses of the United States, 1790 to 1860, volumes on population.

NEWSPAPERS

FILES IN THE STATE LIBRARY.

1. The Richmond Examiner and Argus, August, 1800–February, 1801.
2. The Virginia Argus, Richmond, February, 1804–December, 1805.
3. The Daily Dispatch, Richmond, 1852–1865.
4. The Enquirer, Richmond, May, 1804–December, 1864.

5. The Virginia Gazette, Williamsburg, January, 1767–December, 1768; January, 1771–December, 1777; February, 1779–December, 1779.
6. The Virginia Gazette and General Advertizer, Richmond, March, 1791–December, 1809.
7. The Norfolk and Portsmouth Herald, January–December, 1847.
8. The Constitutional Whig and The Daily Richmond Whig, Richmond, 1824–1865.
9. The Recorder, Richmond, 1802–1803.

FILES IN THE LIBRARY OF CONGRESS.

10. The Virginia Gazette and the American Advertizer, Richmond, January, 1782–December, 1794.
11. The Enquirer, Richmond, 1804–1805 [contain numbers examined to supplement files in Virginia State Library].

MAGAZINES AND PERIODICALS

1. The Virginia Magazine of History and Biography. Edited by R. A. Brock. Vols. i to v. Edited by William G. Stanard, vols. vi–xix. Richmond, 1893–1911.
2. The William and Mary College Quarterly Historical Magazine. Edited by Lyon G. Tyler. Vols. i–xix. Williamsburg, 1892–1911.
3. Calendar of Virginia State Papers. Edited by William P. Palmer. Vols. i–xi. Richmond, 1875.
4. Collections of the Virginia Historical Society, New Series. Edited by R. A. Brock. Vols. i–xx. Richmond, 1882–1891.

   The above serial publications are really source books of Virginia history. They make available in published form many original and valuable manuscripts from collections in the Virginia Historical Society, the Virginia State Archives, county archives, and in the possession of private individuals.
5. The Commercial Review of the South and West. A monthly journal of trade, etc. Edited by J. D. B. DeBow. Vols. i–xxxi. New Orleans, 1846–1861.
6. The Virginia Historical Register and Literary Advertizer. Edited by William Maxwell. Vols. i–vi. Richmond, 1848–1853.

   Contains extracts from "records, journals, diaries, letters, inscriptions and other relics of the 'olden time.'"
7. The Lower Norfolk County Virginia Antiquary. Edited by Edward Wilson James. Vols. i–v. Norfolk, 1897–1906.

   Contains abstracts and gleanings from official records of churches and courts of Lower Norfolk and Princess Anne counties.
8. Virginia County Records. Published quarterly by the Genealogical Association, New York City. William Armstrong Crozier, editor. Vols. i–vii.

   These volumes contain abstracts of wills and extracts from other county and probate court records such as orders, marriage bonds, and land grants.
9. The African Repository and Colonial Journal. Vols. i–xxv. Published by the American Colonization Society. Washington, 1825–1850.

PUBLISHED PARISH RECORDS AND LOCAL HISTORIES

1. The Vestry Book and Register of Bristol Parish, Virginia, 1720–1789. Transcribed and published by C. G. Chamberlayne. Richmond, 1898.
2. Register of Christ's Church, Middlesex County, Virginia, 1653–1812. Published by the National Society of the Colonial Dames of America in the State of Virginia. Richmond, 1897.
3. The Vestry Book of Henrico Parish, Virginia, 1730–1773, from the original MS. By R. A. Brock. Richmond, 1874.
4. Register of St. Peter's Parish, New Kent County, Virginia, 1680–1787. Published by the National Society of the Colonial Dames of America in the State of Virginia. Richmond, 1904.
5. Vestry Book of Saint Peter's Parish, New Kent County, Virginia. Published by the National Society of Colonial Dames of America in the State of Virginia. Richmond, 1904.
6. Papers Relating to the History of the Church in Virginia, 1650–1776. Edited by William S. Perry. Privately printed. 1870.
7. Bagby, Rev. Alfred. King and Queen County, Virginia. New York and Washington, 1908.
8. Bruce, Thomas. Southwest Virginia and the Shenandoah Valley. Richmond, 1891.
9. Burton, Rev. L. W. Annals of Henrico Parish, Diocese of Virginia and especially of St. John's Church, 1611–1884. Richmond, 1904.
10. Cartmell, T. K. Shenandoah Valley Pioneers and Their Descendants. A History of Frederick County, Virginia, from its formation in 1738 to 1908. Compiled mainly from original records of old Frederick County, now Hampshire, Berkeley, Shenandoah, Jefferson, Hardy, Clarke, Warren, Morgan, and Frederick. Privately published by the author, 1909.
11. Goodwin, Rev. W. A. R. Historical Sketch of Bruton Church, Williamsburg, Virginia. Williamsburg, 1903.
12. Wise, Jennings Cropper. Ye Kingdome of Accawmacke; or, the Eastern Shore of Virginia in the Seventeenth Century. Richmond, 1911.
13. Woods, Rev. Edgar. Albemarle County in Virginia, giving some account of what it was by nature, of what it was made by man, and of some of the men who made it. Charlottesville, 1901.

CONTEMPORARY WORKS AND PAMPHLETS

1. Alexander, Archibald. A History of Colonization on the Western Coast of Africa. Philadelphia, 1849.
2. Andrews, E. A. Slavery and the Domestic Slave Trade in the United States. In a series of letters addressed to the executive committee of the American Union for the relief and improvement of the colored race. Boston, 1836.
3. Asbury, Rev. Francis, Bishop of M. E. Church. Journal from Aug. 7, 1771–Dec. 7, 1815. 3 vols. New York, 1821.
4. Ashmum, J. History of the African Colony in Liberia, from December, 1821 to 1823. Compiled from the authentic records of the colony. Washington, 1826.
   Bound in "Slavery Pamphlets," in Virginia State Library.

5. BEVERLY, ROBERT. The History and Present State of Virginia, in four parts. By a native and inhabitant of the place. London, 1705.
6. BULLOCK, WILLIAM, GENT. Virginia impartially examined and left to the publick view to be considered by all iudicious and honest men, etc. London, 1649. Pp. 66.
7. BURK, JOHN. The History of Virginia from its first settlement to the present day. 11 vols. Petersburg, Virginia, 1804–1816.
8. BURNABY, ANDREW. Travels Through the Middle settlements of North America, in the years 1759 and 1760. Pp. 52.
In Pinkerton, J., Voyages, vol. 13.
9. "CALX." Two Great Evils of Virginia and their one Common Remedy.
A pamphlet written September 17, 1859, and printed by John W. Randolph of Richmond. Pp. 18.
One of the evils referred to was the free negro and the other was the seduction of slaves by abolitionists. Bound in "Political Pamphlets," vol. 12, in Virginia State Library.
10. CHASE, A. M., AND SANBORN, CHARLES W. A Statistical View of the Condition of the Free and Slave States. Compiled from official documents. Boston, 1856.
11. CHASTELLUX, FRANÇOIS JEAN. Travels in North America in the years 1780–82. Translated from the French by an English gentleman who resided in America at that period. 2 vols. London, 1787.
12. DABNEY, PROF. ROBERT L. A Defence of Virginia in Recent and Pending Contests against the Sectional Party. New York, 1867.
13. DEW, THOMAS R. Review of the Debates in the Virginia Legislature of 1831–32. Richmond, 1832.
14. FITZHUGH, GEORGE. What shall be done with the Free Negroes. Four essays written for the Fredericksburg Recorder, 1851.
This is a biased argument in favor of reducing free negroes to slavery.
15. — —. Sociology for the South, or The Failure of Free Society. Richmond, 1854.
16. FORCE, PETER. Tracts and Other Papers, relating principally to the Origin, Settlement, and Progress of the Colonies of North America, from the discovery of the country to the year 1776. 4 vols. Washington, 1836–1846.
17. GARLAND, HUGH A. The Life of John Randolph of Roanoke. 2 vols. New York, 1851.
18. GODWYN, MORGAN. Negro's and Indian's Advocate suing for their Admission into the Church: For a persuasive to the instructing and baptizing of the Negroes and Indians in our Plantations, To which is added a brief account of religion in Virginia. London, 1680. Pp. 174.
19. — —. A Supplement to the Negro's and Indian's Advocate, or some further considerations and proposals for the effectual and speedy carrying on of the Negro's Christianity in our plantations without any prejudice to their owners. London, 1681. Pp. 12.
20. GOODELL, WILLIAM. The American Slave Code in theory and practice: Its distinctive features shown by its statutes, judicial decisions, and illustrative facts. Fourth edition. New York, 1853.

21. HAMMOND, JOHN. Leah and Rachel, or the Two Fruitfull Sisters Virginia, and Mary-Land: Their Present Condition, Impartially stated and related. London, 1656.

22. HARTWELL, BLAIR, AND CHILTON. The Present State of Virginia and the College. London, 1727. Pp. 95.

23. HILDRETH, RICHARD. The History of the United States of America from the discovery of the continent to the organization of the government under the Federal Constitution. 1497–1789. Revised edition. 3 vols. New York, 1856.

24. HOWE, HENRY. Historical Collections of Virginia. Charleston, S. C., 1852.

25. HOWISON, ROBERT R. A History of Virginia from its Discovery and Settlement by Europeans to the Present Time. 2 vols. Richmond, 1848.

26. JAY, WILLIAM. Miscellaneous writings on Slavery. Boston, 1853.

27. — —. Slavery in America: or An Inquiry into the character and tendency of the American Colonization and the American Anti-Slavery Societies. London, 1835.

28. JEFFERSON, THOMAS. Writings. Edited by P. L. Ford. 10 vols. New York, 1892–1899.

29. — —. Notes on the State of Virginia with an appendix. Third American edition. New York, 1801.

30. LEIGH, BENJAMIN WATKINS. The letter of Appomattox to the People of Virginia exhibiting a connected view of the recent proceedings in the House of Delegates on the subject of abolition of slavery; and a succinct account of the doctrines broached by the friends of abolition in debate; and the mischievous tendencies of those proceedings and doctrines. Richmond, 1832.

31. — —. Virginia Slavery Debate. Richmond, 1832.

Contains nine of the speeches delivered by members of the House of Delegates of 1831–1832 on the policy of the State in relation to her colored population, and the Letter of Appomattox to the People of Virginia.

32. MADISON, JAMES. Letters and other Writings of James Madison. In four volumes, published by order of Congress, 1769–1836. New York, 1884.

33. MONROE, JAMES. The Writings of James Monroe, including a collection of his public and private papers and correspondence now for the first time printed (1778–1831). Edited by S. M. Hamilton. 7 vols. New York, 1898–1903.

34. NEILL, EDWARD D. History of the Virginia Company of London, with letters to and from the first colony never before printed. Albany, N. Y., 1869.

35. OLMSTEAD, FREDERICK LAW. A Journey in the Seaboard Slave States, with remarks on their economy. New York, 1856.

36. ROWLAND, KATE MASON. The life of George Mason, 1725–1792. Including his Speeches, Public Papers, and Correspondence; with an Introduction by General Fitzhugh Lee. 2 vols. New York, 1892.

37. RUFFIN, EDMUND. African Colonization Unveiled. By Edmund Ruffin. Washington [1859?]. Pp. 32. Virginia State Library.

38. — —. The Political Economy of Slavery, or the institution considered in regard to its influence on public wealth and the

general welfare, with an appendix on the influence of slavery, or of its absence, on manners, morals, and intellect. 1852. Pp. 32.

39. SCHOOLCRAFT, HENRY R. Information respecting the History, Condition and Prospects of the Indian Tribes of the United States. 5 vols. Philadelphia, 1855.
40. SLAUGHTER, PHILIP. Virginia History of African Colonization. Richmond, 1855.
41. SMITH, CAPT. JOHN. Works, 1608–1631. Edited by Edward Arber. Birmingham, England, 1884.
42. STITH, WILLIAM. The history of the first discovery and settlement of Virginia: being an essay towards a general history of this colony. Williamsburg, Virginia, 1747.
43. STRINGFELLOW, B. F. Negro Slavery no Evil; or the North and the South. A report to the Platte county self-defence association, St. Louis: 1854. Pp. 38.

    Bound in "Slavery Pamphlets" in the library of William and Mary College.
44. STROUD, GEORGE M. A Sketch of the Laws Relating to Slavery in the Several States of America. Philadelphia, 1827.
45. TUCKER, GEORGE. Progress of The United States in Population and Wealth in fifty years, as exhibited by the decennial Census from 1790 to 1840. New York, 1855.
46. TUCKER, ST. GEORGE. A Dissertation on Slavery with a proposal for the gradual abolition of it in the State of Virginia. Philadelphia, 1796. Pp. 106.

    A second edition was printed in 1803 as an appendix to the author's Commentaries on Blackstone.
47. A Dialogue Concerning the Slavery of the Africans; Shewing it to be the Duty and Interest of the American States to emancipate all their African Slaves. With an Address to the owners of such Slaves, New York, 1785. Norwich, 1796.

    A rare pamphlet in Virginia State Library.
48. Political Pamphlets.

    A collection of 45 bound volumes of miscellaneous pamphlets, most of which refer to political events immediately preceding or during the Civil War, in Virginia State Library.
49. Views of American Slavery, taken a century ago. Anthony Benzet, John Wesley, etc. Philadelphia, 1858.

    This pamphlet contains a miscellaneous collection of views of slavery in the eighteenth century. It is important on manumission sentiment in Virginia.

INDEX

A CATALOGUE OF SELECTED DOVER BOOKS IN ALL FIELDS OF INTEREST

AMERICA'S OLD MASTERS, James T. Flexner. Four men emerged unexpectedly from provincial 18th century America to leadership in European art: Benjamin West, J. S. Copley, C. R. Peale, Gilbert Stuart. Brilliant coverage of lives and contributions. Revised, 1967 edition. 69 plates. 365pp. of text.
21806-6 Paperbound $2.75

FIRST FLOWERS OF OUR WILDERNESS: AMERICAN PAINTING, THE COLONIAL PERIOD, James T. Flexner. Painters, and regional painting traditions from earliest Colonial times up to the emergence of Copley, West and Peale Sr., Foster, Gustavus Hesselius, Feke, John Smibert and many anonymous painters in the primitive manner. Engaging presentation, with 162 illustrations. xxii + 368pp.
22180-6 Paperbound $3.50

THE LIGHT OF DISTANT SKIES: AMERICAN PAINTING, 1760-1835, James T. Flexner. The great generation of early American painters goes to Europe to learn and to teach: West, Copley, Gilbert Stuart and others. Allston, Trumbull, Morse; also contemporary American painters—primitives, derivatives, academics—who remained in America. 102 illustrations. xiii + 306pp. 22179-2 Paperbound $3.00

A HISTORY OF THE RISE AND PROGRESS OF THE ARTS OF DESIGN IN THE UNITED STATES, William Dunlap. Much the richest mine of information on early American painters, sculptors, architects, engravers, miniaturists, etc. The only source of information for scores of artists, the major primary source for many others. Unabridged reprint of rare original 1834 edition, with new introduction by James T. Flexner, and 394 new illustrations. Edited by Rita Weiss. 6⅝ x 9⅝.
21695-0, 21696-9, 21697-7 Three volumes, Paperbound $13.50

EPOCHS OF CHINESE AND JAPANESE ART, Ernest F. Fenollosa. From primitive Chinese art to the 20th century, thorough history, explanation of every important art period and form, including Japanese woodcuts; main stress on China and Japan, but Tibet, Korea also included. Still unexcelled for its detailed, rich coverage of cultural background, aesthetic elements, diffusion studies, particularly of the historical period. 2nd, 1913 edition. 242 illustrations. lii + 439pp. of text.
20364-6, 20365-4 Two volumes, Paperbound $5.00

THE GENTLE ART OF MAKING ENEMIES, James A. M. Whistler. Greatest wit of his day deflates Oscar Wilde, Ruskin, Swinburne; strikes back at inane critics, exhibitions, art journalism; aesthetics of impressionist revolution in most striking form. Highly readable classic by great painter. Reproduction of edition designed by Whistler. Introduction by Alfred Werner. xxxvi + 334pp.
21875-9 Paperbound $2.25

A CATALOGUE OF SELECTED DOVER BOOKS
IN ALL FIELDS OF INTEREST

VISUAL ILLUSIONS: THEIR CAUSES, CHARACTERISTICS, AND APPLICATIONS, Matthew Luckiesh. Thorough description and discussion of optical illusion, geometric and perspective, particularly; size and shape distortions, illusions of color, of motion; natural illusions; use of illusion in art and magic, industry, etc. Most useful today with op art, also for classical art. Scores of effects illustrated. Introduction by William H. Ittleson. 100 illustrations. xxi + 252pp.
21530-X Paperbound $1.50

A HANDBOOK OF ANATOMY FOR ART STUDENTS, Arthur Thomson. Thorough, virtually exhaustive coverage of skeletal structure, musculature, etc. Full text, supplemented by anatomical diagrams and drawings and by photographs of undraped figures. Unique in its comparison of male and female forms, pointing out differences of contour, texture, form. 211 figures, 40 drawings, 86 photographs. xx + 459pp. 5⅜ x 8⅜.
21163-0 Paperbound $3.00

150 MASTERPIECES OF DRAWING, Selected by Anthony Toney. Full page reproductions of drawings from the early 16th to the end of the 18th century, all beautifully reproduced: Rembrandt, Michelangelo, Dürer, Fragonard, Urs, Graf, Wouwerman, many others. First-rate browsing book, model book for artists. xviii + 150pp. 8⅜ x 11¼.
21032-4 Paperbound $2.00

THE LATER WORK OF AUBREY BEARDSLEY, Aubrey Beardsley. Exotic, erotic, ironic masterpieces in full maturity: Comedy Ballet, Venus and Tannhauser, Pierrot, Lysistrata, Rape of the Lock, Savoy material, Ali Baba, Volpone, etc. This material revolutionized the art world, and is still powerful, fresh, brilliant. With *The Early Work,* all Beardsley's finest work. 174 plates, 2 in color. xiv + 176pp. 8⅛ x 11.
21817-1 Paperbound $3.00

DRAWINGS OF REMBRANDT, Rembrandt van Rijn. Complete reproduction of fabulously rare edition by Lippmann and Hofstede de Groot, completely reedited, updated, improved by Prof. Seymour Slive, Fogg Museum. Portraits, Biblical sketches, landscapes, Oriental types, nudes, episodes from classical mythology—All Rembrandt's fertile genius. Also selection of drawings by his pupils and followers. "Stunning volumes," *Saturday Review.* 550 illustrations. lxxviii + 552pp. 9⅛ x 12¼.
21485-0, 21486-9 Two volumes, Paperbound $6.50

THE DISASTERS OF WAR, Francisco Goya. One of the masterpieces of Western civilization—83 etchings that record Goya's shattering, bitter reaction to the Napoleonic war that swept through Spain after the insurrection of 1808 and to war in general. Reprint of the first edition, with three additional plates from Boston's Museum of Fine Arts. All plates facsimile size. Introduction by Philip Hofer, Fogg Museum. v + 97pp. 9⅜ x 8¼.
21872-4 Paperbound $1.75

GRAPHIC WORKS OF ODILON REDON. Largest collection of Redon's graphic works ever assembled: 172 lithographs, 28 etchings and engravings, 9 drawings. These include some of his most famous works. All the plates from *Odilon Redon: oeuvre graphique complet,* plus additional plates. New introduction and caption translations by Alfred Werner. 209 illustrations. xxvii + 209pp. 9⅛ x 12¼.
21966-8 Paperbound $4.00

DESIGN BY ACCIDENT; A BOOK OF "ACCIDENTAL EFFECTS" FOR ARTISTS AND DESIGNERS, James F. O'Brien. Create your own unique, striking, imaginative effects by "controlled accident" interaction of materials: paints and lacquers, oil and water based paints, splatter, crackling materials, shatter, similar items. Everything you do will be different; first book on this limitless art, so useful to both fine artist and commercial artist. Full instructions. 192 plates showing "accidents," 8 in color. viii + 215pp. 8⅜ x 11¼. 21942-9 Paperbound $3.50

THE BOOK OF SIGNS, Rudolf Koch. Famed German type designer draws 493 beautiful symbols: religious, mystical, alchemical, imperial, property marks, runes, etc. Remarkable fusion of traditional and modern. Good for suggestions of timelessness, smartness, modernity. Text. vi + 104pp. 6⅛ x 9¼.
20162-7 Paperbound $1.25

HISTORY OF INDIAN AND INDONESIAN ART, Ananda K. Coomaraswamy. An unabridged republication of one of the finest books by a great scholar in Eastern art. Rich in descriptive material, history, social backgrounds; Sunga reliefs, Rajput paintings, Gupta temples, Burmese frescoes, textiles, jewelry, sculpture, etc. 400 photos. viii + 423pp. 6⅜ x 9¾. 21436-2 Paperbound $3.50

PRIMITIVE ART, Franz Boas. America's foremost anthropologist surveys textiles, ceramics, woodcarving, basketry, metalwork, etc.; patterns, technology, creation of symbols, style origins. All areas of world, but very full on Northwest Coast Indians. More than 350 illustrations of baskets, boxes, totem poles, weapons, etc. 378 pp.
20025-6 Paperbound $2.50

THE GENTLEMAN AND CABINET MAKER'S DIRECTOR, Thomas Chippendale. Full reprint (third edition, 1762) of most influential furniture book of all time, by master cabinetmaker. 200 plates, illustrating chairs, sofas, mirrors, tables, cabinets, plus 24 photographs of surviving pieces. Biographical introduction by N. Bienenstock. vi + 249pp. 9⅞ x 12¾. 21601-2 Paperbound $3.50

AMERICAN ANTIQUE FURNITURE, Edgar G. Miller, Jr. The basic coverage of all American furniture before 1840. Individual chapters cover type of furniture—clocks, tables, sideboards, etc.—chronologically, with inexhaustible wealth of data. More than 2100 photographs, all identified, commented on. Essential to all early American collectors. Introduction by H. E. Keyes. vi + 1106pp. 7⅞ x 10¾.
21599-7, 21600-4 Two volumes, Paperbound $7.50

PENNSYLVANIA DUTCH AMERICAN FOLK ART, Henry J. Kauffman. 279 photos, 28 drawings of tulipware, Fraktur script, painted tinware, toys, flowered furniture, quilts, samplers, hex signs, house interiors, etc. Full descriptive text. Excellent for tourist, rewarding for designer, collector. Map. 146pp. 7⅞ x 10¾.
21205-X Paperbound $2.00

EARLY NEW ENGLAND GRAVESTONE RUBBINGS, Edmund V. Gillon, Jr. 43 photographs, 226 carefully reproduced rubbings show heavily symbolic, sometimes macabre early gravestones, up to early 19th century. Remarkable early American primitive art, occasionally strikingly beautiful; always powerful. Text. xxvi + 207pp. 8⅜ x 11¼. 21380-3 Paperbound $3.00

ALPHABETS AND ORNAMENTS, Ernst Lehner. Well-known pictorial source for decorative alphabets, script examples, cartouches, frames, decorative title pages, calligraphic initials, borders, similar material. 14th to 19th century, mostly European. Useful in almost any graphic arts designing, varied styles. 750 illustrations. 256pp. 7 x 10. 21905-4 Paperbound $3.50

PAINTING: A CREATIVE APPROACH, Norman Colquhoun. For the beginner simple guide provides an instructive approach to painting: major stumbling blocks for beginner; overcoming them, technical points; paints and pigments; oil painting; watercolor and other media and color. New section on "plastic" paints. Glossary. Formerly *Paint Your Own Pictures.* 221pp. 22000-1 Paperbound $1.75

THE ENJOYMENT AND USE OF COLOR, Walter Sargent. Explanation of the relations between colors themselves and between colors in nature and art, including hundreds of little-known facts about color values, intensities, effects of high and low illumination, complementary colors. Many practical hints for painters, references to great masters. 7 color plates, 29 illustrations. x + 274pp.
20944-X Paperbound $2.50

THE NOTEBOOKS OF LEONARDO DA VINCI, compiled and edited by Jean Paul Richter. 1566 extracts from original manuscripts reveal the full range of Leonardo's versatile genius: all his writings on painting, sculpture, architecture, anatomy, astronomy, geography, topography, physiology, mining, music, etc., in both Italian and English, with 186 plates of manuscript pages and more than 500 additional drawings. Includes studies for the Last Supper, the lost Sforza monument, and other works. Total of xlvii + 866pp. 7⅞ x 10¾.
22572-0, 22573-9 Two volumes, Paperbound $10.00

MONTGOMERY WARD CATALOGUE OF 1895. Tea gowns, yards of flannel and pillow-case lace, stereoscopes, books of gospel hymns, the New Improved Singer Sewing Machine, side saddles, milk skimmers, straight-edged razors, high-button shoes, spittoons, and on and on . . . listing some 25,000 items, practically all illustrated. Essential to the shoppers of the 1890's, it is our truest record of the spirit of the period. Unaltered reprint of Issue No. 57, Spring and Summer 1895. Introduction by Boris Emmet. Innumerable illustrations. xiii + 624pp. 8½ x 11⅝.
22377-9 Paperbound $6.95

THE CRYSTAL PALACE EXHIBITION ILLUSTRATED CATALOGUE (LONDON, 1851). One of the wonders of the modern world—the Crystal Palace Exhibition in which all the nations of the civilized world exhibited their achievements in the arts and sciences—presented in an equally important illustrated catalogue. More than 1700 items pictured with accompanying text—ceramics, textiles, cast-iron work, carpets, pianos, sleds, razors, wall-papers, billiard tables, beehives, silverware and hundreds of other artifacts—represent the focal point of Victorian culture in the Western World. Probably the largest collection of Victorian decorative art ever assembled—indispensable for antiquarians and designers. Unabridged republication of the Art-Journal Catalogue of the Great Exhibition of 1851, with all terminal essays. New introduction by John Gloag, F.S.A. xxxiv + 426pp. 9 x 12.
22503-8 Paperbound $4.50

A HISTORY OF COSTUME, Carl Köhler. Definitive history, based on surviving pieces of clothing primarily, and paintings, statues, etc. secondarily. Highly readable text, supplemented by 594 illustrations of costumes of the ancient Mediterranean peoples, Greece and Rome, the Teutonic prehistoric period; costumes of the Middle Ages, Renaissance, Baroque, 18th and 19th centuries. Clear, measured patterns are provided for many clothing articles. Approach is practical throughout. Enlarged by Emma von Sichart. 464pp. 21030-8 Paperbound $3.00

ORIENTAL RUGS, ANTIQUE AND MODERN, Walter A. Hawley. A complete and authoritative treatise on the Oriental rug—where they are made, by whom and how, designs and symbols, characteristics in detail of the six major groups, how to distinguish them and how to buy them. Detailed technical data is provided on periods, weaves, warps, wefts, textures, sides, ends and knots, although no technical background is required for an understanding. 11 color plates, 80 halftones, 4 maps. vi + 320pp. 6⅛ x 9⅛. 22366-3 Paperbound $5.00

TEN BOOKS ON ARCHITECTURE, Vitruvius. By any standards the most important book on architecture ever written. Early Roman discussion of aesthetics of building, construction methods, orders, sites, and every other aspect of architecture has inspired, instructed architecture for about 2,000 years. Stands behind Palladio, Michelangelo, Bramante, Wren, countless others. Definitive Morris H. Morgan translation. 68 illustrations. xii + 331pp. 20645-9 Paperbound $2.50

THE FOUR BOOKS OF ARCHITECTURE, Andrea Palladio. Translated into every major Western European language in the two centuries following its publication in 1570, this has been one of the most influential books in the history of architecture. Complete reprint of the 1738 Isaac Ware edition. New introduction by Adolf Placzek, Columbia Univ. 216 plates. xxii + 110pp. of text. 9½ x 12¾. 21308-0 Clothbound $10.00

STICKS AND STONES: A STUDY OF AMERICAN ARCHITECTURE AND CIVILIZATION, Lewis Mumford.One of the great classics of American cultural history. American architecture from the medieval-inspired earliest forms to the early 20th century; evolution of structure and style, and reciprocal influences on environment. 21 photographic illustrations. 238pp. 20202-X Paperbound $2.00

THE AMERICAN BUILDER'S COMPANION, Asher Benjamin. The most widely used early 19th century architectural style and source book, for colonial up into Greek Revival periods. Extensive development of geometry of carpentering, construction of sashes, frames, doors, stairs; plans and elevations of domestic and other buildings. Hundreds of thousands of houses were built according to this book, now invaluable to historians, architects, restorers, etc. 1827 edition. 59 plates. 114pp. 7⅞ x 10¾. 22236-5 Paperbound $3.00

DUTCH HOUSES IN THE HUDSON VALLEY BEFORE 1776, Helen Wilkinson Reynolds. The standard survey of the Dutch colonial house and outbuildings, with constructional features, decoration, and local history associated with individual homesteads. Introduction by Franklin D. Roosevelt. Map. 150 illustrations. 469pp. 6⅝ x 9¼. 21469-9 Paperbound $3.50

THE ARCHITECTURE OF COUNTRY HOUSES, Andrew J. Downing. Together with Vaux's *Villas and Cottages* this is the basic book for Hudson River Gothic architecture of the middle Victorian period. Full, sound discussions of general aspects of housing, architecture, style, decoration, furnishing, together with scores of detailed house plans, illustrations of specific buildings, accompanied by full text. Perhaps the most influential single American architectural book. 1850 edition. Introduction by J. Stewart Johnson. 321 figures, 34 architectural designs. xvi + 560pp.
22003-6 Paperbound $3.50

LOST EXAMPLES OF COLONIAL ARCHITECTURE, John Mead Howells. Full-page photographs of buildings that have disappeared or been so altered as to be denatured, including many designed by major early American architects. 245 plates. xvii + 248pp. 7⅞ x 10¾. 21143-6 Paperbound $3.00

DOMESTIC ARCHITECTURE OF THE AMERICAN COLONIES AND OF THE EARLY REPUBLIC, Fiske Kimball. Foremost architect and restorer of Williamsburg and Monticello covers nearly 200 homes between 1620-1825. Architectural details, construction, style features, special fixtures, floor plans, etc. Generally considered finest work in its area. 219 illustrations of houses, doorways, windows, capital mantels. xx + 314pp. 7⅞ x 10¾. 21743-4 Paperbound $3.50

EARLY AMERICAN ROOMS: 1650-1858, edited by Russell Hawes Kettell. Tour of 12 rooms, each representative of a different era in American history and each furnished, decorated, designed and occupied in the style of the era. 72 plans and elevations, 8-page color section, etc., show fabrics, wall papers, arrangements, etc. Full descriptive text. xvii + 200pp. of text. 8⅜ x 11¼.
21633-0 Paperbound $4.00

THE FITZWILLIAM VIRGINAL BOOK, edited by J. Fuller Maitland and W. B. Squire. Full modern printing of famous early 17th-century ms. volume of 300 works by Morley, Byrd, Bull, Gibbons, etc. For piano or other modern keyboard instrument; easy to read format. xxxvi + 938pp. 8⅜ x 11.
21068-5, 21069-3 Two volumes, Paperbound $8.00

HARPSICHORD MUSIC, Johann Sebastian Bach. Bach Gesellschaft edition. A rich selection of Bach's masterpieces for the harpsichord: the six English Suites, six French Suites, the six Partitas (Clavierübung part I), the Goldberg Variations (Clavierübung part IV), the fifteen Two-Part Inventions and the fifteen Three-Part Sinfonias. Clearly reproduced on large sheets with ample margins; eminently playable. vi + 312pp. 8⅛ x 11. 22360-4 Paperbound $5.00

THE MUSIC OF BACH: AN INTRODUCTION, Charles Sanford Terry. A fine, nontechnical introduction to Bach's music, both instrumental and vocal. Covers organ music, chamber music, passion music, other types. Analyzes themes, developments, innovations. x + 114pp. 21075-8 Paperbound $1.25

BEETHOVEN AND HIS NINE SYMPHONIES, Sir George Grove. Noted British musicologist provides best history, analysis, commentary on symphonies. Very thorough, rigorously accurate; necessary to both advanced student and amateur music lover. 436 musical passages. vii + 407 pp. 20334-4 Paperbound $2.25

JOHANN SEBASTIAN BACH, Philipp Spitta. One of the great classics of musicology, this definitive analysis of Bach's music (and life) has never been surpassed. Lucid, nontechnical analyses of hundreds of pieces (30 pages devoted to St. Matthew Passion, 26 to B Minor Mass). Also includes major analysis of 18th-century music. 450 musical examples. 40-page musical supplement. Total of xx + 1799pp.
(EUK) 22278-0, 22279-9 Two volumes, Clothbound $15.00

MOZART AND HIS PIANO CONCERTOS, Cuthbert Girdlestone. The only full-length study of an important area of Mozart's creativity. Provides detailed analyses of all 23 concertos, traces inspirational sources. 417 musical examples. Second edition. 509pp. (USO) 21271-8 Paperbound $3.50

THE PERFECT WAGNERITE: A COMMENTARY ON THE NIBLUNG'S RING, George Bernard Shaw. Brilliant and still relevant criticism in remarkable essays on Wagner's Ring cycle, Shaw's ideas on political and social ideology behind the plots, role of Leitmotifs, vocal requisites, etc. Prefaces. xxi + 136pp.
21707-8 Paperbound $1.50

DON GIOVANNI, W. A. Mozart. Complete libretto, modern English translation; biographies of composer and librettist; accounts of early performances and critical reaction. Lavishly illustrated. All the material you need to understand and appreciate this great work. Dover Opera Guide and Libretto Series; translated and introduced by Ellen Bleiler. 92 illustrations. 209pp.
21134-7 Paperbound $1.50

HIGH FIDELITY SYSTEMS: A LAYMAN'S GUIDE, Roy F. Allison. All the basic information you need for setting up your own audio system: high fidelity and stereo record players, tape records, F.M. Connections, adjusting tone arm, cartridge, checking needle alignment, positioning speakers, phasing speakers, adjusting hums, trouble-shooting, maintenance, and similar topics. Enlarged 1965 edition. More than 50 charts, diagrams, photos. iv + 91pp. 21514-8 Paperbound $1.25

REPRODUCTION OF SOUND, Edgar Villchur. Thorough coverage for laymen of high fidelity systems, reproducing systems in general, needles, amplifiers, preamps, loudspeakers, feedback, explaining physical background. "A rare talent for making technicalities vividly comprehensible," R. Darrell, *High Fidelity*. 69 figures. iv + 92pp. 21515-6 Paperbound $1.00

HEAR ME TALKIN' TO YA: THE STORY OF JAZZ AS TOLD BY THE MEN WHO MADE IT, Nat Shapiro and Nat Hentoff. Louis Armstrong, Fats Waller, Jo Jones, Clarence Williams, Billy Holiday, Duke Ellington, Jelly Roll Morton and dozens of other jazz greats tell how it was in Chicago's South Side, New Orleans, depression Harlem and the modern West Coast as jazz was born and grew. xvi + 429pp.
21726-4 Paperbound $2.00

FABLES OF AESOP, translated by Sir Roger L'Estrange. A reproduction of the very rare 1931 Paris edition; a selection of the most interesting fables, together with 50 imaginative drawings by Alexander Calder. v + 128pp. 6½x9¼.
21780-9 Paperbound $1.25

AGAINST THE GRAIN (A REBOURS), Joris K. Huysmans. Filled with weird images, evidences of a bizarre imagination, exotic experiments with hallucinatory drugs, rich tastes and smells and the diversions of its sybarite hero Duc Jean des Esseintes, this classic novel pushed 19th-century literary decadence to its limits. Full unabridged edition. Do not confuse this with abridged editions generally sold. Introduction by Havelock Ellis. xlix + 206pp. 22190-3 Paperbound $2.00

VARIORUM SHAKESPEARE: HAMLET. Edited by Horace H. Furness; a landmark of American scholarship. Exhaustive footnotes and appendices treat all doubtful words and phrases, as well as suggested critical emendations throughout the play's history. First volume contains editor's own text, collated with all Quartos and Folios. Second volume contains full first Quarto, translations of Shakespeare's sources (Belleforest, and Saxo Grammaticus), Der Bestrafte Brudermord, and many essays on critical and historical points of interest by major authorities of past and present. Includes details of staging and costuming over the years. By far the best edition available for serious students of Shakespeare. Total of xx + 905pp. 21004-9, 21005-7, 2 volumes, Paperbound $5.25

A LIFE OF WILLIAM SHAKESPEARE, Sir Sidney Lee. This is the standard life of Shakespeare, summarizing everything known about Shakespeare and his plays. Incredibly rich in material, broad in coverage, clear and judicious, it has served thousands as the best introduction to Shakespeare. 1931 edition. 9 plates. xxix + 792pp. (USO) 21967-4 Paperbound $3.75

MASTERS OF THE DRAMA, John Gassner. Most comprehensive history of the drama in print, covering every tradition from Greeks to modern Europe and America, including India, Far East, etc. Covers more than 800 dramatists, 2000 plays, with biographical material, plot summaries, theatre history, criticism, etc. "Best of its kind in English," *New Republic*. 77 illustrations. xxii + 890pp. 20100-7 Clothbound $7.50

THE EVOLUTION OF THE ENGLISH LANGUAGE, George McKnight. The growth of English, from the 14th century to the present. Unusual, non-technical account presents basic information in very interesting form: sound shifts, change in grammar and syntax, vocabulary growth, similar topics. Abundantly illustrated with quotations. Formerly *Modern English in the Making*. xii + 590pp. 21932-1 Paperbound $3.50

AN ETYMOLOGICAL DICTIONARY OF MODERN ENGLISH, Ernest Weekley. Fullest, richest work of its sort, by foremost British lexicographer. Detailed word histories, including many colloquial and archaic words; extensive quotations. Do not confuse this with the Concise Etymological Dictionary, which is much abridged. Total of xxvii + 830pp. 6½ x 9¼. 21873-2, 21874-0 Two volumes, Paperbound $5.50

FLATLAND: A ROMANCE OF MANY DIMENSIONS, E. A. Abbott. Classic of science-fiction explores ramifications of life in a two-dimensional world, and what happens when a three-dimensional being intrudes. Amusing reading, but also useful as introduction to thought about hyperspace. Introduction by Banesh Hoffmann. 16 illustrations. xx + 103pp. 20001-9 Paperbound $1.00

POEMS OF ANNE BRADSTREET, edited with an introduction by Robert Hutchinson. A new selection of poems by America's first poet and perhaps the first significant woman poet in the English language. 48 poems display her development in works of considerable variety—love poems, domestic poems, religious meditations, formal elegies, "quaternions," etc. Notes, bibliography. viii + 222pp.
22160-1 Paperbound $2.00

THREE GOTHIC NOVELS: THE CASTLE OF OTRANTO BY HORACE WALPOLE; VATHEK BY WILLIAM BECKFORD; THE VAMPYRE BY JOHN POLIDORI, WITH FRAGMENT OF A NOVEL BY LORD BYRON, edited by E. F. Bleiler. The first Gothic novel, by Walpole; the finest Oriental tale in English, by Beckford; powerful Romantic supernatural story in versions by Polidori and Byron. All extremely important in history of literature; all still exciting, packed with supernatural thrills, ghosts, haunted castles, magic, etc. xl + 291pp.
21232-7 Paperbound $2.00

THE BEST TALES OF HOFFMANN, E. T. A. Hoffmann. 10 of Hoffmann's most important stories, in modern re-editings of standard translations: Nutcracker and the King of Mice, Signor Formica, Automata, The Sandman, Rath Krespel, The Golden Flowerpot, Master Martin the Cooper, The Mines of Falun, The King's Betrothed, A New Year's Eve Adventure. 7 illustrations by Hoffmann. Edited by E. F. Bleiler. xxxix + 419pp. 21793-0 Paperbound $2.25

GHOST AND HORROR STORIES OF AMBROSE BIERCE, Ambrose Bierce. 23 strikingly modern stories of the horrors latent in the human mind: The Eyes of the Panther, The Damned Thing, An Occurrence at Owl Creek Bridge, An Inhabitant of Carcosa, etc., plus the dream-essay, Visions of the Night. Edited by E. F. Bleiler. xxii + 199pp. 20767-6 Paperbound $1.50

BEST GHOST STORIES OF J. S. LEFANU, J. Sheridan LeFanu. Finest stories by Victorian master often considered greatest supernatural writer of all. Carmilla, Green Tea, The Haunted Baronet, The Familiar, and 12 others. Most never before available in the U. S. A. Edited by E. F. Bleiler. 8 illustrations from Victorian publications. xvii + 467pp. 20415-4 Paperbound $2.50

THE TIME STREAM, THE GREATEST ADVENTURE, AND THE PURPLE SAPPHIRE—THREE SCIENCE FICTION NOVELS, John Taine (Eric Temple Bell). Great American mathematician was also foremost science fiction novelist of the 1920's. *The Time Stream,* one of all-time classics, uses concepts of circular time; *The Greatest Adventure,* incredibly ancient biological experiments from Antarctica threaten to escape; The *Purple Sapphire,* superscience, lost races in Central Tibet, survivors of the Great Race. 4 illustrations by Frank R. Paul. v + 532pp.
21180-0 Paperbound $2.50

SEVEN SCIENCE FICTION NOVELS, H. G. Wells. The standard collection of the great novels. Complete, unabridged. *First Men in the Moon, Island of Dr. Moreau, War of the Worlds, Food of the Gods, Invisible Man, Time Machine, In the Days of the Comet.* Not only science fiction fans, but every educated person owes it to himself to read these novels. 1015pp. 20264-X Clothbound $5.00

LAST AND FIRST MEN AND STAR MAKER, TWO SCIENCE FICTION NOVELS, Olaf Stapledon. Greatest future histories in science fiction. In the first, human intelligence is the "hero," through strange paths of evolution, interplanetary invasions, incredible technologies, near extinctions and reemergences. Star Maker describes the quest of a band of star rovers for intelligence itself, through time and space: weird inhuman civilizations, crustacean minds, symbiotic worlds, etc. Complete, unabridged. v + 438pp. 21962-3 Paperbound $2.00

THREE PROPHETIC NOVELS, H. G. WELLS. Stages of a consistently planned future for mankind. *When the Sleeper Wakes,* and *A Story of the Days to Come,* anticipate *Brave New World* and *1984,* in the 21st Century; *The Time Machine,* only complete version in print, shows farther future and the end of mankind. All show Wells's greatest gifts as storyteller and novelist. Edited by E. F. Bleiler. x + 335pp. (USO) 20605-X Paperbound $2.00

THE DEVIL'S DICTIONARY, Ambrose Bierce. America's own Oscar Wilde—Ambrose Bierce—offers his barbed iconoclastic wisdom in over 1,000 definitions hailed by H. L. Mencken as "some of the most gorgeous witticisms in the English language." 145pp. 20487-1 Paperbound $1.25

MAX AND MORITZ, Wilhelm Busch. Great children's classic, father of comic strip, of two bad boys, Max and Moritz. Also Ker and Plunk (Plisch und Plumm), Cat and Mouse, Deceitful Henry, Ice-Peter, The Boy and the Pipe, and five other pieces. Original German, with English translation. Edited by H. Arthur Klein; translations by various hands and H. Arthur Klein. vi + 216pp.
20181-3 Paperbound $1.50

PIGS IS PIGS AND OTHER FAVORITES, Ellis Parker Butler. The title story is one of the best humor short stories, as Mike Flannery obfuscates biology and English. Also included, That Pup of Murchison's, The Great American Pie Company, and Perkins of Portland. 14 illustrations. v + 109pp. 21532-6 Paperbound $1.00

THE PETERKIN PAPERS, Lucretia P. Hale. It takes genius to be as stupidly mad as the Peterkins, as they decide to become wise, celebrate the "Fourth," keep a cow, and otherwise strain the resources of the Lady from Philadelphia. Basic book of American humor. 153 illustrations. 219pp. 20794-3 Paperbound $1.25

PERRAULT'S FAIRY TALES, translated by A. E. Johnson and S. R. Littlewood, with 34 full-page illustrations by Gustave Doré. All the original Perrault stories—Cinderella, Sleeping Beauty, Bluebeard, Little Red Riding Hood, Puss in Boots, Tom Thumb, etc.—with their witty verse morals and the magnificent illustrations of Doré. One of the five or six great books of European fairy tales. viii + 117pp. 8⅛ x 11. 22311-6 Paperbound $2.00

OLD HUNGARIAN FAIRY TALES, Baroness Orczy. Favorites translated and adapted by author of the *Scarlet Pimpernel.* Eight fairy tales include "The Suitors of Princess Fire-Fly," "The Twin Hunchbacks," "Mr. Cuttlefish's Love Story," and "The Enchanted Cat." This little volume of magic and adventure will captivate children as it has for generations. 90 drawings by Montagu Barstow. 96pp.
(USO) 22293-4 Paperbound $1.95

THE RED FAIRY BOOK, Andrew Lang. Lang's color fairy books have long been children's favorites. This volume includes Rapunzel, Jack and the Bean-stalk and 35 other stories, familiar and unfamiliar. 4 plates, 93 illustrations x + 367pp.
21673-X Paperbound $1.95

THE BLUE FAIRY BOOK, Andrew Lang. Lang's tales come from all countries and all times. Here are 37 tales from Grimm, the Arabian Nights, Greek Mythology, and other fascinating sources. 8 plates, 130 illustrations. xi + 390pp.
21437-0 Paperbound $1.95

HOUSEHOLD STORIES BY THE BROTHERS GRIMM. Classic English-language edition of the well-known tales — Rumpelstiltskin, Snow White, Hansel and Gretel, The Twelve Brothers, Faithful John, Rapunzel, Tom Thumb (52 stories in all). Translated into simple, straightforward English by Lucy Crane. Ornamented with headpieces, vignettes, elaborate decorative initials and a dozen full-page illustrations by Walter Crane. x + 269pp. 21080-4 Paperbound $2.00

THE MERRY ADVENTURES OF ROBIN HOOD, Howard Pyle. The finest modern versions of the traditional ballads and tales about the great English outlaw. Howard Pyle's complete prose version, with every word, every illustration of the first edition. Do not confuse this facsimile of the original (1883) with modern editions that change text or illustrations. 23 plates plus many page decorations. xxii + 296pp.
22043-5 Paperbound $2.00

THE STORY OF KING ARTHUR AND HIS KNIGHTS, Howard Pyle. The finest children's version of the life of King Arthur; brilliantly retold by Pyle, with 48 of his most imaginative illustrations. xviii + 313pp. 6⅛ x 9¼.
21445-1 Paperbound $2.00

THE WONDERFUL WIZARD OF OZ, L. Frank Baum. America's finest children's book in facsimile of first edition with all Denslow illustrations in full color. The edition a child should have. Introduction by Martin Gardner. 23 color plates, scores of drawings. iv + 267pp. 20691-2 Paperbound $1.95

THE MARVELOUS LAND OF OZ, L. Frank Baum. The second Oz book, every bit as imaginative as the Wizard. The hero is a boy named Tip, but the Scarecrow and the Tin Woodman are back, as is the Oz magic. 16 color plates, 120 drawings by John R. Neill. 287pp. 20692-0 Paperbound $1.75

THE MAGICAL MONARCH OF MO, L. Frank Baum. Remarkable adventures in a land even stranger than Oz. The best of Baum's books not in the Oz series. 15 color plates and dozens of drawings by Frank Verbeck. xviii + 237pp.
21892-9 Paperbound $2.00

THE BAD CHILD'S BOOK OF BEASTS, MORE BEASTS FOR WORSE CHILDREN, A MORAL ALPHABET, Hilaire Belloc. Three complete humor classics in one volume. Be kind to the frog, and do not call him names . . . and 28 other whimsical animals. Familiar favorites and some not so well known. Illustrated by Basil Blackwell. 156pp. (USO) 20749-8 Paperbound $1.25

EAST O' THE SUN AND WEST O' THE MOON, George W. Dasent. Considered the best of all translations of these Norwegian folk tales, this collection has been enjoyed by generations of children (and folklorists too). Includes True and Untrue, Why the Sea is Salt, East O' the Sun and West O' the Moon, Why the Bear is Stumpy-Tailed, Boots and the Troll, The Cock and the Hen, Rich Peter the Pedlar, and 52 more. The only edition with all 59 tales. 77 illustrations by Erik Werenskiold and Theodor Kittelsen. xv + 418pp. 22521-6 Paperbound $3.00

GOOPS AND HOW TO BE THEM, Gelett Burgess. Classic of tongue-in-cheek humor, masquerading as etiquette book. 87 verses, twice as many cartoons, show mischievous Goops as they demonstrate to children virtues of table manners, neatness, courtesy, etc. Favorite for generations. viii + 88pp. 6½ x 9¼.
22233-0 Paperbound $1.25

ALICE'S ADVENTURES UNDER GROUND, Lewis Carroll. The first version, quite different from the final *Alice in Wonderland,* printed out by Carroll himself with his own illustrations. Complete facsimile of the "million dollar" manuscript Carroll gave to Alice Liddell in 1864. Introduction by Martin Gardner. viii + 96pp. Title and dedication pages in color. 21482-6 Paperbound $1.25

THE BROWNIES, THEIR BOOK, Palmer Cox. Small as mice, cunning as foxes, exuberant and full of mischief, the Brownies go to the zoo, toy shop, seashore, circus, etc., in 24 verse adventures and 266 illustrations. Long a favorite, since their first appearance in St. Nicholas Magazine. xi + 144pp. 6⅝ x 9¼.
21265-3 Paperbound $1.75

SONGS OF CHILDHOOD, Walter De La Mare. Published (under the pseudonym Walter Ramal) when De La Mare was only 29, this charming collection has long been a favorite children's book. A facsimile of the first edition in paper, the 47 poems capture the simplicity of the nursery rhyme and the ballad, including such lyrics as I Met Eve, Tartary, The Silver Penny. vii + 106pp. 21972-0 Paperbound $1.25

THE COMPLETE NONSENSE OF EDWARD LEAR, Edward Lear. The finest 19th-century humorist-cartoonist in full: all nonsense limericks, zany alphabets, Owl and Pussycat, songs, nonsense botany, and more than 500 illustrations by Lear himself. Edited by Holbrook Jackson. xxix + 287pp. (USO) 20167-8 Paperbound $1.75

BILLY WHISKERS: THE AUTOBIOGRAPHY OF A GOAT, Frances Trego Montgomery. A favorite of children since the early 20th century, here are the escapades of that rambunctious, irresistible and mischievous goat—Billy Whiskers. Much in the spirit of *Peck's Bad Boy,* this is a book that children never tire of reading or hearing. All the original familiar illustrations by W. H. Fry are included: 6 color plates, 18 black and white drawings. 159pp. 22345-0 Paperbound $2.00

MOTHER GOOSE MELODIES. Faithful republication of the fabulously rare Munroe and Francis "copyright 1833" Boston edition—the most important Mother Goose collection, usually referred to as the "original." Familiar rhymes plus many rare ones, with wonderful old woodcut illustrations. Edited by E. F. Bleiler. 128pp. 4½ x 6⅜. 22577-1 Paperbound $1.25

TWO LITTLE SAVAGES; BEING THE ADVENTURES OF TWO BOYS WHO LIVED AS INDIANS AND WHAT THEY LEARNED, Ernest Thompson Seton. Great classic of nature and boyhood provides a vast range of woodlore in most palatable form, a genuinely entertaining story. Two farm boys build a teepee in woods and live in it for a month, working out Indian solutions to living problems, star lore, birds and animals, plants, etc. 293 illustrations. vii + 286pp.
20985-7 Paperbound $2.50

PETER PIPER'S PRACTICAL PRINCIPLES OF PLAIN & PERFECT PRONUNCIATION. Alliterative jingles and tongue-twisters of surprising charm, that made their first appearance in America about 1830. Republished in full with the spirited woodcut illustrations from this earliest American edition. 32pp. 4½ x 6⅜.
22560-7 Paperbound $1.00

SCIENCE EXPERIMENTS AND AMUSEMENTS FOR CHILDREN, Charles Vivian. 73 easy experiments, requiring only materials found at home or easily available, such as candles, coins, steel wool, etc.; illustrate basic phenomena like vacuum, simple chemical reaction, etc. All safe. Modern, well-planned. Formerly *Science Games for Children.* 102 photos, numerous drawings. 96pp. 6⅛ x 9¼.
21856-2 Paperbound $1.25

AN INTRODUCTION TO CHESS MOVES AND TACTICS SIMPLY EXPLAINED, Leonard Barden. Informal intermediate introduction, quite strong in explaining reasons for moves. Covers basic material, tactics, important openings, traps, positional play in middle game, end game. Attempts to isolate patterns and recurrent configurations. Formerly *Chess*. 58 figures. 102pp. (USO) 21210-6 Paperbound $1.25

LASKER'S MANUAL OF CHESS, Dr. Emanuel Lasker. Lasker was not only one of the five great World Champions, he was also one of the ablest expositors, theorists, and analysts. In many ways, his Manual, permeated with his philosophy of battle, filled with keen insights, is one of the greatest works ever written on chess. Filled with analyzed games by the great players. A single-volume library that will profit almost any chess player, beginner or master. 308 diagrams. xli x 349pp.
20640-8 Paperbound $2.50

THE MASTER BOOK OF MATHEMATICAL RECREATIONS, Fred Schuh. In opinion of many the finest work ever prepared on mathematical puzzles, stunts, recreations; exhaustively thorough explanations of mathematics involved, analysis of effects, citation of puzzles and games. Mathematics involved is elementary. Translated by F. Göbel. 194 figures. xxiv + 430pp. 22134-2 Paperbound $3.00

MATHEMATICS, MAGIC AND MYSTERY, Martin Gardner. Puzzle editor for Scientific American explains mathematics behind various mystifying tricks: card tricks, stage "mind reading," coin and match tricks, counting out games, geometric dissections, etc. Probability sets, theory of numbers clearly explained. Also provides more than 400 tricks, guaranteed to work, that you can do. 135 illustrations. xii + 176pp.
20338-2 Paperbound $1.50

MATHEMATICAL PUZZLES FOR BEGINNERS AND ENTHUSIASTS, Geoffrey Mott-Smith. 189 puzzles from easy to difficult—involving arithmetic, logic, algebra, properties of digits, probability, etc.—for enjoyment and mental stimulus. Explanation of mathematical principles behind the puzzles. 135 illustrations. viii + 248pp.
20198-8 Paperbound $1.25

PAPER FOLDING FOR BEGINNERS, William D. Murray and Francis J. Rigney. Easiest book on the market, clearest instructions on making interesting, beautiful origami. Sail boats, cups, roosters, frogs that move legs, bonbon boxes, standing birds, etc. 40 projects; more than 275 diagrams and photographs. 94pp.
20713-7 Paperbound $1.00

TRICKS AND GAMES ON THE POOL TABLE, Fred Herrmann. 79 tricks and games—some solitaires, some for two or more players, some competitive games—to entertain you between formal games. Mystifying shots and throws, unusual caroms, tricks involving such props as cork, coins, a hat, etc. Formerly *Fun on the Pool Table.* 77 figures. 95pp. 21814-7 Paperbound $1.00

HAND SHADOWS TO BE THROWN UPON THE WALL: A SERIES OF NOVEL AND AMUSING FIGURES FORMED BY THE HAND, Henry Bursill. Delightful picturebook from great-grandfather's day shows how to make 18 different hand shadows: a bird that flies, duck that quacks, dog that wags his tail, camel, goose, deer, boy, turtle, etc. Only book of its sort. vi + 33pp. 6½ x 9¼. 21779-5 Paperbound $1.00

WHITTLING AND WOODCARVING, E. J. Tangerman. 18th printing of best book on market. "If you can cut a potato you can carve" toys and puzzles, chains, chessmen, caricatures, masks, frames, woodcut blocks, surface patterns, much more. Information on tools, woods, techniques. Also goes into serious wood sculpture from Middle Ages to present, East and West. 464 photos, figures. x + 293pp.
20965-2 Paperbound $2.00

HISTORY OF PHILOSOPHY, Julián Marias. Possibly the clearest, most easily followed, best planned, most useful one-volume history of philosophy on the market; neither skimpy nor overfull. Full details on system of every major philosopher and dozens of less important thinkers from pre-Socratics up to Existentialism and later. Strong on many European figures usually omitted. Has gone through dozens of editions in Europe. 1966 edition, translated by Stanley Appelbaum and Clarence Strowbridge. xviii + 505pp. 21739-6 Paperbound $2.75

YOGA: A SCIENTIFIC EVALUATION, Kovoor T. Behanan. Scientific but non-technical study of physiological results of yoga exercises; done under auspices of Yale U. Relations to Indian thought, to psychoanalysis, etc. 16 photos. xxiii + 270pp.
20505-3 Paperbound $2.50

Prices subject to change without notice.
Available at your book dealer or write for free catalogue to Dept. GI, Dover Publications, Inc., 180 Varick St., N. Y., N. Y. 10014. Dover publishes more than 150 books each year on science, elementary and advanced mathematics, biology, music, art, literary history, social sciences and other areas.